Birds of Derbyshire

Birds of Derbyshire

R. A. Frost

Moorland Publishing Company

British Library Cataloguing in Publication Data
Frost, Roy
    Birds of Derbyshire.
    1. Birds—England—Derbyshire
    I. Title
    598.2′9425′1   QL690.G7
    ISBN 0–903485–46–X

For Sheila

ISBN 0 903485 46 X

© R. A. Frost 1978

Printed in Great Britain by
Redwood Burn Limited
Trowbridge & Esher

For the Publishers
Moorland Publishing Company
The Market Place, Hartington,
Buxton, Derbyshire SK17 0AL

Contents

Illustrations

Acknowledgements

This book could not have been written without a great deal of help from many people, to whom I am extremely grateful. In particular I must thank the officials of the Derbyshire Ornithological Society, and also of the Derbyshire Naturalists' Trust and Sheffield Bird Study Group for allowing me to quote their records and for assistance in other ways; Gordon and Pat Hollands for very kindly loaning me their extensive notes and making many helpful suggestions; Don Bramwell for his excellent article on fossil bird remains in Derbyshire; Harold A. Hems, Stephen Jackson, James Russell and Derick Scott for the photographs; Mrs Carolyn Marriott for ably typing the manuscript from my indifferent handwriting; for much assistance in a variety of ways, Dick Appleby, Tom Cockburn, John Ellis, David Gosney, David Herringshaw and Michael Stoyle; and not least to my wife, Sheila, for a tremendous amount of practical encouragement and forbearance.

I also thank the following for helping me: A. Adams, D. Alsop, D. Amedro, D. Atter, J. W. Atter, P. J. Bacon, F. N. Barker, T. Hedley Bell, A. Bennett, P. Betts, H. Braunton, D. Budworth, F. Bunton, A. P. E. Cain-Black, Dick and Mollie Carr, Richard and Elizabeth Carr, K. Clarkson, S. H. Clowes, F. Constable, G. Curtis, Dr A. J. Deadman, S. Dexter, S. Dobson, R. Doncaster, R. Fern, T. A. Gibson, W. Gibson, T. Goodley, E. Hardy, L. Harris, F. Harrison, D. V. Haslam, A. Hepworth, Miss K. M. Hollick, P. Hollingworth, G. Howe, K. Hughes, W. S. Jacklin, A. W. Jones, A. Kelly, A. Kent, R. W. Key, M. Leonard, P. D. R. Lomas, A. G. Macey, Captain W. K. Marshall, T. Marshall, M. Marsland, G. P. Mawson, D. F. McPhie, Marcus and Betty Moore, Dr I. Newton, N. W. Orford, R. Overton, H. A. Pigott, B. C. Potter, F. Price, T. Riley and the staff of Sheffield Museum, D. A. Robinson, J. E. Robson, Miss H. C. Rodgers, T. Rodgers, Mrs H. E. Roe, P. C. Roworth, G. Sellors, Alan Shaw, Mrs Anne Shaw, Dr A. H. V. Smith, K. Smith, T. G. Smith, C. J. Stokes, M. E. Taylor, L. Tipple, T. W. Tivey, P. Tooley, Mrs G. T. Walker, M. J. Wareing, A. W. Ward, A. B. Wassell, C. H. Wells, C. N. Whipple, D. R. Wilson, J. S. Wooddisse, and Dr D. W. Yalden.

Preface

The last Derbyshire avifauna was written by F. B. Whitlock over eighty years ago and, not surprisingly, is out of date, out of print, and difficult to obtain. At that time ornithology was mainly the pastime of an élite few, and commonly conducted along a gunbarrel. Subsequently birdwatching has become a popular pursuit, and improved and greatly increased observation has led to the addition of many new species to the county list, while many others which were previously considered rare vagrants are now known to be of regular occurrence. Our knowledge of the numbers and distribution of breeding birds is also greatly improved, especially as a result of the BTO Atlas investigation of 1968–72. This book attempts to assimilate all the published and much unpublished information since 1893 – at present available only from widely-scattered sources – and considers the effect on the avifauna of the great habitat changes this century, such as urbanisation, improved agricultural practices, wetland drainage, gravel digging, stone quarrying and reservoir construction.

A history of modern Derbyshire ornithology

The only previous avifauna of Derbyshire was written by F. B. Whitlock and published in 1893 under the title *Birds of Derbyshire*. Whitlock lived at Beeston, a few miles inside Nottinghamshire, and did most of his bird-watching in the Trent Valley along the Derbyshire–Nottinghamshire border. Considering the paucity of ornithologists then and consequent gaps in ornithological knowledge, Whitlock's ideas seem generally sound and the book quite well-written. He was greatly aided by the taxidermist, A. S. Hutchinson, and he also corresponded with several other ornithologists, most of them resident in south Derbyshire. Whitlock compiled a check-list of Nottinghamshire birds, also in 1893. His egg collection is at the Wollaton Hall Museum in Nottingham.

Whitlock utilised several published references to Derbyshire's birds. The earliest of importance was J. Pilkington's *View of the Present State of Derbyshire* (1789) in which one chapter is devoted to birds. This was upgraded in 1829 in S. Glover's *The History and Gazeteer of the County of Derby*. Again one chapter of this two volume work deals with ornithology but Whitlock rightly found some of the records unacceptable.

J. J. Briggs of King's Newton seems to have been an indefatigable ornithologist. He contributed many notes to *The Zoologist* between 1843 and 1875 including an interesting series of articles entitled 'Birds of Melbourne' in the 1849–50 volumes.

Natural History of Tutbury and Neighbourhood is the title of a book written by Sir Oswald Mosley. It was published in 1863, and a considerable portion written by Mosley and Edwin Brown deals with birds. Shortly afterwards, in 1866, came a small book, *Wild Flowers of Repton and Neighbourhood* which contains a bird list compiled by A. O. Worthington. The book was revised in 1881 with the bird list undertaken by

W. Gurneys. Still concerning the southern regions of the county were notes by G. W. Pullen entitled 'The Birds of Derby and Neighbourhood', published in *The Young Naturalist* of 1883–4. Two years later Whitlock wrote an article on Peakland birds (based mainly on observations in the Kinder Scout area) for *The Naturalist*.

In the *Journal of the Derbyshire Archaeological and Natural History Society (DAJ)* for 1892 the Reverend Charles Molineux published a fascinating article on the birds shot by a previous rector of Staveley, Francis Gisborne, between 1761 and 1784. Those who know the Staveley area now will find the paper interesting not only for its ornithological value but also for an insight into the landscape of that parish before the impact of industry.

Following the publication of *Birds of Derbyshire* several notes relating to Derbyshire birds appeared in such journals as the *DAJ*, *The Zoologist* and *The Field*. 1905 saw the appearance of part one of the *Victoria County History of Derbyshire*. A thirty-page chapter is given over to birds, based largely upon Whitlock's work, and written by the county's most famous ornithologist, the Reverend Francis Jourdain. Born at Derwent, where his father was vicar of a church now submerged under the reservoir, Jourdain was vicar of Clifton from 1894 to 1914. He was above all an oologist, active not only in Derbyshire but also in Europe and North Africa. He wrote many papers and some books; most notably he was wholly or partly responsible for the sections on display and posturing, breeding, food, and overseas distribution in the epic *Handbook of British Birds* (1938–41). His diaries are at the Edward Grey Institute in Oxford and make fascinating reading.

An almost annual bird report appeared in the *DAJ* from 1904 to 1954. Jourdain was editor of the report until he moved to Berkshire in 1914. The editor for the following year was Dr W. Shipton, who was succeeded by N. H. Fitzherbert of Somersal from 1916–25. The reports for 1923–4 contain interesting open letters between Fitzherbert and Jourdain regarding the latter's oological activities. No report was published for the years 1926–9 and few references to this period can be traced elsewhere. Jourdain, by then resident in Bournemouth but often visiting Clifton, resumed as editor for 1930–9, relinquishing the task shortly before his death in 1940.

Captain W. K. Marshall of Radbourne became county recorder from 1940 and he, together with Stanton Whitaker who became its first chairman, was largely responsible for initiating the formation of Derbyshire Ornithological Society in December 1954. Since 1955 this Society (DOS) has been responsible for publishing the annual bird report. Captain Marshall continued to act as recording secretary until he moved to Monmouthshire in 1957. D. R. Wilson of Sheffield was elected recorder for the years 1957–9, resigning shortly after he took up the post of secretary of the British Trust for Ornithology. D. C. Hulme (1960–2), N. A. Kerridge (1963–4), C. N. Whipple (1965–8) and D. Amedro (1969 onwards) comprise a succession of southern Derbyshire recorders. The dates refer to the relevant bird reports rather than years of office.

In its first year Derbyshire Ornithological Society showed its serious scientific intent in publishing a *Bird Distribution Survey*, organised by F. G. Hollands. Since those days the Society has encouraged research into the bird populations of specific areas, or more commonly, into the status of various species; these have included Great Crested and Little Grebes, Golden Plover, Curlew, Dunlin, Lesser Black-backed Gull, Little Owl, House Martin, Rook, Nuthatch, Dipper, and Ring Ouzel. Additionally DOS has organised winter wildfowl counts for the Wildfowl Trust and has assisted the British Trust for Ornithology with its enquiries, most notably the Atlas project of 1968–72.

The great recent increase in ornithology in the county is reflected in a commensurate increase in the number of observers submitting records to the annual bird report. There were forty-nine contributors in 1955, 128 in 1964 and 192 in 1975. Derbyshire Ornithological Society has clearly succeeded in its chief aim – the furtherance of bird study in the field.

Meanwhile an ever-increasing number of local societies and groups contributes to our knowledge of birdlife in their areas. These include Buxton Field Club, Matlock Field Club, Sorby Natural History Society, Sheffield Bird Study Group, Burton upon Trent Natural History and Archaeological Society, Ogston Hide Group, Whitwell Wood Study Group and a few ringing groups. Some publish their own annual report. Liaison with DOS is generally good and it is to be hoped that this state of affairs will continue.

That part of Derbyshire lying within twenty miles of Sheffield City Museum is dealt with in *The Birds of the Sheffield area* (1974), a small book edited by Dr Harold Smith. Earlier lists with the same title were compiled by D. R. Wilson in 1958 and, earlier, in 1929, by the oologist Arthur Whitaker, who spent much of his time in Derbyshire.

Since the publication of Whitlock's book several references to the county's birds have been published in such journals as *British Birds*, *The Zoologist*, *The Derbyshire Countryside* and *Birds*. For the purposes of this book, these have been abstracted, reputable ornithologists working in isolation from local societies have been contacted, and the diaries of such excellent field naturalists as Jourdain, W. Storrs-Fox and G. T. Walker have been studied.

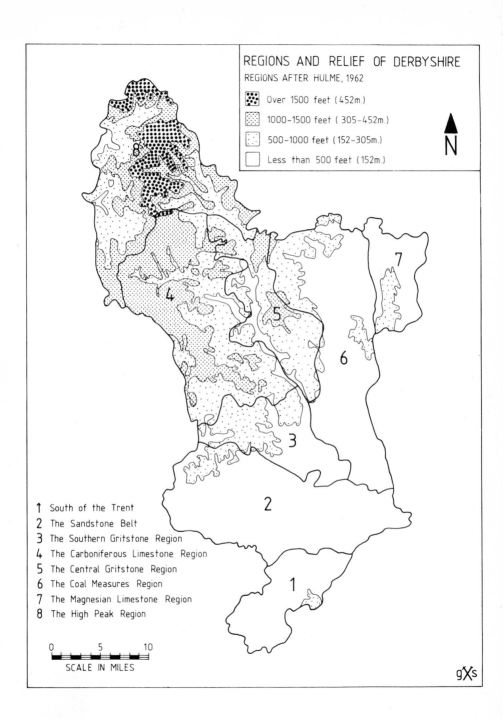

REGIONS AND RELIEF OF DERBYSHIRE

REGIONS AFTER HULME, 1962

Over 1500 feet (452m.)

1000–1500 feet (305–452m.)

500–1000 feet (152–305m.)

Less than 500 feet (152m.)

N

1 South of the Trent
2 The Sandstone Belt
3 The Southern Gritstone Region
4 The Carboniferous Limestone Region
5 The Central Gritstone Region
6 The Coal Measures Region
7 The Magnesian Limestone Region
8 The High Peak Region

0   5   10

SCALE IN MILES

gXs

The County

Derbyshire contains 1,035 square miles or 649,781 acres within its maximum dimensions of sixty miles long and thirty-five miles wide. It is bounded to the east by Nottinghamshire, to the south-east by Leicestershire, to the south-west and west by Staffordshire, by Cheshire and Greater Manchester to the north-west, and by West and South Yorkshire to the north. Most of the 542 square mile Peak District National Park, designated in 1950, lies within the county boundaries.

The great variety of scenery corresponds largely with the geological structure. In the National Park is much of the Millstone Grit which in the north typically gives rise to moorland, of either heather or cotton grass communities or eroding peat, while the Carboniferous Limestone dome is largely a grassy plateau dissected by dales, justly famed for their beauty. On the eastern flank of the county is the coalfield, an area greatly modified by urbanisation, mining, and other forms of industry, while in the far north-eastern corner arable farming mixes with some of the county's larger woodlands on the Magnesian Limestone plateau. In the more tranquil south, where the Keuper series dominates, is the Trent Valley with its chain of aquatic habitats, bordered on either side by an attractive area of farmland, woods, and large parks.

Altitude varies from 90 feet by the River Trent to 2,088 feet in the Pennines, and naturally affects the climate to a considerable degree. Rainfall varies from twenty-two inches a year in parts of the extreme south to over sixty-three inches on Kinder Scout; and naturally the highest land also has the greatest incidence of snow, strong winds and fog. The Trent system drains nine-tenths of the county, only some north-western and north-eastern streams flowing elsewhere.

Farming land accounts for some seventy-four per cent of the surface area, including sixty-two per cent grassland for dairying (compared with an average forty-eight per cent in England and Wales). However, Derbyshire is only 5.5 per cent wooded, compared with the national average of eight per cent. Just over a quarter of the total 35,190 acres of woods are coniferous.

The county is rich in minerals, including coal, Magnesian and Carboniferous Limestone, dolomite, sand, gravel, fluorspar and clay. All of these are worked, and if deep-mined coal is excluded, Derbyshire produces more minerals than any other British county.

In 1971 the population was 886,605, over seventy per cent of which lived in the eastern half of the county. Within thirty-five miles of Derbyshire's borders lives a population of fourteen and a half million. Thus it is not surprising that many people seek weekend recreation in the Derbyshire countryside, especially the Peak District, and human pressure on certain areas is considerable.

Since Whitlock's *Birds of Derbyshire* was published in 1893 there have been several minor changes to the county boundary, as follows:

1894	Part of Stapenhill and Winshill were transferred to Staffordshire.
1895	Croxall was wholly transferred to Staffordshire.
1895	Most of Pinxton and part of Kirkby in Ashfield were transferred from Nottinghamshire to Derbyshire.
1897	Appleby, Oakthorpe and Donisthorpe, Willesley, Chilcote, Measham and Stretton en le Fields were transferred to Leicestershire.
1897	Netherseal, Overseal and part of Ashby Woulds and Blackfordby were transferred from Leicestershire to Derbyshire.
1936	Ludworth, Mellor and part of New Mills were transferred to Cheshire.
1936	Parts of Yeardsley cum Whaley,

1	Alport Castles	52	Kinder Reservoir
2	Alport Hill	53	Kinder Scout
3	Axe Edge	54	Ladybower Reservoir
4	Barbrook Reservoir	55	Langley Mill Flash
5	Beeley Moor	56	Lathkill Dale
6	Beresford Dale	57	Leash Fen
7	Birdholme Wildfowl Reserve	58	Linacre Reservoir
8	Black Hill	59	Locko Park
9	Bleaklow	60	Long Eaton
10	Bolsover	61	Longendale
11	Bolsover Colliery Marsh	62	Longshaw Estate
12	Bradford Dale	63	Manners Wood
13	Brampton East Moor	64	Mapleton
14	Brinsley Flash	65	Matlock Moor
15	Broadhurst Edge Wood	66	Melbourne Pool
16	Butterley Reservoir	67	Mercaston Gravel Pits
17	Calke Park	68	Middleton Moor
18	Carr Wood	69	Millers Dale
19	Catton Park	70	Monks Dale
20	Chapel-en-le-Frith	71	Monsal Dale
21	Chatsworth Park	72	Moss Valley
22	Chee Dale	73	Norbury
23	Church Wilne Reservoir	74	Ogston Reservoir
24	Clay Mills Gravel Pits	75	Old Whittington Sewage Farm
25	Combs Moss	76	Osmaston Park
26	Combs Reservoir	77	Padley Wood
27	Cressbrook Dale	78	Peak Dale Quarries
28	Cromford Canal Wharf	79	Pebley Pond
29	Derwent Reservoir	80	Pleasley Park
30	Dove Dale	81	Radbourne Estate
31	Drakelow Wildfowl Reserve	82	Ramsley Reservoir
32	Dronfield	83	Renishaw Park
33	Drum Hill	84	Repton Shrubs
34	Earl Sterndale Quarries	85	Ringinglow Bog
35	Eckington	86	Ripley
36	Egginton Sewage Farm	87	Robin Wood
37	Elvaston Castle Country Park	88	Scarcliffe Woods
38	Errwood Reservoir	89	Shiningcliff Wood
39	Fernilee Reservoir	90	Shipley Lake
40	Flash Dam	91	Spondon Sewage Farm
41	Foremark Reservoir	92	Staunton Harold Reservoir
42	Golden Brook Storage Lagoon	93	Staveley
43	Hardwick Park	94	Staveley Sewage Farm
44	Hathersage	95	Sudbury Lake
45	Heanor	96	Swadlincote
46	Hilton Gravel Pits	97	Swarkestone Gravel Pits
47	Hoo Moor	98	Tibshelf
48	Howden Reservoir	99	Toddbrook Reservoir
49	Ilkeston	100	Via Gellia
50	Kedleston Park Lake	101	Whitwell Wood
51	Killamarsh Meadows	102	Williamthorpe Colliery Reservoir

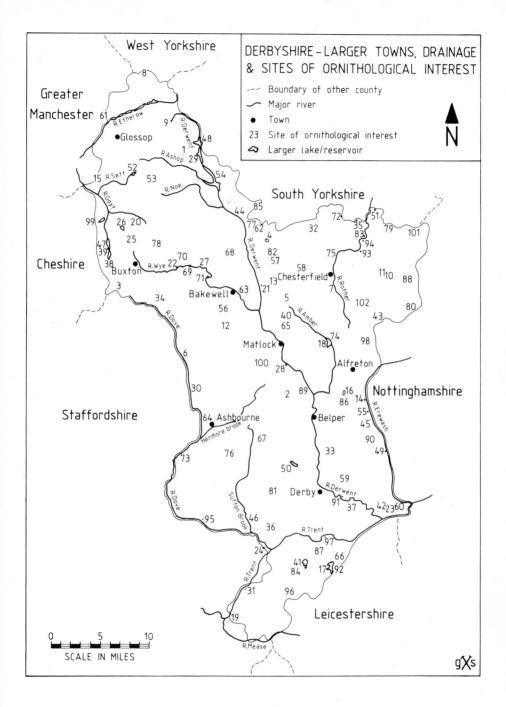

DERBYSHIRE – LARGER TOWNS, DRAINAGE
& SITES OF ORNITHOLOGICAL INTEREST

- - - Boundary of other county
——— Major river
● Town
23 Site of ornithological interest
⌒ Larger lake/reservoir

N

West Yorkshire

Greater Manchester

Cheshire

Staffordshire

South Yorkshire

Nottinghamshire

Leicestershire

8

61
●Glossop
9
48
1
29
52
15 53
54
44 85
77
62 4
32
72
51
35
83 94
79
101
99
26 20
25 78
68
82
57
75
93
47
39
38 Buxton
R.Wye 22 70 27
69
71
63
13 Chesterfield
58
11 10
88
3
34
R.Dove
Bakewell
56
12
21
5
40
65
R.Amber
74
102
43
80
6
30
Matlock
100 28
2 89
18
98
16
86 14
55
Belper
45
90
49
64 Ashbourne
67
33
59
73 76
50
81 Derby
91 37
42 23 60
95 46 36
24
87 97
66
41 9
84 17 92
31 96
19

SCALE IN MILES
0   5   10

Disley, Kettleshulme and Taxal were transferred from Cheshire to Derbyshire.

1968 Beighton, Dore, Totley and Beauchief were transferred to Yorkshire.

1974 Tintwistle was transferred from Cheshire to Derbyshire.

In 1905 Linton, in his section on botany in the *Victoria County History of Derbyshire*, divided Derbyshire into eight botanical districts, which, however, met with considerable criticism. In 1962 Derek C. Hulme in the *Index of Derbyshire Localities* modified Linton's list though still retaining eight areas, numbered from south to north and based largely on geological structure. DOS immediately adopted his system for recording purposes and continues to use it. Each area is now considered in greater detail.

South of the Trent

Only a small portion of Derbyshire lies south of the River Trent. It is a region of diverse geology and is delineated by the river and the county boundary with Staffordshire and Leicestershire. Most of it belongs to the Keuper series in common with much of south Derbyshire, but there are formations of Millstone Grit, Carboniferous Limestone and Coal Measures. Thus this region contains all of Derbyshire's major rock formations with the exception of Magnesian Limestone.

Morphologically the region is much more unified than its geological structure would suggest. Away from the flatter areas by the Trent (only 120 feet above sea level at King's Newton) and Mease, is a series of small valleys and ridges which rise to 604 feet at Pistern Hill. Hulme (1962) describes the climate as mild and damp with an average rainfall of about twenty-five inches. The scenery lacks dramatic beauty but is for the most part diverse and in parts extremely pleasant. There are fine deciduous woodlands and parklands, conifer plantations, quarries of gravel, sand and limestone, several small ponds, and two large reservoirs.

The only sizeable scar is the Swadlincote complex where coal mining and clay extraction have produced the saddest industrial landscape in Derbyshire. The degraded area seems larger than it really is owing to its high position on a series of ridges.

With its arable land and woods and the proximity of heavy industry the region has some similarities with the Magnesian Limestone area but is altogether less open, and more undulating and intimate.

The region has a long history of ornithological recording, and perusal of the older literature shows that its woods were particularly well-studied. Nowadays with nearby gravel pits, reservoirs and the like to claim the bird-watcher's attention, the woods are not so well-known. Some, such as Repton Shrubs, and Robin Wood, near Ingleby, have been largely felled and replanted since the war. At Repton Shrubs Wood Warblers breed at least occasionally and Hawfinches may also do so. A careful census of birds was carried out at Robin Wood during the 1960s but there are rather few recent records from this site. Nightjar, Grasshopper and Sedge Warblers, and Woodcock were all heard on one night in 1970 — with Quail in an adjacent field. One wonders how many of these species regularly breed there.

Some of the parklands and woodlands associated with private estates are virtually unknown now. Calke Park has many fine mature deciduous trees including some stagheaded oaks reminiscent of those of Sherwood Forest (and, like them, harbouring many nesting Tree Sparrows). At the edge of Calke Park is Ticknall Limeyards, whose ugly name belies an intriguing mixture of ponds, scrub and woodland — the only place in the county where Traveller's Joy is rampant. Spring Wood by Staunton Harold Reservoir attracts large numbers of Redpolls to its birches in a good passage year. At the southern extremity of Derbyshire Catton Park had a small heronry until 1971, whilst another potentially productive wood with few or no recent records is Grange Wood near Overseal. All of the above woods, and those in the Foremark and Newton Park

1   *Farmland scene near Repton. (S. Jackson)*

2   *Calke Park contains some fine woodlands, which are ornithologically little known. (S. Jackson)*

3 *Staunton Harold Reservoir is an important site, especially for wintering wildfowl.*
(S. Jackson)

areas, would repay closer attention.

All of the water bodies south of the Trent are ornithologically overshadowed by Staunton Harold Reservoir and Drakelow Wildfowl Reserve. Staunton Harold Reservoir, south of Melbourne and covering 208 acres, has been well-watched since flooding in 1964, though coverage does not rival that of Ogston. Staunton Harold has strong claims to being one of the county's top ornithological reservoirs in terms of the number and variety of water birds it attracts. It is by far the most important site in Derbyshire for Great Crested Grebes. Though only a few grebes attempt to breed the population is large at all seasons with up to 164 recorded, and in winter, when most waters lose their grebes, numbers here may still exceed triple figures. There are fewer Mallard now than in the late 1960s but Wigeon, Coot and diving ducks often occur in large flocks. Mud is frequently exposed and waders are regular on passage. Several locally rare species have been seen: these include Great Northern and Red-throated Divers, all of the rarer grebes,

Long-tailed Duck, Smew, Purple Sandpiper, Razorbill, Little Auk, Arctic Skua and White-winged Black Tern. Unfortunately, the days when reservoirs seemed to be reserved for birds alone are over and fishing and sailing are recent innovations, though there are restrictions on both activities in winter and a commendably large area has been designated a nature reserve. A 245 acre reservoir has recently been flooded three miles further west, near Foremark, and already promises to be an important site for waterfowl.

Drakelow Wildfowl Reserve lies on Central Electricity Generating Board property between Drakelow Power Station and the Trent. About fifty acres of flyash lagoons and gravel pits have been carefully planned as a nature reserve. The scheme to ensure an attractive all-year habitat for water birds has been very successful and the active group of ornithologists there has recorded 180 species including Slavonian Grebe, Ring-necked Duck, Ferruginous Duck, Spotted Crake, Temminck's Stint, Pectoral Sandpiper,

4 *Drakelow Wildfowl Reserve, where the Central Electricity Generating Board has created an exciting wetland habitat. Black Redstarts have nested at the adjacent power station. (S. Jackson)*

Pomarine Skua and Caspian Tern. In particular Drakelow attracts large flocks of diving duck, a large autumnal gull roost, and an excellent variety of waders on both spring and autumn migration. Black Redstarts bred at the power station in 1970.

Prior to the construction of Staunton Harold Reservoir the ornamental Melbourne Pool was the most important water south of the Trent. A mass of Yellow Water-lilies in summer, it is often thronged with ducks and Coots. The region has many smaller ponds, occasionally productive of interesting records – such as the first county Mandarin in 1963, and a Red-crested Pochard in one recent winter.

Farming in the area is varied. In the south and north-west arable predominates. Near Swadlincote is a dairying region, while the most intensive horticultural area in Derbyshire is around Melbourne. More than 3,000 acres hereabouts are given over to the production of brassicas, salad crops, peas, beans, potatoes and small fruit. However, whether such specialised farming produces a distinct

avifauna seems to be unknown. The gently rolling country bounded by Ticknall, Ingleby, Milton and Repton is a traditional Quail area while no fewer than eleven were heard calling further south, at Grangewood, during the summer of 1977.

The Sandstone Belt

This is a large southern region, covering 184 square miles and stretching the breadth of the county to the borders of Staffordshire and Nottinghamshire. From Sandiacre its northern boundary runs roughly west to Allestree and then west-north-westerly to Clifton. Hulme's southern boundary is the Trent and Dove from Long Eaton to Newton Solney. For the purposes of this account I have included the whole of the flood plains of these rivers where these lie in Derbyshire.

The whole area is of the Keuper series so characteristic of the English Midlands. Keuper marl dominates but there is an area of Keuper Sandstone and Bunter Sandstone

5 *The River Trent near Newton Solney. The river is now, as in Whitlock's day, a major highway for migratory birds. (S. Jackson)*

in the north-west, and broad alluvial belts along the valleys of the Trent, Dove and Derwent. The altitudinal limits are 602 feet at Snelston and 90 feet by the Trent at Long Eaton, while rainfall amounts vary from twenty-two to thirty-one inches a year.

That part of the region west of a line from Etwall to Brailsford is characterised by low, well-dissected hills. This is chiefly an area of dairy farming, the fields being quite small and bounded by hedges dotted with oaks — truly part of the Midlands Plain. Settlements are generally small and unspoilt. Most of the bird records in this quietly pleasant countryside come from parklands such as those at Osmaston and Sudbury.

To the east of the Etwall-Brailsford line the hills are smaller, and the valleys broader and whilst dairying is still important, the farming becomes more mixed. Derby and its expanding suburbs dominate this sub-region, and the area between the county town and the Nottinghamshire border is quite heavily populated.

Some of the private estates and parklands of the Sandstone Belt are ornithologically important. In the west, near Ashbourne is the picturesque Osmaston Estate — a mixture of agricultural land, parkland, woods and water. The rhododendron-fringed lakes usually hold grebes and duck, including breeding Ruddy Duck in 1975. Unusually far south in Derbyshire, Dippers and Grey Wagtails probably breed on the streams. Nuthatches are common and Sparrowhawks nest annually in the Larch woods. Herons have recently bred, but many mature trees were felled a few years ago and rhododendron clearance has caused a large finch roost to diminish. Not far from Osmaston, a private woodland at Norbury contains Derbyshire's largest active heronry.

Better known than Osmaston is Kedleston Park, only three miles north-west of the centre of Derby. Here the Markeaton Brook has been dammed to form a long, narrow lake harbouring good numbers of duck, including Goosander in some winters. The

6   *Osmaston Park. The variety of birds rivals the fine scenery. (S. Jackson)*

7   *The colony of Canada Geese in Kedleston Park is the second largest in Britain. (R. A. Frost)*

Canada Goose colony is Britain's second largest, only Holkham in Norfolk exceeding it. Up to 1,400 of these semi-ornamentals have been counted though at least part of the population is prone to wandering. Sometimes returning Canada Geese bring other species of feral or escaped geese with them. Herons have nested at Kedleston in recent years.

The Radbourne and Sudbury Estates were frequently mentioned in the annual bird reports when Captain W. K. Marshall was ornithological recorder for Derbyshire. Now little information is received from either, though Reed Warblers are known to breed in *phragmites* patches at both places. These estates, and others at Longford, Snelston and elsewhere, might repay more extensive study. Conversely S. Jackson has recently conducted an outline survey of the birds of Locko Park near Spondon. The lake here has produced a number of interesting wildfowl records disproportionate to its eleven acres – such as the first Derbyshire breeding of Gadwall in 1957, and the first Red-crested Pochard sighting in 1960. Four miles southeast of Derby Cathedral is Elvaston Castle Country Park which is an excellent spot for observing Siskins, Redpolls, woodpeckers and other arboreal species.

Rising in Staffordshire and flowing to the Humber, the River Trent is in its upper reaches in Derbyshire, yet it is a broad river commanding a flood plain one and a half to two miles wide. It is also a quiet river, bridged only in a few places, and flowing through agricultural land which it still occasionally floods (when the valley becomes a vast shallow lake). The Trent is generally shallow and its pebbly beaches attract waders, gulls, wagtails and many other species, while Sand Martins breed in the sandy banks. Close to the river are small oxbow lakes attractive to wildfowl. In prolonged cold winter weather the Trent, warmed by water returned from a string of giant power stations, becomes a retreat for wildfowl driven from frozen lakes and reservoirs. In the icy 1962–3 winter great numbers of duck and waders wintered on the Trent and many rare species were observed,

including Garganey, Scaup, Velvet Scoter, Merganser, Smew, Knot, Sanderling, wild swans and five species of geese.

Whitlock wrote in 1893 of the importance of the Trent to migrating birds and this is every bit as true now as it was then. However, although there is no boating or barge traffic above Shardlow, the Trent's birdlife is disturbed by the many fishermen. As it is such an important ornithological highway perhaps the river authority might be persuaded to leave at least a small stretch free from disturbance.

The gravel terraces of the Trent have been quarried to produce pits in several places, mainly north of the river. In most places a thin alluvial layer overlies the gravel which averages some twenty feet thick. During excavation water is pumped away, though the quarry bed usually retains small pools attractive to breeding Little Ringed Plovers and passage waders. The cessation of excavation usually results in permanent flooding since most of the gravel lies below the water table.

The gravel pits at Elvaston, Swarkestone, Willington, Egginton, Clay Mills and Hilton contain a variety of wetland habitats. There are large stretches of open water, some with islets where duck, Canada Geese, Black-headed Gulls and Common Terns nest. Willows invade some pits – one such willow bed became a roost for up to 500 Snipe. Hilton gravel pits have been acquired as a reserve by the Derbyshire Naturalists' Trust; here are seventy-five acres of open water, willow beds and Greater Reedmace marsh. Water Rails have nested here, Reed Warblers do so regularly and interesting migrants occur from time to time. In 1967 the site was surveyed by M. W. Pienkowski who found the commonest species to be Sedge Warbler, Blackbird, Song Thrush and Willow Warbler in that order. Part of Swarkestone pits have been taken over by both a yachting club and a radio-controlled boat club. Others have been drained or filled with domestic rubbish. However, a more usual fate at present is infilling with pulverised flyash burned at the local power stations. This practice is not

8 *Hilton gravel pits are now a reserve of the Derbyshire Naturalists' Trust, supporting breeding grebes, a variety of wildfowl and Reed and Sedge Warblers. (S. Jackson)*

wholly detrimental to birds since passage waders often frequent the areas where sediment is being pumped. Following infilling and drying-out topsoil is usually added and the land returned to agricultural use.

With gravel much in demand and resources in the Trent Valley said to be considerable, there should be enough of these artificial wetlands to satisfy the needs of both

bird and birdwatcher for a considerable time to come. In November 1974 planning permission existed for some 2,000 acres of future workings in the eastern Trent Valley. Whether these gravel pits will be as free from disturbance as in the past, however, remains to be seen.

Egginton sewage farm lies a little more than a mile from the Trent. It has been known as a haunt of migrant waders for over eighty years. At first sight it appears to be merely a collection of large fields with a few tiny pools – but tiny pools are all that are needed to attract waders here. Rare birds recorded here have included Avocet, Pectoral Sandpiper, Killdeer, Red-footed Falcon and Cattle Egret. Finches find the weedy fields much to their liking and flocks of some thousands occur regularly. Part of the area has now been returned to agriculture and another part quarried for gravel. A much smaller sewage farm, on the Trent-side at Willington, only discovered by ornithologists in 1962, was at times highly suitable for sandpipers, shanks and other waders, until it was reclaimed in 1977.

In the south-eastern corner of the county near Sawley is Church Wilne Reservoir. Excavation began in the mid 1960s and eighty-three acres were flooded in 1971, with a similar area at present partially flooded and due to come into use as the second half of the reservoir in the late 1970s. The existing reservoir has vertical concrete sides and is free from disturbance. Duck, especially Wigeon,

9   *The Trent Valley contains a number of small pools with marshy vegetation, like this one near Sawley. (S. Jackson)*

congregate in large numbers; terns and Little Gulls call regularly and the gull roost is usually the largest in the county. Several rare species have been seen already including Slavonian Grebe, Great and Arctic Skuas and Red-footed Falcon. Close to Church Wilne Reservoir, at Breaston, is the Golden Brook Storage Lagoon, a waterlogged rushy field, sometimes productive of interesting water birds.

One of the most interesting wetlands of the Sandstone Belt and, indeed, of the whole county, is the large sewage farm by the River Derwent near Spondon. A Black-headed Gull colony, first recorded in the 1930s, still persists on a few shallow lagoons. The farm's potential was only rediscovered in the late 1960s: regular observations since have established this as an important site for duck, especially wintering Teal and Shoveler, waders, pipits and finches.

With many ornithologists among its population of 220,000 Derby itself often features in ornithological literature. Even in the town centre Goldfinches and Grey Wagtails may be seen and duck and grebes have oc-

10   *Spondon sewage farm has the only regular Derbyshire colony of Black-headed Gulls in its lagoons. (S. Jackson)*

casionally been reported on the River Derwent. A Black Redstart sang in an urban back-street in 1963 and there have been other recent sightings of this bird in the breeding season. Suburban gardens, here and elsewhere in the county, may hold very high densities of birds in summer and in winter. A Firecrest seen in disused allotments at Sunnyhill and a Bluethroat in a Mickleover garden, both in the spring of 1977, are further reminders that bird-watching in built-up areas can be most profitable.

The Southern Gritstone region

Of all Hulme's regions of Derbyshire this is the second smallest, occupying only seventy-nine square miles of land between the Coal Measures, Carboniferous Limestone and the Sandstone regions. It is very roughly triangular, with its apex in the west at Ashbourne, and Morley and Sandiacre at the north and south of its base. Apart from an inlier of Carboniferous Limestone around Kniveton and some Bunter Sandstone in the south-west the underlying rock is Millstone Grit. The Derwent near Derby is only 160 feet above sea level whereas Alport Hill, famed for its monolith and striking views, stands at 1,034 feet. Rainfall is in the order of thirty to thirty-five inches a year.

Small, deep valleys, gorse patches in the rough fields, narrow, steep-banked lanes and a lack of industry make this a picturesque and rural region, especially west of the Derwent. Dairy farming dominates, except in the south of the area where the farming is more mixed. The small fields have hedges or more rarely stone walls as their boundaries. The region's woodlands are generally small except in the east where Shiningcliff and Drum Hill are large by Derbyshire standards. Ornithologically the Southern Gritstone region is the least known region of the whole county. There are few resident ornithologists, and birdwatchers from other regions rarely spend much time here. Only the environs of Ashbourne and the two woods already mentioned have had adequate coverage.

P. D. R. Lomas conducted an admirable census of farmland bird communities at Mapleton from 1963 to 1972. His plot was 294 acres of largely pastoral land comprising sixty-four small fields, two small woods, five farms, village houses, and the village church. A stream formed a boundary across one corner. The British Trust for Ornithology's analysis of Lomas' work in 1965–71 showed that the most numerous species (in order) were Blackbird, Willow Warbler, Chaffinch, Starling, Dunnock, and Robin. Lapwings were surprisingly scarce, averaging only a pair a year.

The best known site in the region, in fact one of the county's better known woodlands, is Shiningcliff Wood on the western bank of the Derwent at Alderwasley. Sessile Oak, Birch and Sycamore dominate though there has been some planting of conifers. Ornithologists find the wood rewarding at all times of the year. In a survey of fifty-six acres during the late 1960s T. A. Gibson showed Willow Warbler to be by far the commonest species, followed by Blackbird, Robin, Blue and Great Tits and Wren. Wood Warblers regularly breed and the beautiful Pied Flycatcher sometimes does so. In winter a dense Rhododendron thicket clothing a steep slope has the largest roost of finches known in Derbyshire – some ten thousand were counted in 1966, over half of them Bramblings. Subsequent counts have been smaller. Redpolls, Siskins, Goldcrests and tits are often numerous in Shiningcliff Wood at this season.

Another woodland of some importance is at Drum Hill, near Little Eaton. Only four miles from the centre of Derby, this wood is composed mainly of birch, with some good stands of Oak, Beech and conifers. Drum Hill was not adequately watched until the early 1960s, when Wood Warbler and Redstart were found there. These species still breed with a good range of woodland birds including Sparrowhawk, Woodcock and woodpeckers. Redpolls often throng the birches, especially on spring passage.

There are no large woods in the region apart from Drum Hill and Shiningcliff, but

11   *Alport Hill, with its striking monolith, gives extensive views over the unspoilt country-side of the Southern Gritstone region. (R. A. Frost)*

small woods and spinneys, often of conifers, are well scattered. Such areas need not lack interest, and one careful observer has submitted many records of interest from Bradley Wood, only about twenty acres in extent, near Ashbourne.

The Southern Gritstone region is devoid of large water bodies, though this situation will be drastically changed if governmental approval is given to plans to construct a 600 acre regulating reservoir between Carsington and Hognaston. There are however a few small lakes in parklands and on private estates. Bradley Dam usually holds small numbers of wildfowl whilst Bear Pond at the edge of Shiningcliff Wood, has breeding Canada Geese. The River Derwent, like the Trent, attracts duck, especially in hard weather. Scaup and Velvet Scoter were seen in the 1962–3 winter when a flock of some

350 duck lived on Belper River Gardens. Quarrying of the Bunter sand and gravel around Mercaston has taken place largely above the water table though a few pools have been created. Little Ringed Plovers may have bred in at least one year and small numbers of duck occur.

The Carboniferous Limestone region

Carboniferous or Mountain Limestone forms a distinctive region in the central west of the county. The western boundary is the Staffordshire border (formed by the River Dove) and Hulme's other boundary encompasses Burbage, Peak Forest, Great Hucklow, Stoney Middleton, Bakewell, Matlock, Wirksworth and Fenny Bentley. Hulme's region covers 186 square miles. The rock, pale

12 *Near Foolow, where the pastures are divided by typical limestone walls, though the ridge in the distance is of gritstone. (S. Jackson)*

grey in colour, is some 2,400 feet thick, at least in the west. Most of the Carboniferous Limestone region is an open plateau 1,000 feet or more above sea level. However, though they occupy only a tiny fraction of the total area it is the superb dales – to many the epitome of Derbyshire – which are better known.

Most of the area is controlled by the Peak Park Joint Planning Board, though the quarrying regions around Buxton and Wirksworth have been excluded.

Rainfall in the area varies between thirty-five and fifty inches a year depending largely upon altitude. Buxton, England's highest market town, averages 48.4 inches a year. Other weather records from this station exemplify the rather severe climate. The mean January temperature is 36.6°F, while the corresponding figure for July is only 57.7°F. On average there are 211 days a year with some rain, and 111 with ground frost.

The plateau is lower in the south, generally 900–1,000 feet with some hills rising to 1,200 feet. In the north it is more rolling with a few hills over 1,400 feet while Eldon Hill reaches 1,543 feet. The lowest point is 260 feet by the Derwent. The plateau landscape is dominated by permanent grassland divided into fields by pale drystone walls and crossed by narrow roads and several ancient trackways. Cattle and sheep graze the fields, though some are used for hay production. Fields often contain small dewponds to counteract the porous nature of the ground and the deep water-table. The characteristic breeding birds are Skylarks and Lapwings, with much smaller numbers of Curlews. Whinchats may use the walls as song-posts, and Wheatears are not uncommon. In places where cereal growing has been attempted a few Corn Buntings may be found. Foraging Fieldfares and Redwings often occur in large flocks, especially in spring.

The generally open nature of the plateau is accentuated by the lack of timber. Woodland is all but absent. The well-spaced farmsteads are often sheltered by belts of trees, usually

13 *Monk's Dale, part of a National Nature Reserve. The dale is dry except after heavy rainfall. (S. Jackson)*

Sycamore, which hold small numbers of typical woodland species. Some Hawthorn and Elder scrub is found in those places where the edge of the Limestone is marked by scarp-like features. Long-eared Owls nest sparingly in these areas.

At Bradwell Moor, Longstone Moor and in a few other places there are small heather moorlands, probably as a result of leaching which led to the formation of podsols. Such moorlands hold Red Grouse, Meadow Pipits, Curlews and other species typical of the gritstone moors. A fuller comparison between the birds of Millstone Grit and Carboniferous Limestone moorlands would be useful.

The dales are nationally famous for their scenic beauty, which attracts hordes of tourists at summer weekends. Many dales contain streams or rivers but still more are dry: the former are usually the more interesting for birds, and ornithologists have found such places as Beresford Dale, Dove Dale and Monsal, Miller's and Chee Dales on the Wye particularly rewarding. Parts of Lathkill

Dale and Monk's Dale have been established as National Nature Reserves, though largely on account of their botanical communities.

On the rivers in such dales Little Grebes, Mallards and Moorhens nest, and in places where the flow of water is slow sometimes Coot and Tufted Duck may be found. Dippers are commonly seen perched on rocks in midstream or more usually as dark shapes speeding away just above the water surface. Pied and Grey Wagtails use the same rocks as launches for their insect-catching sallies. Kingfishers are not uncommon but Common Sandpipers are few, generally avoiding the more populous spots. The dale sides are often clothed with Ash woodland which supports many of the commoner species of woodland birds, with perhaps Chaffinch and Willow Warbler most numerous of all. To add variety there are Green and Great Spotted Woodpeckers, Redstarts, Bullfinches, Marsh Tits, Spotted Flycatchers and occasional Pied Flycatchers, Wood Warblers and Hawfinches. Recently Nuthatches have spread to

14 *Monsal Dale on the River Wye. Little Grebes, Coots, Tufted Ducks, Kingfishers, Dippers and Grey Wagtails are among the breeding birds. (S. Jackson)*

many of the dales and Herons have nested in one of the larger blocks of woodland. House Martins breed on several of the crags and buttresses towering above the woodlands.

Six kilometres of the River Wye, centred on Miller's Dale, were assessed in 1974–5 by the Waterways Bird Survey, organised by Mrs Betty A. Moore. The population density was greater than that of the River Derwent (on the gritstone), averaging sixty-four territories a year. In order the most numerous species were Moorhen, Mallard, Coot, Little Grebe, and Tufted Duck and Dipper equally.

In winter Little Grebes often gather in small groups on the rivers and small flocks of duck may be seen. In severe weather the limestone rivers do not freeze as the water comes from underground sources. In consequence unusual species of duck sometimes occur, along with occasional rare water birds. Those dales without surface water vary greatly in size from tiny clefts in the plateau's surface to much larger valleys such as

Deep Dale (near Taddington), Combs Dale and upper Lathkill Dale. Some occasionally hold running water after very heavy rain. Ash woodland may be present or it may be replaced by scrub Hawthorn or Elder. However, the majority have rough grassy sides (grazed by animals if not too steep) with scree or rocky outcrops. Such dales are characterised by Kestrels, Jackdaws, Little Owls and Wheatears.

At present there is considerable argument about the future of quarrying in the Peak District. Preservationists complain of the ugliness of the quarries and the amounts of noise and dust produced. Industrialists point out the great demand for Carboniferous Limestone and that quarrying is now the chief source of employment in the National Park. Quarries are well scattered throughout the region, most obtrusively in the Earl Sterndale/Buxton/Peak Dale area. In addition rake mining is used to obtain certain minerals, as at Longstone Edge, where

15 *The Via Gellia is a thickly wooded limestone valley with a wealth of bird life which includes Nuthatches, Redstarts, Wood Warblers and Sparrowhawks. (S. Jackson)*

16 *Topley Pike, near Buxton. Limestone quarries cover a huge acreage in the Peak District, and hold breeding Kestrels, Stockdoves and Jackdaws. (S. Jackson)*

fluorspar is extracted. Limestone quarries hold large colonies of Jackdaws, and quite considerable populations of Stockdoves, while most disused faces of any size have a pair of breeding Kestrels. House Martins have not been slow to colonise those quarries which lie close to rivers, and Little Ringed Plovers have nested on at least one quarry floor.

At Middleton Moor and Peak Dale, and to a lesser degree at Harborough, lagoons associated with mineral waste have proved attractive to concentrations of gulls and migrant water birds. Rarer species have included Shelduck, Turnstone, Little Stint, Knot, Purple Sandpiper and Little Gull.

The Central Gritstone region

This relatively small region of 92 square miles lies in central north Derbyshire on either side of the River Derwent between Bamford in the north and Ambergate in the south. Except for small inliers of Carboniferous Limestone at Ashover and Crich the rock is Millstone Grit – so called because millstones for grinding corn were made from it. Most of the region is encompassed by the Peak District National Park (a triangular section from Rowsley to Press to Crich lying outside it), on account of its fine scenery with appealing woodland and moorland landscapes on either side of the relatively lush Derwent Valley. The area outside the National Park is by no means unattractive, with upland farming generally replacing moorland.

The lowest ground is 220 feet by the Derwent at Ambergate, the highest 1,418 feet at Sir William Hill, while east of the river Totley Moss reaches 1,296 feet. Altitude greatly affects climate; for example Chatsworth in the Derwent Valley has an average rainfall of 34.7 inches a year, yet adjacent moorland receives over forty inches. Because of the climate and the generally damp nature of the ground, settlement in the central gritstone region is largely confined to low ground and valley bottoms.

The eastern moors stretch unbroken from Totley Moss in the north almost as far as Matlock, whereas west of the Derwent is a single large moorland block comprising Abney, Eyam and Offerton Moors. Of these two areas, the East Moors are ornithologically much the better known. Scarcely over 1,000 feet high they generally dip eastwards but overlook the Derwent in a series of striking, west-facing escarpments known as edges. The East Moors were once wooded but centuries of burning, sheep grazing, and more recently the effects of atmospheric pollution, have changed them. Now the area is largely composed of Heather communities, with some grassland dominated by Purple Moor grass and tracts of Bilberry. Where there is a thicker covering of peat, cottongrass moorland occurs at relatively low altitudes as on Leash Fen and Totley Moss. East Moor is largely treeless though some scattered birches and a few stunted hawthorns grow up to 1,250 feet.

The bird life of the moors varies greatly according to season. In winter a birdwatcher may spend a full day walking through the heather and cotton grass seeing little more than a few Red Grouse and Carrion Crows. More usually, though, a few Reed Buntings and Wrens, odd lingering Meadow Pipits and Skylarks, and perhaps one or two Stonechats will be encountered. Hen Harriers are seen most winters, usually between Big Moor and Brampton East Moor. Often Hen Harriers are accompanied by Merlins, the falcon appearing to 'wait on' its larger relative. Rarely Snow Buntings may be flushed from stony or burnt-out stretches.

These moors become much more interesting in spring. In mild weather Skylarks return from the lowlands from February onwards, always a little before Meadow Pipits. By mid or late April both species are in full numbers, the pipit being easily the most numerous breeding species on the heather moors. Skylarks may also be found in heather but prefer more grassy stretches. Reed Buntings, small numbers of Linnets and Twites, and Whinchats take up territory in April and May. Evening visits may reveal

17   *The East Moors near Beeley. Whinchats nest in the Bracken beds, with Ring Ouzels and formerly Merlins along the rocky edges. (S. Jackson)*

18   *Big Moor is part of the East Moors, which are well known for their wintering Hen Harriers and Merlins. (S. Jackson)*

a quite high Snipe population when the male birds make their remarkable bleating. Curlews may be slowly declining however, and Golden Plover are very scarce breeding birds in this region. At one time nesting Merlins were not so uncommon but this engaging falcon has decreased rapidly in recent times. Short-eared Owls sometimes nest in the more isolated parts.

In autumn the moors hold quite large populations of birds for a time: in particular in the rocks, and in a few quiet areas breed a few pairs of Ring Ouzels and Kestrels. The areas below the edges, dominated by Bilberry, Heather and Bracken hold good populations of Whinchats and in a very few places, Nightjars too.

Further north in England and in Scotland large areas of moorland have been afforested with softwoods. In Derbyshire this has not happened on any large scale except on Matlock Moor where some hundreds of acres of

19 *Matlock Forest is the Derbyshire stronghold of Nightjars, which nest among the young plantations. Sparrowhawks and Long-eared Owls inhabit some of the older stands of trees. (S. Jackson)*

Meadow Pipits and Twite may form big flocks, but these and most other species quickly retreat to lower ground with the coming of cold weather, and the moors will then become relatively deserted until the Skylarks return the following spring.

The rocky edges are better known to rock climbers than ornithologists. Indeed the presence of hundreds of climbers at weekends must have a detrimental effect upon the breeding success of certain sensitive species. Jackdaws nest colonially in holes and fissures

young conifers are admixed with a few taller stands. This is the county's Nightjar stronghold with up to a dozen churring males in recent years. Long-eared Owls and Sparrowhawks nest in some of the older plantations.

The dominant tree of the Millstone Grit valleys and cloughs is the Sessile Oak which grows up to about 800 feet. Especially interesting oakwoods occur around Holloway, Abney and on the Chatsworth Estate: however, most birdwatchers would regard Padley Wood (also known as Padley Gorge) near

20 *Padley Gorge is the Derbyshire headquarters of the Pied Flycatcher. Woodpeckers, Wood Warblers and Hawfinches also breed here. (S. Jackson)*

Grindleford as outstanding. With its old Oaks, Birches and Rowans and its stream tumbling over great boulders it is a pleasant place at any time of year. In spring and early summer Padley Wood is alive with the songs and calls of numerous tits, warblers including Wood Warblers, Green and Great Spotted Woodpeckers, Redstarts and notably several Pied Flycatchers. Padley was the first breeding site in Derbyshire for this diminutive beauty; in recent years it has begun to breed in several other woods.

Excepting the new Matlock Forest discussed above there are several areas of coniferous woodland of which Longshaw is perhaps the most interesting. With its clumps of pines and open heathland, Longshaw is a favourite resort of irrupting Crossbills which

small acreage of arable crops is aimed largely at home consumption. Hedges are scarce except where there are underlying shales, drystone walls being much more usual. Most fields are small. Many have been reseeded and 'improved' since the last war but there remain many fields of rough grass with rushes beloved of nesting Lapwings, Curlews and, if wet enough, Snipe too. Miss H. C. Rodgers and others have carried out a common birds census on 120 acres near Hathersage since 1967. The land, ranging from 500 to 1,000 feet in altitude, is mainly pastoral but includes a bracken-covered bank, a little heather moorland, pine woodland, and boggy ground. The commonest species are Blackbird, Chaffinch and Wren, followed by Willow Warbler, Robin and

21 *Longshaw, where open heathland intermixes with clumps of conifers, which regularly attract Crossbills in eruption years. (S. Jackson)*

have stayed to nest at least once. Siskins may also be breeding there. Buzzards may nest regularly in another wood in the Central Gritstone region.

In the non-moorland parts of this region farming is dominated by dairying and the

Meadow Pipit.

This region is not well-endowed with waters. The only one of major importance is Barbrook Reservoir on Big Moor, covering 30 acres and standing at 1,070 feet. A few duck and waders breed but its chief interest is in autumn when a falling water level usually proves suitable for the reception of migrating water birds. A large gull roost forms at this season. Nearby Ramsley Reservoir is much less important though duck are often present and waders fairly regular when the water level is low. Both Barbrook and Ramsley were constructed around the turn of the century. Flash Dam near Matlock and Press Reservoirs near Ashover occasionally produce interesting wildfowl records.

A good number of duck are usually present on the lakes in the magnificent Chatsworth Park, and Mallard and Tufted in some numbers, and a few Teal, stay to nest. Many of the ducks from Chatsworth's lakes visit the Derwent, here flowing quite passively, and in really hard weather unusual species are sometimes found. Grey Wagtails, Dippers and Common Sandpipers nest by the river. The wagtail and Dipper breed freely on several other streams and small rivers in the Central Gritstone region, but Common Sandpipers are more localised.

The breeding birds of the River Derwent from Bamford at 500 feet to Beeley at 350 feet were censussed in 1974–5 by the Waterways Bird Survey. The river, lined in many places with Alders, flows through pastures and mixed woodlands. An average of 171 bird territories were found on this nineteen kilometre stretch, with Mallard and Moorhen accounting for slightly more than half overall; next in order were Pied Wagtail, Dipper, Grey Wagtail, Tufted Duck and Common Sandpiper.

Cromford Canal, in the extreme south of the area, runs alongside the Derwent and, passing through some pleasant oak and birch woodland, is a popular spot with ornithologists. Grey Wagtails and Dippers breed, as do interesting passerines including Pied Flycatcher and Hawfinch. Siskins visit the Alders in some numbers in winter.

The Coal Measures region

Coal Measures sandstones, clays, shales and coal seams cover a large area of eastern Derbyshire, from the South Yorkshire boundary near Sheffield in the north as far south as Stanton by Dale. In the east the Coal Measures stretch into Nottinghamshire though from Ault Hucknall northwards they dip under the Magnesian Limestone. The western boundary is less easily defined as the coal underlies part of the Millstone Grit of the lower Peak District. Hulme's boundary cuts across the East Moors, and part of Leash Fen and Brampton East Moor are therefore placed in the Coal Measures region. However these moorland areas have more obvious topographical and ornithological connections with the Central Gritstone region, and are therefore described there. Further south this western boundary also encompasses Wingerworth, South Wingfield, Belper and Smalley.

Though geomorphologically modified by mining, industry and settlement, the 200 square miles covered by the Coal Measures is very much a 'ridge and valley' region, the long ridges composed of sandstones and the valleys shales. Most of the ridges run north to south though some spurs of land extend eastwards from the Peak District hills. The higher ground is 1,296 feet at Flask Edge and the lowest 148 feet in the Rother Valley. Altitude naturally affects climate, parts of the hills having some 35 inches of rain a year, whilst most of the lowlands average between 27 and 30 inches. Similarly the higher ground has the greatest snowfall, the highest incidence of fog and the strongest winds.

East of a line drawn through Chesterfield, Clay Cross and Ripley there are few sizeable areas unaffected by mining and one cannot travel far without seeing colliery tips and headstocks or farmland bearing the legacies of opencast mining. Mining, associated manufacturing industries and settlement have given rise to a high level of scenic complexity. Even so there remain a few villages whose character is agricultural rather than industrial and some unmodified woods, small valleys and other features. Mining has not so metamorphosed the area west of the line: there are more hills, a good proportion of woodland and some fast flowing, clear streams. The Cordwell and Moss Valleys and the hills around Holymoorside remind one that the Coal Measures region must have been one of very fine scenery before the need for coal.

Coal has been mined from mediaeval times. At first it was obtained only where it outcropped or lay very near the surface. Pilkington (1789) considered a shaft of 222 feet near West Hallam exceptional. By about 1800 there were eighty-six active mines in the region with many more already abandoned. For about a century thereafter mining flourished but this century has seen a marked decline and only eleven collieries and a few small mines in eastern Derbyshire are now active. Although reserves in the region are said to be considerable the most productive mines in this coalfield are now further north and east in Yorkshire and Nottinghamshire.

Coal itself forms only a very small proportion of the rock layer called Coal Measures. Several brickyards have produced their goods from the coal shales, and local iron ores led to the establishment of many small iron and steel industries. Like the coal mines these two latter industries have diminished, and though a few large iron and steel concerns still exist in the Chesterfield and Ilkeston areas, almost all of the iron ore is now imported from elsewhere.

In many places where the good quality coal seams were too thin to be worked economically underground they have been won by opencast mining. Since 1940, 25,000 acres of Derbyshire land have been thus affected. In effect this means that large quarries are usually present for a few years until the rock and soil not required is returned. Usually the site is then reinstated to agricultural land though in a few places small scale forestry or recreational parks have been found to be better substitutes.

All in all mining and its implications have profoundly changed the local landscape and bird populations. Colliery head buildings rarely attract birds other than House Sparrows and Starlings, though Barn Owls and Kestrels may find suitable nesting sites in them. All collieries have adjacent tips of coal waste, which increase the already broken nature of the relief. Where shales have been fired by spontaneous combustion these tips are strikingly reddish; otherwise they are usually grey in colour. The older tips were generally the smallest both in area and height (though occasionally exceeding 200 feet), and while the newer ones rarely exceed 100 feet they may cover thirty acres or more. J. H. Johnson has described in detail the vegetation of undisturbed tips in *The Flora of Derbyshire* (1969). Birch and other trees readily colonise and with plants such as Rosebay Willowherb and Gorse these tips are attractive to several species of birds, notably Redpolls, Whitethroats and Yellowhammers. More interesting in some ways are the newer, largely unvegetated tips which are similar to those of the Magnesian Limestone region in attracting breeding Little Ringed Plovers, both species of partridge and Meadow Pipits albeit little else. Colliery tips are undoubtedly eyesores and many have been removed or levelled in recent years. However, they do hold the bulk of the county's Little Ringed Plover population and additionally form superb viewpoints over the surrounding land.

Where opencast mining takes place the top soil is removed and stored nearby in large bare mounds which initially form loafing spots for gulls, particularly Lesser Blackbacks. Usually they become overgrown with grasses and tall weeds which then often attract large numbers of Linnets and other finches. Otherwise opencast mining sites are unproductive places for the ornithologist. Furthermore, following restoration to farming land, ugly wire fences are erected where hedges once stood, many hedge and tree nesting species thereby being deprived of sites. No birds nest on wire fences.

One of the better ornithological side effects of coal mining has been the creation of shallow lakes – known locally as flashes – owing to subsidence. When coal is extracted the land surface can subside by up to two thirds of the thickness of the seam. If this occurs where the water table is near the land

22　*A typical subsidence lake in the Erewash Valley, near Brinsley. Such sites support good populations of wildfowl, migrant waders and breeding Reed and Sedge Warblers. (S. Jackson)*

surface, permanent flooding may result. Small stretches of water have been created in this way in the valleys of Erewash, Doe Lea, and Rother – the latter two, sadly, listed amongst Britain's filthiest rivers. However, by far the most interesting subsidence lake existed at Westhouses from the early 1950s until the late 1960s when it was drained. About eight acres of shallow water and mud attracted large numbers of water birds, especially waders – twenty-seven species were recorded in the few years from 1965. The future of most other subsidence lakes, where conditions are often ideal for dabbling ducks and waders, is similarly uncertain.

The Coal Measures region is quite well endowed with other waters. There are large drinking water storage reservoirs at Ogston and Linacre and several canal feeder reser-voirs, notably at Butterley, Codnor Park and Mapperley. Ogston Reservoir, near Clay Cross, is undoubtedly the most popular spot in Derbyshire for ornithologists. Covering 206 acres with pleasant pastoral and wooded surroundings, it was flooded in 1958, largely to supply the N.C.B. Carbonisation Plant at Wingerworth. Over 190 species of birds have been recorded there, though fishing and yachting now cause a great deal of disturb-ance. A Wilson's Phalarope in 1965 was the pick of the bird list; other species have in-cluded all three divers, Ferruginous Duck, Green-winged Teal, Temminck's Stint and White-winged Black Tern. Its main interest now is in winter when a large wildfowl popu-lation vies with thousands of roosting gulls for the attention of the many birdwatchers. Iceland and Glaucous Gulls appear with some degree of regularity in the gull roost. Terns are regular – once, over a hundred were seen – and migrant waders frequently call and are sometimes numerous.

Butterley Reservoir is very much older than Ogston, having been built to feed the canal running from Cromford to the Erewash valley. It has long been known as one of the county's chief haunts of the Great Crested Grebe. As at Ogston, though, fishing

shaw Park, and the small wildfowl reserve at Birdholme.

The clays and alluvial soils hold several smaller marshes though many have been drained. Sometimes Snipe and Redshank nest in them, and Lapwings are often more numerous close to such damp areas. If colonised by Reed or Greater Reedmace these marshes become roosting sites for Buntings, Wagtails, and so on. Particularly important

23   Ogston Reservoir is undoubtedly the most popular birdwatching site for Derbyshire's ornithologists. (S. Jackson)

and more recently sailing have disturbed the grebes and other wildfowl. Terns are often seen in the spring or autumn but the reservoir banks are not suitable for waders. There are smaller canal feeder reservoirs occasionally productive of interesting records at Mapperley and Codnor Park. Other waters worth at least an occasional visit are the reservoirs at Linacre and Crowhole, the attractive lakes at Stubbing Court and Reni-

in this respect are the marshes at Old Whittington and Williamthorpe Colliery Reservoir; at the latter site up to 180 Corn Buntings, 300 Pied Wagtails, and 5,000 Swallows have been recorded. This small water was once noted for its rare migrants but is now greatly disturbed by the residents of Holmewood, and waders and duck, though calling regularly, rarely linger.

Before leaving the Coal Measures

wetlands mention should be made of two sewage farms, both in the north of the region, at Staveley and Old Whittington. Here the sludge lagoons attract a variety of small birds and a few waders, though in much smaller quantity than those at Egginton and Willington in the Trent Valley.

Industry has had a considerable effect on farming patterns in the Coal Measures region, and consequently on birds of agricultural habitats. Much land has been taken for building, trespass has increased, subsidence has caused drainage problems and pollution has had its effects. On the other hand, farms are now nearer urban services and there is a ready market for perishable products. Dairying is the main type of farming. This, together with the rather clayey soils has resulted in a preponderance of permanent grassland, though a considerable acreage is under arable. In the west of our region, on the higher ground falling from the Pennines, the farms may be only twenty acres or so, and any arable land is usually given over to cereals or root crops for the dairy herd. Further east, in the more urbanised areas, the incidence of arable land increases and the farming is more mixed, with some cash crops such as potatoes, wheat and barley.

An interesting account of a typical year's birdwatching on a Coal Measures farm is found in *Bird Watcher's Year* (1973) in which M. J. Wareing describes the relationship between birds and land use on his 200 acre farm known as The Breck at Barrowhill, near Staveley, one of the most industrial parishes in Derbyshire. This farm may be considered typical of many in this region (except that part of it is prone to regular flooding and thus attracts water birds). A common birds census carried out there by Mrs B. A. Moore and others showed Skylark and Blackbird to be easily the commonest species, with Dunnock, Yellowhammer and Partridge sub-dominant. The results of this census and those from Mr W. S. Jacklin's farm at Tibshelf, part of which lies in Derbyshire, are utilised in the systematic list.

Many ornithologists would consider farmland an unexciting habitat. While this is largely true there is nevertheless no lack of interest for ornithologists with enquiring minds. The Golden Plover flocks visiting the Coal Measures lowlands in winter seem to have decreased, while those on the nearby Magnesian Limestone have held their own or increased in recent years. Is this a case of population shift? Could it be that the bird prefers the larger fields created by hedgerow removal on the limestone? Both species of partridge are found but here the Red-legged is much scarcer than its relative, despite introductions for sporting purposes. The countrywide decline of Grey Partridges is alarming both ornithologists and shooters. Changes in agricultural methods, such as stubble burning and early cutting of silage, seem to be the most likely reasons. Yet in the Coal Measures their numbers seem little altered. Grey Partridges are very often found on colliery tips: could these ugly hills in some ways have helped our local partridges to survive? What effect does air pollution from collieries and chemical works have on farmland birds, if any? These and many more questions remain to be answered.

Woodland on the Coal Measures has been greatly fragmented by mining and settlement. The larger woods are now mainly in the hillier western part of the region. Oak is probably the climax tree and some of the more interesting oakwoods are Hardwick Wood near Wingerworth and Carr Wood at Ogston, with others at Linacre and in the Cordwell and Moss Valleys. In addition to the more widespread breeding species there are small numbers of Redstarts, Wood Warblers, and three species of Woodpecker. Pied Flycatchers have held territories in some of these woods but have so far failed to win mates.

In some places, for example around Unstone, birch is dominant, at least temporarily. Birchwoods lack the variety of species found in oakwoods but harbour larger numbers of Redpolls and Bullfinches in particular. Hawthorn thickets are scattered throughout the region, often quite close to urbanisation; they usually hold good numbers of breeding and winter species.

A few coniferous woods have been established to replace deciduous woodland or unproductive farmland, or on reinstated opencast land. Unlike the Magnesian Limestone region, where Corsican Pine predominates, a variety of coniferous species has been planted. These woods will become more interesting as they mature. The older conifer woods in the area have attracted nesting Redpolls and Goldcrests, whilst Sparrowhawks also nest in a few of them, especially those containing tall Larches.

The Magnesian Limestone region

In the north-eastern corner of the county is found a narrow band of Magnesian Limestone belonging to the Permian System. It is part of a long strip of limestone running from Nottingham to North Yorkshire. Thus it is bounded in the north and east by the South Yorkshire and Nottinghamshire county boundaries. Technically its western boundary is the foot of an impressive escarpment running from Hardwick in the south to Barlborough in the north. However, Hulme in the 'Index of Derbyshire Localities' (1962) used the rivers Doe Lea and Rother as the boundary, and I have followed suit.

Scenically the Magnesian Limestone region with a total area of fifty-two square miles, is quite different from the coal measures country to the west. Apart from the escarpment where only a thin capping of limestone covers coal shales, the whole area lies on a dip slope running towards the Bunter Sandstone of Nottinghamshire. The land is gently undulating and intensively cultivated: there are large blocks of woodland and small steep-sided valleys, often with low cliffs. These features, combined with the relative lack of heavy industry, give the region a pleasant, rural character. The altitudinal limits are 140 feet near Killamarsh and 613 feet at Palterton, and rainfall is usually between twenty-five and thirty inches a year.

The reddish, slightly alkaline, soils are well-drained (though in places stony), and

eminently suited to the farming of cereals, potatoes and beef. Sheep rearing was once important but attacks by uncontrolled dogs from nearby villages have led to a decline. Both farmsteads and fields tend to be large, and many fields are still increasing in size as a result of the cutting-out of Hawthorn hedges. In some places drystone walls are found instead of hedges. Of terrestrial birds, the Skylark is easily the most common nesting in large numbers on headlands and among crops. Both species of Partridge are widespread, a recent census at Scarcliffe suggesting that Grey Partridges outnumber Red-legged Partridges by about three to one. Their small relative, the Quail, is heard somewhere in the region in most summers and would probably be proved an annual visitor with more observation. Isolated small trees and telegraph wires form song posts for Corn Buntings which breed widely but tend to occur in small concentrations. Turtle Doves are more numerous hereabouts than anywhere else in the county, feeding on weeds growing among cereals and breeding in Hawthorn clumps or nearby woodlands. Lapwings still breed in the fields but the demand for more efficient farming has led to a rather low density.

In winter the local Lapwings are either replaced or augmented by immigrants from the north and east and large flocks occur. At the same time these are joined by Golden Plovers, most of which are probably of Scandinavian origin, as by April many show the bold plumage of the Northern race. Elmton, Whitwell and Hardwick are particularly favoured by these attractive waders. In winter, too, flocks of pigeons, thrushes and finches add life to the silent fields, and partridges occur in sizeable coveys.

The region contains several interesting woods, especially those at Scarcliffe and Whitwell, which have been well worked by ornithologists. In addition there is a large, lesser-known wood at Pleasley and several small blocks and fox-coverts. In some ways these woodlands have similarities to the well-known Sherwood Forest of Nottinghamshire, with which they were presumably con-

24 *Scarcliffe Park, which held a large population of Hawfinches until the 1960s. (S. Jackson)*

tinuous at one time. Scarcliffe parish contains three large woods amounting to about a thousand acres. Until the early 1960s these were mainly deciduous with much Birch and Hazel scrub and no single dominant climax species. They held a great wealth of bird life including an estimated fifty pairs of Hawfinches, probably the greatest concentration in Britain. However in the past decade thinning and clear-felling and subsequent replanting with Corsican pine has greatly transformed them. Now only a few Hawfinches remain in the taller stands and many other woodland birds have declined. But in their places have come more Redpolls, Whitethroats, Grasshopper Warblers and other species attracted to the young pine plantations. The two Forestry Commission plantations of Whitwell Wood and Pleasley Park are both rather even-aged, but

support good numbers of Turtle Doves, Redpolls, Woodcock and many commoner species. In winter all of these woodlands hold good numbers of feeding and roosting birds.

All of the few streams and small rivers run roughly west to east. They are mainly unpolluted, and a few ducks and Moorhens nest by them. On the more sluggish stretches a few Snipe may be seen and Water Rails skulk in willowherb patches in winter. In places some of the streams have cut into the rock to form small, steep-sided valleys with rocky outcrops which are locally known as 'grips', and at Creswell the Millwood Brook flows between fifty foot cliffs called Creswell Crags. Stock Doves and Spotted Flycatchers characterise such areas. Apart from streams, and colliery lagoons, dealt with below, surface water is scarce. The only waters of any size are at Hardwick Park and Pebley. Hardwick has

25　*Woodland and arable farmland mix on the Magnesian Limestone plateau near Elmton.*
(S. Jackson)

two small lakes and half a dozen ponds. Early this century C. B. Chambers recorded a variety of visiting water birds but since then ornithological interest has declined owing to silting and disturbance. The lakes have recently been dredged, and since this part of the Hardwick Estate is now a Country Park with swimming, canoeing and fishing to be catered for, it is unlikely that the lakes will revert to their former level of interest. More rewarding is Pebley Pond, near Barlborough, a small feeder reservoir for the Chesterfield Canal. Its islet usually supports a pair of Canada Geese (the only regular breeding pair in north Derbyshire) and Tufted Ducks and Great Crested Grebes breed in most years. The winter wildfowl population is fairly small and migrant waders, terns, and the like, are occasional.

Ornithologists have found much interest at two marshes in the west of the region just below the scarp. Much the larger, until it was destroyed by opencast coal-mining in 1976, was at Killamarsh Meadows, where the boggy ground supported a large bed of Reedmace with some Reed-grass and scattered clumps of willows. The rare Water Rail bred here along with Snipe, and Sedge and Grasshopper Warblers. Water Rails and Snipe were relatively common in winter when they were joined by a few Jack Snipe, and at times large numbers of hirundines, thrushes, wagtails and buntings roosted in the Reedmace. The other marsh is improbably sandwiched between Bolsover Colliery and a large chemical works. Here about one and a half acres of shallow water have been colonised by the Common Reed. This is a favourite roosting plant of certain species and up to 300 Reed Buntings, 270 Corn Buntings and 250 Pied Wagtails have used the marsh. However the site's future is being jeopardised by infilling with coal waste.

As previously mentioned the impact of industry is less on the Magnesian Limestone than on the Coal Measures. A few collieries have drilled through the limestone to reach coal below and nearly all of the consequent waste heaps hold breeding Little Ringed Plovers. The only other regular breeding species of these artificial grey hills is the Meadow Pipit, though Red-legged Partridges are often seen. A few ducks and gulls frequent colliery lagoons and migrant waders occasionally call, but a lack of food prevents any of them from staying long. Magnesian Limestone has been extensively quarried at Steetley, Whitwell and Bolsover Moor. At Steetley the large quarry floor, dotted with small pools, has played host to up to six pairs of Little Ringed Plovers since 1958. Little Stint and Sanderling are among the migrant waders which have been seen at this site, but recent infilling with coal waste has reduced its ornithological value.

The High Peak region

This is by far the most rugged region of the county, occupying about 174 square miles in the north-western corner. It is roughly triangular, with a line from Hathersage through Edale to Axe Edge as its base. Its other boundaries are formed by the borders of Staffordshire, Cheshire, Lancashire and Yorkshire. The rock is Millstone Grit, which has produced the dominating high plateaux of Kinder Scout, Bleaklow and Black Hill, which reach 2,088, 2,061 and 1,908 feet. Axe Edge, close to the Staffordshire border, stands at 1,810 feet. The lowest ground is 370 feet at New Mills in the rather densely populated lowlands of the extreme northwest.

The rainfall on Kinder Scout is high, averaging some 63 inches a year, whereas some of the valleys only a few miles away receive less than 40 inches. Axe Edge averages over 50 inches a year. Rain falls on at least 225 days in the year, about fifty more than in southern Derbyshire, and of course snow cover persists longer than anywhere else in the county. Low cloud, hill fog and strong winds are frequent. The high rainfall has led to the creation of numerous reservoirs, most

of them of limited ornithological value. Settlement and agriculture are largely confined to valleys and lower ground.

Most ornithologists would think first and foremost of moorland when considering this region. The high moorlands, of which Bleaklow has been the best-studied, have a distinctive avifauna which includes Red Grouse, Golden Plover, Snipe, Dunlin, Curlew, Twite, Wheatear, Ring Ouzel, Merlin and Short-eared Owl. The tops of Kinder Scout, Bleaklow and Black Hill are capped with peat which has been eroded to form hillocks supporting little vegetation other than Crowberry. Such areas have very limited birdlife – usually only a few Red Grouse and Meadow Pipits and an occasional pair of Golden Plover. Below the summits but generally at about 1,500 feet the flatter stretches of moorland are dominated by cotton-grass which appears to have largely replaced *sphagnum* within the last 150 years, perhaps as a result of sheep grazing and trampling. In this zone birdlife is more abundant with the plaintive piping of Golden Plover and the reeling of Dunlin frequent sounds in some places. Heather dominates the region between 1,250 (sometimes lower) and 1,500 feet. Heather moorland, often systematically burned in the principles of good grouse management, has still greater bird densities with Red Grouse and Meadow Pipits often abundant, and Twite favour this zone. Below 1,250 feet most moors are of Mat-grass on damp soils or Common Bent-grass and Sheep's Fescue in drier conditions.

The moors are extensively grazed by sheep. Grazing rights on the various moors are often ancient and sheep belonging to several owners may be found in the same area. Often it is difficult to distinguish any boundary between moorland and farmland, of such poor quality is some of the latter. Cultivation extends in places to 1,000 feet and exceptionally to 1,500 feet on Win Hill. High altitude root fields are often popular with winter finches. Field boundaries are usually stone walls with some hedges on the shales.

The most recent quantitative information on the birdlife of a High Peak farm has

26　*Hoo Moor in the Goyt Valley is one of only two or three sites where Black Grouse may now be found. (S. Jackson)*

kindly been provided by A. W. Jones who in 1972 surveyed 200 acres of farmland between 850 and 1,100 feet on the eastern slopes of Fernilee Reservoir. Jones found Skylarks, with 40 pairs, the commonest species, followed by Meadow Pipits (28 pairs) and Lapwings at the high density of 26 pairs. The eight pairs of Curlew and five pairs of Wheatear also represented good populations of those species.

Often as interesting (or more so) than the moorlands themselves are the moorland valleys, which are known as cloughs if steep and rocky enough. These vary from narrow defiles to such grandiose valleys as Alport Dale. Ring Ouzels are characteristic birds of rocky valley sides, using rocks and stunted trees as songposts. Whinchats may often be found in the same areas, especially if Bracken beds are present, with Wheatears in suitably barren places. A very few pairs of the now rare Merlin frequent remote localities.

Twites occur in bracken and heather areas in broader valleys. The rocky gritstone edges, very popular with climbers like those in the Central Gritstone region, hold Ring Ouzels, Wheatears and Kestrels. Isolated cliffs and tors may also hold these three species, and Peregrine and Raven have bred on one of them in the past twenty-five years. The fast flowing streams hold Dippers, Pied and Grey Wagtails and Common Sandpipers.

Winter brings desolation to the high moorlands of this region. On the rare days when a breeze is absent the silence may be most striking. As on the East Moors a full day may reveal little more than the ubiquitous Red Grouse unless the observer is lucky enough to stumble across a few Snow Buntings or spot an occasional Hen Harrier or Hooded Crow.

The High Peak region is poorly endowed with woodland. A few semi-natural oak-birch woodlands exist in Longdendale,

27 *Longdendale, with some huge boulders on the moor edges. (S. Jackson)*

28 *Howden Reservoir. Only small numbers of wildfowl utilise the reservoir but the surrounding conifer woods are more interesting. (S. Jackson)*

around Ladybower and in a few other places. Though harbouring tits, warblers, Tree Pipits, Redpolls and so on, they are not so species-rich as those of the Central Gritstone. Pied Flycatchers have occasionally nested in certain oakwoods but apparently nowhere with any regularity. The Goyt Valley woodlands, Shire Hill near Glossop and the Kinder Valley woodlands east of Hayfield appear worthy of investigation. There are stretches of hawthorn scrub, for example, near Bamford, Hathersage and Padfield, which attract winter thrushes and sometimes large numbers of Waxwings.

Since 1974 Anne Shaw has surveyed a plot of about thirty acres near New Mills. Broadhurst Edge Wood, most of which is a reserve of the Derbyshire Naturalists' Trust, comprises nineteen acres of Sessile Oak and Birch woodland, with a mixture of other species

and an understorey of Heather and Bilberry. Willow Warbler was easily the most numerous species, followed by Blackbird, Robin, Wren and, surprisingly, Redpoll. The rest of the census area consisted of a rough damp field with a streamlet, about eleven acres in size. Skylark was the dominant species in this habitat.

Coniferous woodland now occupies a much greater acreage than broad-leaved woodland, though it is largely confined to valley sides. There are large tracts of spruce, Lodgepole Pine and other conifers in the Derwent and Goyt Valleys and the Snake area. Smaller plantations have been established elsewhere. After planting such areas tend to retain the species of the replaced habitat for a while, often gaining others like Whinchats and Grasshopper Warblers. As the trees grow, true moorland birds such as Red

Grouse, Curlew and Meadow Pipit disappear, and for many years thereafter such plantations may be very dull ornithologically.

They again become more interesting towards maturity. The older closed canopy fir woodlands of the High Peak usually hold Goldcrests, Coal Tits, Chaffinches, Wood-pigeons, thrushes and a few other species. Where these mature conifers are more open, or admixed with other trees, as in parts of the Derwent valley, birdlife is much more varied and abundant and includes such species as Great Spotted Woodpeckers, Treecreepers, Tawny and Long-eared Owls, Woodcocks and Sparrowhawks. Black Grouse retain a very tenuous hold on the Goyt Valley woodlands and one or two other areas.

Although there are many reservoirs in this part of Derbyshire, the elevation and acidity of many of them limits their attractiveness to birds. The six large reservoirs in Longdendale, mentioned in Whitlock, were constructed between 1849 and 1877. The largest is 160 acres. Black-headed Gulls have recently bred at these reservoirs and there are a few pairs of Mallard and Common Sandpipers. Mallard numbers sometimes attain three figures outside the breeding season, when other species of wildfowl may be seen.

Just south-east of Longdendale lies the Derwent chain of reservoirs – Howden, Derwent and the great Ladybower with its thir-teen-mile shoreline. All three have retaining walls between 114 and 140 feet high and up to 1,250 feet long. Small numbers of Mallard are regular with lesser numbers of Teal and occasional diving ducks including sawbills in hard weather. Rarer visitors have included Red-throated Diver, Gannet, Velvet Scoter and Glaucous Gull. Further west, Combs Reservoir near Chapel-en-le-Frith is the major reservoir for the ornithologists of the Buxton–Chapel area. Despite heavy fishing and yachting many interesting observations have been made. Combs is a very old reservoir constructed between 1794 and 1800 as a canal feeder, like nearby Toddbrook. It is less acidic than most of the other reservoirs hereabouts and has gently-sloping banks. The two reservoirs in the Goyt Valley, Fernilee and Errwood (flooded in 1937 and 1967) have been well-watched by Buxton ornithologists who have noted such rare species as Puffin and Leach's Petrel and breeding Mergansers.

There are few other wetlands of interest in the High Peak region. The small sewage farms at Hathersage, Hayfield, New Mills and Glossop may hold good numbers of wagtails and pipits. Gulls are sometimes numerous at rubbish tips in the area, the constituent species of the flocks often differing markedly from those in the lowland regions.

The Systematic List

The list includes all modern-day species recorded in Derbyshire: for details of prehistoric birds, see Appendix 3. Order, British and Latin names are those in BTO Guide 13, *A Species List of British and Irish Birds* except in the case of the Tree Swallow where I followed Gruson (1976). Current status generally accords with that in *The Derbyshire Bird Report 1975*, though modification was necessary in some cases. Place names generally follow Ordnance Survey usage. Plant names here and elsewhere in the book, are those found in Clapham, Tutin and Warburg's *Flora of the British Isles* (1952); lists of Latin names of plants and other orders comprise Appendices 4 and 5.

Observations from localities no longer within the county boundary are included if the record referred to Derbyshire at the time. All published records up to 31 December 1977 have been taken into account. In modern times 273 species have been recorded in the county up to that date.

References are omitted if the record was originally published in the *DAJ* or DOS reports. Observers' names are generally supplied only for first sightings or for species recorded five times or fewer this century; or for first breeding records or first this century; or for hitherto unpublished records. The source of ringing recoveries is not given: most of these were obtained from the ringers or ringing groups concerned, or from *British Birds*.

From 1958 the *British Birds* Rarities Committee has adjudicated on records of nationally rare species. Unless otherwise stated, all relevant records in the list have gained the committee's acceptance. The few records rejected by the committee have been excluded. The same applies to local rarities, records of which are judged by the DOS Rare Birds Committee.

For most breeding species there is information on habitat, distribution and numbers or densities (where known). For wintering or summering species or passage migrants, typical and extreme dates are supplied. Records of those birds which have occurred fewer than five times this century are stated in full. Ringing recoveries of interest are noted, as is any other relevant information such as flocking or visible movement.

Black-throated Diver
Gavia arctica
Rare winter visitor.

There are eight records of single birds between 1897 and 1975. Both the first and last were at Combs Reservoir, in January or February 1897 and October and November 1975. In between these dates there were records from Beauchief Dam, Sheffield, in February and March, 1938; Staveley on 3 April 1947; Buxton in November 1951; Bakewell in October 1955 and probably the same bird at Allestree Lake the following month; and in December 1972 at Ogston Reservoir.

Great Northern Diver
Gavia immer
Rare winter visitor.

In the nineteenth century there were five dated records and several other possible occurrences from the Trent, the lower reaches of the Dove and Derwent, Darley, Ockbrook and between Peak Forest and Tideswell. This century there are but five records – from Williamthorpe in December 1931 (C. B. Chambers), the Derwent at Rowsley in January and February 1942 (R. Eglinton), Staunton Harold Reservoir on 15–23 May 1968 (R. W. Key, T. G. Smith), Ogston Reservoir on 21–25 December 1969 (M. F. Stoyle *et al*) and again on 2–24 November 1977 (many observers). All were seen between November and February with the exception of the May bird in 1968 and one on 1 August (1899).

Red-throated Diver
Gavia stellata
Rare winter visitor.

Red-throated Divers are the most frequent of the divers to visit Derbyshire although it seems likely that they are not as regular as formerly. Several records were quoted by Whitlock: many, including 'quite a little flock' were seen on the Trent in severe weather in 1848. Seventeen singles have occurred since 1893, in all months between 13 September (1974) and 29 April (1969) with most in January. Localities include the Rivers Trent, Dove and Derwent, Repton Park pool, the reservoirs at Barbrook, Ramsley, Derwent, Ladybower, Fernilee, Toddbrook, Staunton Harold and Ogston, the gravel pits at Egginton and Swarkestone, with dead birds picked up near Derby and at Ashford and Duffield. One flew over Hadfield on 16 January 1968 to Arnfield Reservoir, (then in Cheshire), where it stayed for several days (L. Harris, *pers comm*). Most remain for a few days only, although in 1969 one stayed from 3–29 April.

Great Crested Grebe
Podiceps cristatus
Fairly common summer visitor, passage migrant and winter visitor.

Great changes have occurred since Whitlock said that this large grebe was 'chiefly known as a passing migrant or winter visitor to Derbyshire'. Only a few pairs bred on private ponds in the south of the county. At that time the species was persecuted for its feathers from which 'grebe furs' were made. Jourdain wrote frustratedly about the defiance of the Wild Birds Protection Act and the fact that five were killed in 1900–01. He thought the three pairs at Shipley, where the species was protected, constituted the entire county breeding population at that time.

Perhaps some good came of Jourdain's words since by 1914 small numbers of Great Crested Grebes were established on many lakes and ponds of central and southern Derbyshire and the first northern nesting record came from Combs Reservoir in 1918. A national census in 1931 showed the Derbyshire population to be twenty-one pairs at

29   *In a census in summer 1975 there was a total of 134 adult Great Crested Grebes at twenty-five sites in Derbyshire. (Derick Scott)*

fourteen waters. In 1953 S. J. Weston found eighty to eighty-four adults on sixteen waters and in the following year ninety-six at eighteen sites. Weston found only seventy-one birds in 1958 but around this time the acreage of open water was increasing rapidly owing to the creation of reservoirs and gravel pits, and the national census of 1965 revealed ninety-one to ninety-eight birds, with forty-two at the new Staunton Harold Reservoir. In 1972 a private survey revealed 186 adults on thirty-one waters (Bacon, 1972) and a national census in May and June 1975 gave an estimated total of 134 adults on twenty-five of fifty-two sites counted (P. J. Bacon, *pers comm*). Bacon found breeding success lower than the national average, most likely because of a lack of nest sites.

Great Crested Grebes usually appear back at their nesting grounds between February and April, and vacate them, according to breeding activities, in the autumn. Many lakes, gravel pits, and reservoirs now hold this fine bird, though few breed in the Peak District. Butterley Reservoir was the bird's Derbyshire headquarters from at least 1933 to 1962. In July of the latter year this water held forty-three adults, nine of them incubating. Vast numbers of fish died when the reservoir was frozen in 1962–3: since then grebe numbers have been much lower. Staunton Harold now has the largest number at any time of year: up to 164 have occurred in autumn, and even in winter when most waters lose their grebes well over 100 are sometimes seen. It will be interesting to see the long-term effects of sailing and fishing upon this population.

In winter small numbers of Great Crested Grebes may occur at any sizeable water, but invariably in parties of under ten. In hard weather a few may be found on the Trent.

Red-necked Grebe
Podiceps grisegena
Rare winter visitor.

Whitlock quotes two nineteenth-century records and another was shot in 1887 (*VCH*). There have been ten sightings this century, three of them in 1972. Records have come from Burton on Trent, the River Derwent near Derby, a brook near Chapel en le Frith, Hardwick, Eyam and Repton. One was shot at Catton in 1922 (Catton Game Book). All recent records are from reservoirs, at Ogston, Church Wilne and Staunton Harold. Of ten dated occurrences, five were in February, two in January and one in September (27th, 1977), October, and April (1849).

Slavonian Grebe
Podiceps auritus
Rare winter visitor and passage migrant.

Singles were shot at Newton Solney in 1860 (Whitlock) and at Allestree in 1898 (*VCH*). Since 1912 eighteen have been recorded in all months between the extreme dates of 13 October (1973) and 30 April (1976), with six first seen in the month of February. Slavonian Grebes have been seen on the Trent, at Williamthorpe, Ogston, Combs, Staunton Harold and Church Wilne Reservoirs, Hilton gravel pits and Drakelow Wildfowl Reserve. In November 1953 a storm-driven but unharmed bird was picked up at Edale (D. T. Wilks, *in litt*).

Black-necked Grebe
Podiceps nigricollis
Rare passage migrant.

Since they have occurred in eight of the last ten years, usually in autumn, Black-necked Grebes may be regarded as rare but regular passage migrants. Although Whitlock knew of only one convincing record, from Draycott in 1860, about thirty-two have been recorded since 1924. Most have been between July and October, though there are records for all months except June. A few have been in breeding dress but most are in the drabber immature or winter plumages. Usually Black-necked Grebes visit us in ones or twos, though four were at Ogston Reservoir in December 1968. Other localities where Black-necked Grebes have been seen are Williamthorpe, Shipley, the gravel pits at Egginton and Hilton, and the reservoirs at Barbrook, Church Wilne, Staunton Harold and Fernilee. At Church Wilne Reservoir an adult stayed for sixty-three days in the autumn of 1972 and likewise for fifty-eight days in 1973.

Little Grebe
Tachybaptus ruficollis
Fairly common resident.

Little Grebes may occasionally be found

Twenty of Derbyshire's twenty-seven ten kilometre squares held Little Grebes in at least one year between 1968–72. Bacon (1972) found ninety-two adults in the summer of 1972 but he thought this an under-estimate, as many potentially suitable rivers and canals were not visited. Many breed on the Wye and other limestone rivers: the

30 *Little Grebes breed on slow-flowing rivers as well as gravel pits, ponds and larger waters.*
(Derick Scott)

breeding at the edges of large lakes and reservoirs, but generally prefer smaller stretches of water including pools, gravel pits and rivers. The water's size is not so important to these birds as is the presence of aquatic vegetation to which the nest may be anchored. Subsidence pools with their partially submerged trees and bushes often form ideal habitats.

Waterways Bird Survey of 1975 found eight territories on six kilometres of the River Wye, and, on the gritstone, six or seven territories on nineteen kilometres of the River Derwent. Some breeding congregations are rather ephemeral: for example at Stubbing Court eleven nests were found in one day in 1957 (F. Price, *in litt*) but very few have bred since, while there were three or four pairs at

Locko Park in 1971 but not more than a single pair since then (S. Jackson). It seems unlikely that there has been much change since Whitlock wrote that the bird was common in Derbyshire and very common around Bakewell. Pollution of some lowland rivers and marshland drainage seem to have been offset by the increase of gravel pit and subsidence pool habitats.

Outside the breeding season these grebes do not appear to leave their breeding grounds to the same extent as Great Crested Grebes, and birds are found at some sites all year. Even so there are certain favourite gathering grounds where flocks build up in late autumn and winter. Forty were at Langley Mill in January 1972 and at Egginton in July 1975. Good numbers winter in limestone dales; for example there were thirty-eight at Miller's Dale on 4 November 1977. Any count of twenty or more is worth recording.

Black-browed Albatross
Diomedea melanophris
Rare vagrant.

One was captured at Staveley a few days prior to 21 August 1952, after it had become entangled in telegraph wires. It was thought to be exhausted and was released at Skegness in Lincolnshire.

At the time this was only the second British record. It was recorded in square brackets in *DAJ* 'because of the possibility of it having been caught by a sailor and released in home waters'. However the record is fully accepted by the national ornithological bodies (see Macdonald, 1953).

Fulmar
Fulmarus glacialis
Rare vagrant

One was shot at Melbourne on 25 October 1847 (Whitlock). Another was found in Lathkill Dale on 18 December 1949 but died during the night (Dr A. P. Eaton). One roosted overnight at Ogston Reservoir on 23–4 June 1973 (R. A. Frost, M. F. Stoyle). At Walton Dam, Chesterfield, two were seen on 16 January 1974 (L. Oldfield) and one on 6 July 1974 (A. P. Hattersley).

Manx Shearwater
Puffinus puffinus
Rare vagrant.

The status of this oceanic species is unchanged since Whitlock's day: it remains an occasional vagrant, always found dead, dying or exhausted. Twenty-three have been found since 1879, always singly. Of eighteen dated records no fewer than seventeen were in September, with the oddity on 3 October. Most of these birds arrived during westerly gales and three ringing recoveries give some indication of their origins: a young bird ringed at Skokholm, Pembrokeshire on 31 August 1950 was recovered at Chesterfield four weeks later; one ringed at Skokholm, again, on 31 August 1967 was found at Riddings Park six days later; and one found at Eckington on 7 September 1963 had been ringed at Copeland Bird Observatory, County Down, the previous day.

Storm Petrel
Hydrobates pelagicus
Rare vagrant.

Five sources informed Whitlock of undated birds and *VCH* added three more; of these the only dated record is for December. All were found exhausted or dead. One was obtained at Whitwell in the early years of this century (Walker diaries) and one was picked up in Derby on the curious date of 14 June 1919 (A. F. Adsetts). T. G. Smith watched one circling a fly-ash lagoon at Clay Mills on 11 September 1967 and G. Howe recorded a corpse on a golf course at Buxton on 27 May 1972. The last two, and quite possibly all the others, followed severe gales.

Leach's Petrel
Oceanodroma leucorhoa
Rare vagrant.

Whitlock quotes five nineteenth-century records for the south and south-east of the county, all apparently of distressed birds. Two were dated November and one December. The next records came in October 1952 when there was a nation-wide 'wreck' of Leach's Petrels. In the final three days of that month specimens were picked up in seven localities in Derbyshire; undated corpses from two other places would doubtless refer to the same period (Boyd, 1954; Ellis 1973). The only subsequent record concerns one at Fernilee Reservoir on 15–16 and possibly 17 September 1957.

Gannet
Sula bassana
Rare vagrant.

About eight occurred last century (Whitlock, *VCH*) and this century there have been seventeen records, involving nineteen birds. Some of these were picked up exhausted but several were seen in flight, including two birds together over Fenny Bentley on 18 April 1919 and Parwich on 8 December 1943. Four out of seventeen dated records were in March, three in April and September, two in October and November, and one in May, August and December. Records not published in *DAJ* are of a juvenile found dying at Hackenthorpe about 1923 (F. N. Barker, *pers comm*) and one shot at Doe Hill between 1914 and 1918 (*Birds of the Alfreton area 1870–1970*).

Cormorant
Phalacrocorax carbo
Scarce passage migrant and winter visitor.

Whitlock and Jourdain said that Cormorants were irregular visitors to southern Derbyshire, usually in autumn. This century Cormorants have been seen throughout the county on all kinds of waters, from the larger reservoirs to quite small rivers. Sometimes birds are seen passing over open country. Usually seen in ones and twos, there are records of up to thirteen together (at Church Wilne Reservoir in November 1971 and Newton Solney in December 1977). A strange record was of two on Derby Cathedral tower for several days in September 1943.

In the autumn of 1970 there was an influx of several Cormorants to the upper reaches of the Trent, and at least five stayed all winter. Since then Cormorants have shown signs of becoming regular visitors to the same region, with up to thirteen noted. It is presumed that these are offshoots from the regular wintering populations at some of the West Midland reservoirs.

Omitting records likely to concern wintering birds, September, October and April have seen most occurrences of Cormorants. There are records for all months, but few in June and July. Birds with much grey on the nape, possibly of the Continental race, *P.c. sinensis*, have been seen in at least three recent springs.

Shag
Phalacrocorax aristotelis
Rare vagrant.

Four nineteenth-century records are quoted in Whitlock and *VCH*. This century there have been about thirty-two records involving some forty individuals. Seven records were in September with five in March and some in all other months except August, November and December, though three were seen 'at the end of 1902' (*VCH*). Unpublished records concern one at Bamford Millpond in February 1967 and one in Longdendale in June and July 1972 (C. E. Exley and J. E. Robson, *pers comm*). Up to three Shags have also been recorded at Ogston, Butterley, Church Wilne, Staunton Harold and Ladybower Reservoirs, Bakewell, Monsal Dale, Spondon, Derby, Cromford, Ambergate, Hasland, Borrowash, Belper, Kedleston, Drakelow and Egginton gravel pits. Some of these were picked up exhausted and it seems likely that a high proportion of the others were brought in by gales. Most are seen on only one or a very few days, though one stayed for five or six months at Cromford in 1952–3.

One found dead at Ambergate in February 1954 had been ringed as a chick on the Farne Islands, Northumberland, in the previous June. This bird would be in immature plumage, like the majority of Shags seen in Derbyshire.

Grey Heron
Ardea cinerea
Fairly common resident and winter visitor.

Though it was not always adequately

documented, the Heron has had an unsettled history as a Derbyshire breeding bird. Whitlock wrote of heronries at Eaton Wood (near Doveridge), Kedleston, and Sutton Scarsdale. The first two continued to 1921 and 1927 but the northern colony had become extinct soon after 1884. Longford Carr was occupied from about 1900 to 1926, and Hopton Hall for several years early this century. (Nicholson, 1929.) Catton Park was in use from at least 1933 to 1971 with up to twenty pairs at times. The first mention of the Calke Park colony was in 1941 when there were twenty-four nests, so obviously it had existed for some time, and breeding continued until 1964, with forty-four nests in 1944. Up to four pairs bred in the Goyt Valley in 1951–62 while the only regular heronry at present is at Norbury. This colony was established in 1968 and in 1976 held perhaps fifteen nests.

In addition to these more stable sites, the Heron has nested erratically or for a very short time at many other places in the past century, including Anchor Church, Clifton, Shirley, Haddon, Hassop, Hope, Dovedale, Farnah Hall, Sudbury, Stubbing Court, Chatsworth, Ambaston, Sheldon, Grindleford and Ogston. However the most unlikely site was at an electricity sub-station at Spondon where in 1948 two nests were found on top of a lattice steel structure.

It is possible that the bird may be breeding in unrecorded sites, especially in conifers in

31   *Herons may be seen at almost any water in Derbyshire, but currently breed in only one regular colony. (H. A. Hems)*

which the nest is quite easy to miss. At most of the localities mentioned above the nests were in tall deciduous trees, often in parkland. The species is unpopular with many fishermen, and human persecution has been responsible for the destruction of some colonies.

The Heron may be seen anywhere in Derbyshire, visiting waters of all kinds provided they hold fish. Ogston, where up to thirty-nine have occurred (August, 1962), Hathersage and the Newton Solney area are regular flocking grounds. Congregations may be seen between July and March, but numbers in the intervening months are much lower.

That the bird visits us regularly as a winter visitor is suggested by four ringing recoveries, all of birds ringed as nestlings abroad. These came from Pomerania, Germany, to Derby (recovered in April), Norway to Ashbourne and Bakewell (both in March) and Holland to Bamford (August).

Purple Heron
Ardea purpurea
Rare vagrant.

One was killed on the Trent at Wetmore on 1 July 1856 and another at Newton Solney prior to 1881 (Whitlock). Single adults were seen on oxbow lakes at Shardlow on 18–19 April 1968 (R. W. Key, T. G. Smith) and at nearby Sawley on 27 August 1975 (R. A. Frost). One or two were in the Brinsley–Langley Mill area of the Erewash Valley on 2–4 May 1977 (S. Jackson *et al*) and one flew over Shipley Lake on 15 May 1977 (R. Taylor). These two latter records are subject to acceptance by the *British Birds* Rarities Committee.

Little Egret
Egretta garzetta
Rare vagrant.

One frequented a Trent backwater at Repton 18–24 May 1967 (R. H. Appleby, R. Salt, N. Till *et al*). This was approximately the seventy-third British and Irish record.

Great White Egret
Egretta alba
Rare vagrant.

A single bird seen in the Newton Solney–Clay Mills area on 19 May 1974 (R. H. Appleby, E. and P. Warren) was only the eleventh recorded in Britain and Ireland and the first since 1951.

Squacco Heron
Ardeola ralloides
Rare vagrant.

Whitlock records a male shot on the banks of the Dove on 17 May 1874 by Mr Archer of Coton.

Cattle Egret
Bubulcus ibis
Rare vagrant.

An immature visited Egginton sewage farm on 12 July 1966 (T. A. Gibson, A. N. Stephens) and an adult was at Shardlow from 15–18 September 1968 (R. W. Key, T. Lindsey *et al*). Both were perhaps as likely to have been escapes as genuine vagrants.

Night Heron
Nycticorax nycticorax
Rare vagrant.

An adult was shot at Combs Reservoir in the 1860s (*VCH*). One shot near Castle Donington in 1846 would probably have been in Leicestershire (Whitlock). On 13 June 1931 an adult was 'obtained' on the Derbyshire side of the River Dove between Norbury and Calwich Abbey. In 1976 an immature was seen in the Erewash valley near Langley Mill from 9 September–2 October. It reappeared at Shipley on 28 November (P. Bagguley *et al*).

Little Bittern
Ixobrychus minutus
Rare vagrant.

There are some half a dozen claimed sightings or shootings but for only two is the evidence satisfactory. A female was shot at Draycott in August 1872 (Whitlock) and a male suffered the same fate on some trout ponds at Langwith in the spring of 1889 (*VCH*).

Bittern
Botaurus stellaris
Rare winter visitor.

Bitterns obviously visit Derbyshire much less often now than in the nineteenth century. Whitlock and Jourdain knew of thirty records, Whitlock mentioning that 'thirty or forty years ago they came pretty frequently to the neighbourhood of Wilne, a certain favourite haunt being seldom untenanted during the winter months.' Strangely, after 1902 none was seen until 1924, since when about nineteen have been recorded, all singly. This includes previously unpublished records from the Catton area in 1924, 1931 and 1945 (Catton Game Book) and Heath in December 1974 (T. Rodgers, *pers comm*). All have been in the period 25 October (1950) to 11 March (1971) with the majority in January. Usually Bitterns are recorded on single dates only but in 1971 one stayed at Renishaw for over seven weeks, and one at Mercaston in 1972 may have been there for six weeks. Most have been recorded from the Trent and Dove Valleys, while there has not been a definite record from the Peak District since 1937. One ringed as a chick at Minsmere, Suffolk, in June 1950 was recorded in October of the same year at Walton on Trent.

White Stork
Ciconia ciconia
Rare vagrant.

Several were recorded by Robert Garner in his *Natural History of Staffordshire* (1844) as being seen or shot on the Dove (Whitlock).

Spoonbill
Platalea leucorodia
Rare vagrant.

There are five records. Whitlock knew of birds killed at Butterley 'many years ago' and in the Erewash valley in 1847. Three flew over Lea on 'Whit Monday' 1942 (R. Eglinton). One was by the Trent at Wil-

lington on 18 June 1966 (R. H. Appleby, T. G. Smith, C. N. Whipple) and an immature called briefly at Ogston Reservoir on 9 November 1969 (A. Bennett, L. M. Plater, M. F. Stoyle).

Glossy Ibis
Plegadis falcinellus
Rare vagrant.

Birds were shot at Chellaston, Walton on Trent and Derby, all probably in the mid-nineteenth century (*VCH*). One was shot at Sawley on 24 January 1923.

Mallard
Anas platyrhynchos
Common resident and winter visitor.

Whitlock stated that Mallard were fairly common breeding birds, but he made little mention of the situation in winter, merely mentioning that great numbers were found on the Longdendale reservoirs at that season. Jourdain said that considerable numbers bred, especially on the banks of the Dove: he thought the bird was increasing as a result of new legislation.

In common with so many numerous species the Mallard was scarcely mentioned in the annual bird reports during the first half of this century. However by the mid 1950s about five places held triple figure flocks and the construction of three large reservoirs since then has been at least partly responsible for a further increase.

The bird's favourite haunts at present include the reservoirs at Staunton Harold (where up to 1,200 have occurred), Ogston (maximum 520), Church Wilne and Fernilee, and Drakelow Wildfowl Reserve, Chatsworth, Kedleston and the River Wye around Bakewell. In really severe weather the bird moves to the rivers and a flock of 700 frequented the Trent at Newton Solney in the 1962–3 winter. The average county maximum on the National Wildfowl Count for the five seasons 1971–2 to 1975–6 was 2,630 though 3,382 were counted in November 1970: maximum numbers most often occur in the latter month. Even in May and June flocks of 100 plus, practically all of them males, may be seen in some areas. Numbers increase from August onwards, usually building up to a maximum in late October and November. Numbers remain high until February, falling quickly in March and April.

Mallard commonly nest in wet areas of all kinds, often well away from water, and sometimes in woodland. Though there is little information the breeding population must be of at least several hundred pairs. The Waterways Bird Survey of 1974–5 showed an average total of sixty-three pairs on twenty-five kilometres of the Derwent and Wye combined. In a few areas the species is artificially reared for sporting purposes.

One at Loscoe in October 1975 was found to have been ringed at the Ballinrobe Duck Decoy in Co Mayo, Ireland, fifteen months previously, while a bird shot at Glossop in the early winter had been ringed near Hanover, Germany, in the previous spring.

Teal
Anas crecca
Common winter visitor. Rare breeder.

As breeding birds in Derbyshire, Teal are less widespread than formerly. Whitlock and Jourdain reported likely breeding from the Trent Valley, Sutton Scarsdale, Castleton and the grouse moors at the head of the Derwent Valley. In 1916 a few pairs were said to be breeding along the River Etherow in the north-west, and in the 1940s breeding was reported from eight areas including 'fair numbers' in the Derwent area. Since the 1950s, though, only a few pairs have nested annually with Weston on Trent, Heath, Scarcliffe and Whitwell (Ellis, 1973) the only lowland sites. In the Peak the most regular nesting places now are Chatsworth, Barbrook Reservoir and the Derwent Reservoirs. Further evidence in support of diminished numbers came from E. H. Peat who said in 1956 that very few then nested at Derwent where there had been many twenty years previously.

Any midsummer gathering of more than five is noteworthy and there is at first only a gradual increase in numbers from July onwards, with usually a substantial arrival from September. The largest Wildfowl Count is usually made in February, with 625 the average maximum for the county from 1971–2 to 1975–6: the highest count of all was 2,282 in December 1968. Numbers quickly decrease from March onwards with only small numbers by late April. In winter Teal are well-scattered on lowland waters and marshes with large concentrations regularly at Ogston Reservoir, Spondon sewage farm and on the River Trent, where maxima have been 400, 450 and 1,250.

Teal found in the county in late autumn or winter were found to have been ringed in Northamptonshire, Essex, Cumberland and Holland.

A drake showing characters of the American race, *A.c. carolinensis*, known as the Green-winged Teal, was at Ogston Reservoir from 14–22 November 1976 (R. A. Frost, A. G. Macey, M. F. Stoyle *et al*). This was the ninety-eighth record for Britain and Ireland. A Mallard × Teal hybrid was at Ogston Reservoir in 1975 and a Teal × Wigeon hybrid at Birdholme in 1974.

Garganey
Anas querquedula
Scarce summer visitor and passage migrant.

Whitlock considered the Garganey to be an uncommon winter visitor to Derbyshire on the strength of five authorities, though neither he nor Jourdain apparently saw the bird for himself. There were but two records between 1893 and 1944 since when Garganeys have been proved to be much more regular. They are now scarce but annual migrants. A few are seen most springs from March (earliest date 12th, 1977) to May, and rather more on autumn passage from July to September, with occasional stragglers in October and November. Most of these passage birds occur in the south and east, singly or in groups of up to seven. Very few are seen on high ground. In the severe winter of January 1963 a female remained on the Trent at Newton Solney for at least a week.

Since 1962 Garganeys have been seen quite often in late spring and early summer in the Erewash and Trent valleys, especially near Sawley. Birds have stayed all summer in at least one year and sometimes a pair has been seen early in spring and a lone drake later. This strongly suggests breeding but proof is still lacking.

Gadwall
Anas strepera
Scarce visitor, mainly in winter.

Three seen by C. B. Chambers at Hardwick Park in 1920 comprised the first county record. One was at Osmaston in 1936 and from 1943 to 1948 one or two visited south-west Derbyshire each year. One was shot at Catton in 1954 (Catton Game Book). No more were seen until 1956 since when Gadwall have been recorded annually in generally increasing numbers; they may now occur on practically any stretch of water and at any time of year, but mainly in winter. At present their favoured localities are Renishaw, Melbourne Pool and the Ogston and Staunton Harold Reservoirs: up to nineteen have been seen at the latter site.

In 1957 a pair bred successfully at Locko Park near Spondon and in view of their increase further breeding in the county seems likely. It is understood that wildfowling associations and shooting clubs have released Gadwall in Derbyshire and adjoining counties, and many of our birds may have come from this source.

Wigeon
Anas penelope
Fairly common winter visitor. Rare in summer.

In the late nineteenth and early twentieth century this duck was fairly numerous on the Trent in winter, Whitlock reporting flocks of up to 100. The reservoirs at Butterley and in Longdendale were often visited, as were the lakes at Sutton Scarsdale, and 'some of the wet moors and streams near Castleton'. The pattern has changed considerably, since Wigeon are now uncommon and only brief visitors to the reservoirs mentioned and no longer visit wet moorland. Sutton Scarsdale lakes no longer exist, though the bird is still regular on the Trent.

This century there were no records of more than twenty-four together until 200 were reported from Repton in March 1948. Since the formation of DOS much more information has been received and a regular pattern established. Wigeon winter in numbers at relatively few places, but small gatherings winter or pass through several other sites. Much the favoured locality is Church Wilne Reservoir where in February 1977 there were 1,191. There is a much smaller regular flock at Ogston Reservoir (maximum 180) and also, more erratically, at Staunton Harold Reservoir (up to 335). Though there were possibly 2,000 on the Trent in the severe winter of 1962–3 subsequent numbers have been much lower. 918 is the average maximum of the Wildfowl Counts from 1971–2 to 1975–6; peak counts are invariably made in February, and the last flocks are seen in April.

Very small numbers have been seen in all months of the year, with birds summering at Church Wilne Reservoir in 1974–7. In 1949 a pair summered at Howden 'but no young were seen'. (*DAJ*) The first arrivals are sometimes in July but more usually in August and September, with a steady build-up in numbers thereafter.

One ringed at Blithfield Reservoir, Staffordshire in December 1969 was recovered in Swadlincote in January 1974.

Pintail
Anas acuta
Scarce winter visitor and passage migrant.

Obviously Pintail are more regular now than they were last century when Whitlock described them as being 'of uncertain appearance' and then apparently only in severe weather.

No records followed until 1942. Only since 1959 have these elegant duck been regarded as annual winter visitors; even in the mildest winter weather, they are usually present somewhere in the county, though numbers are generally small. Any gathering of double figures is noteworthy, and the forty-six which flew over Drakelow in March 1972 was an exceptional record. As in Whitlock's day the Trent Valley is still the favoured area, though any large water body, marsh, or flood, is likely to be visited.

Though recorded in all months, they are rare between May and July and uncommon in August and September, though the period of arrival is rather variable. Larger numbers usually occur late in the winter.

In 1943 R. J. Raines followed the course of a distinctive group of five through Nottinghamshire, from Rufford to Salterford to Moorgreen, and finally to Shipley Reservoir, Derbyshire.

Shoveler
Anas clypeata
Scarce visitor. Rare breeder.

Only small numbers of Shoveler winter with us, with a rather variable increase in spring from February onwards, whilst a few are usually to be found somewhere in the county in summer. A steady build-up in numbers from July onwards leads to maximum numbers between September and November, especially in October. Fifty-eight in September 1973 was the largest of any National Wildfowl Count with the average maximum count from 1971–2 to 1975–6 as low as thirty-three. However, fifty-nine were seen at Staunton Harold Reservoir (September 1972) and gatherings of thirty to fifty have recently been reported from Church Wilne and Ogston Reservoirs, Renishaw, Langley Mill, Melbourne Pool and Spondon sewage farm. These duck are not rare elsewhere at subsidence lakes, gravel pits and ornamental waters, but Peak District records are relatively few, the majority of them from Combs Reservoir.

Shoveler have always been rare breeding birds in Derbyshire and in only thirteen years between 1928–76 has this certainly taken place with no more than two pairs in any year: neither Whitlock nor Jourdain knew of a definite record. All of the six breeding records in 1928–44 came from the Heath and Whitwell areas, and probably involved offshoots from the Nottinghamshire breeding stock. Since 1955 breeding has been reported from Kedleston, Ingleby, Westhouses, Staunton Harold Reservoir and Staveley.

Mandarin Duck
Aix galericulata
Rare vagrant.

A male was seen on a pond at Repton on 14 December 1963 (T. G. Smith). Subsequently single males were recorded from Ogston Hall in March 1964, Darley Abbey in March 1974, Allestree Lake in October 1975 and Ramsley Reservoir in December 1977. A female was at Markeaton Park in November 1974. At Walton Dam, Chesterfield, a male remained from early April to late May, 1973. It was said to have mated with a female Mallard, the pair making two unsuccessful attempts to nest in a hollow tree (L. Oldfield).

Mandarins breed ferally in a few parts of England and our birds may have been of this stock or, equally likely, escapes from waterfowl collections.

Red-crested Pochard
Netta rufina
Rare winter visitor and passage migrant.

The first Derbyshire record was of a female at Locko Park from 27 July–12 October 1960 (R. H. Appleby *et al*). There are ten subsequent records involving a pair at Ogston Reservoir and nine singles at Ogston, Staunton Harold, Toddbrook and Church Wilne Reservoirs, Bretby, Swarkestone and Elvaston gravel pits, and Killamarsh where there was a drake on 11 April 1970 (SNHS Newsletter). There are records for all months except May and June. Seven of the birds were immatures or females, and five males. Some of these birds may have been escapes from waterfowl collections: those at Bretby and Locko were considered most likely to be from this source. S. Jackson has been informed of recent breeding by a captive pair in south Derbyshire; the young fledged and were allowed to disperse.

Scaup
Aythya marila
Rare passage migrant and winter visitor.

Several Scaup occurred on the Trent last century and were 'not uncommon' in the great frost of 1890 and 1891. However Whitlock knew of only one record away from the Trent. Scaup were subsequently recorded in 1904, 1912, 1924, 1928, three times in the 1940s and fairly regularly since the 1950s. As in Whitlock's day a significant proportion of these birds arrive in response to cold weather, though Scaup may be seen in any weather conditions and there are records for all months, with most in the period November to January. Scaup have been reported from many reservoirs, lakes, gravel pits, and the larger rivers.

In 1963–4 a flock of seventeen or so wintered at Ogston Reservoir. The following winter a smaller party spent the winter at Staunton Harold Reservoir and individuals or small groups have wintered in the county in recent years, especially at Church Wilne Reservoir.

It has been suggested (Gillham *et al*, 1964–5) that isolated 'Scaup' wintering inland with other species of *aythya* may be hybrids. In Derbyshire a variety of *aythya* hybrids has been seen in recent years but most of the Scaup critically examined have been pedigrees. Scaup are not uncommon coastal birds and it seems reasonable to suppose that a few occasionally stray inland.

Tufted Duck
Aythya fuligula
Fairly common resident and common winter visitor.

Whitlock was able to report breeding at three sites from 1854 onwards, though nowhere regularly; Jourdain said that this duck established itself as a breeding bird late in the nineteenth century, with its stronghold in the south-west of the county. Its subsequent increase was quite rapid and in 1906 three nests (one with a clutch of twenty-eight eggs) were found on a small islet at Osmaston Lakes while twelve pairs bred at Ashford lake, near Bakewell. In 1934 *DAJ* stated that the bird had colonised nearly all pools and lakes in Derbyshire, though this seems to have referred to its presence in summer rather than to positive breeding. The increase continued to the 1960s, facilitated by

the creation of new gravel pits and other waters, but the population is now more stable with some forty to fifty broods of ducklings seen each year, although the number of summering pairs is much higher than this. As well as at gravel pits, the Tufted Duck breeds at reservoirs, lakes, subsidence flashes and on rivers, at least in the Peak District.

The number of wintering birds, presumed immigrants, between about September-October and April, has also shown a marked increase, no doubt at least partly because of the creation of three large reservoirs since the mid 1950s. In winter both Whitlock and Jourdain found the bird quite common, especially in the Trent Valley during severe weather. However the first three-figure count recorded was in 1943 at Shipley and since then many waters have held such flocks, with three of the new waters having most – at Staunton Harold there were 520 in August 1973, and Church Wilne Reservoir held 490 in February 1976 with 500 at Drakelow Wildfowl Reserve in January 1977. However there were 800 on the Trent on 22 January 1963. Wildfowl counts show that this is now the third most numerous species in the county, with an average county maximum of 921 between 1971–2 and 1975–6, the largest counts usually being made between December and February.

Ring-necked Duck.
Aythya collaris
Rare vagrant.

T. Cockburn and J. C. Eyre-Dickinson identified a drake at Drakelow Wildfowl Reserve on 27 December 1977. This record is subject to verification by the *British Birds* Rarities Committee.

Pochard
Aythya ferina
Fairly common winter visitor. Rare breeder.

In Whitlock's time Pochard were quite common in southern Derbyshire, and apparently easy to shoot, since 'of all duck locally obtained and sold on Nottingham Market they were amongst the most frequent'. Many were seen on the Trent in the great frost of

1890–91. However it seems unlikely that they occurred in flocks as large as those witnessed today.

Up to the mid 1950s small numbers were reported from many places, though with no flock larger than fifty-eight. The first three-figure flock was seen at Ogston Reservoir in 1958, shortly after its flooding, and this reservoir has remained a favourite site with 391 in January 1977 the largest recorded gathering in the county. The two other major new reservoirs, at Church Wilne and Staunton Harold, and Drakelow Wildfowl Reserve, have all supported gatherings of around 300, with 200-plus seen at other gravel pits in the south, and at Shipley Lake.

The average county maximum of 625 during the National Wildfowl counts of 1971–2 to 1975–6 made this the fifth most numerous species of wildfowl, equal with Teal. Maximum numbers occur between November and March, but with a rapid dispersal after the latter month. A few Pochard may be found almost anywhere in summer but invariably in very small numbers with ten or more together rare at that season. Numbers build up from July and the tendency is for an earlier increase than formerly with, for example, 140 at Staunton Harold Reservoir in August 1972.

In 1941 two pairs and four young were reported from Bradley on 2 August but it is not clear whether the young had been reared there. However in 1972, three broods of young were seen on a large pond not far from Bradley (T. Goodley, *pers comm*) and in 1976 a brood was successfully reared at Brinsley 'flash' in the Erewash valley (P. Bagguley *et al.*).

Ferruginous Duck
Aythya nyroca
Rare winter visitor.

A pair was reported from Butterley Reservoir during the 1950–51 winter (W. J. Milne). The same locality produced a female on 29 February–7 March 1964. A drake was at Ogston Reservoir on 8 March 1964. Drakelow Wildfowl Reserve held a drake from 6–27 February 1972 and 31 January–11 March 1973. An immature was identified on 9 November 1975 at Egginton gravel pits, and a pair was reported from Shipley Lake on 25 January 1976.

Goldeneye
Bucephala clangula
Scarce winter visitor and passage migrant. Rare in summer.

Whitlock said that the Goldeneye was not uncommon in southern Derbyshire but apparently he knew of no northern sightings, though Jourdain quoted a record from Baslow. A note in *British Birds* 1927 of one at Combs Reservoir in that year prompted a reply in 1928 from A. W. Boyd that he had seen one at Derwent in 1927 also, and that they were frequent on Pennine reservoirs outside Derbyshire. Nowadays the Goldeneye may visit any sizeable stretch of water in the county, including reservoirs, lakes, gravel pits and the larger rivers. On some barren, upland waters it may be the only species of duck present in winter.

There are two September records, the earlier on 16th (1975) but October is usually the month for first sightings. Arrival continues into November; although there is some movement between waters, numbers are fairly static in December and January. Spring passage, from February to April, invariably supplies the largest counts and at this time up to forty-one have been seen at Church Wilne Reservoir (March, 1976) and up to twenty-six at Staunton Harold Reservoir (March, 1968). However the largest Derbyshire flock was of fifty birds on the Trent at King's Mills in January, 1963. On the National Wildfowl Count the average maximum for Derbyshire in 1971–2 to 1975–6 was 52, with March usually having the highest numbers.

Stragglers have been seen in all of the summer months, and on 13 June 1954 D. R. Wilson recorded an adult female making short, circular display flights over Barbrook Reservoir.

Long-tailed Duck
Clangula hyemalis
Rare winter visitor.

Pilkington, Glover and Mosley all recorded Long-tailed Ducks in southern Derbyshire (Whitlock). An immature female was at Shipley in December 1943 and since November 1963 fifteen have been seen, at Ogston, Staunton Harold, Barbrook, Crowhole and Ladybower Reservoirs, Clay Mills gravel pits, Brough clay pits and on the Trent at Ingleby. Seven have been seen in December, six in November, one in February and October and one on the unusual date of 28 May.

Velvet Scoter
Melanitta fusca
Rare winter visitor and passage migrant.

Velvet Scoters were shot at Willington and Draycott last century (Whitlock). Others on the Trent befell the same fate in 1932 and 1935. Since 1953 about fourteen have been seen. In severe weather early in 1963 at least three frequented the Rivers Derwent, Dove and Trent. Others have occurred at Allestree Lake, Fernilee, Ladybower, Ogston, and Butterley Reservoirs, and Old Whittington. There are records for all months between October (earliest, 6th 1963) and February.

Common Scoter
Melanitta nigra
Scarce passage migrant.

These distinctive sea ducks are regular visitors to Derbyshire's larger waters. They may occur at any time of year but peak numbers are in April, July and August, with fewest records for January and February. Though ones and twos are usually involved there are several records of double figures, with the largest flock twenty-eight at Howden Reservoir in July 1971.

Whitlock found Common Scoters frequent visitors to the Trent Valley, but while these ducks are seen in that area most years, especially at the two large reservoirs there, they are more frequent on northern reservoirs, chiefly Ogston and Barbrook. It seems likely that the late summer records are of birds crossing the country to the west or south-west, some of them perhaps originating from the Humber district.

Eider
Somateria mollissima
Rare vagrant.

E. H. Peat saw a pair at Derwent about thirty years prior to 1966 but the record does not appear to have been published. (DOS Bulletin no. 119.) Two females were at Clay Mills gravel pits on 25 April 1971 (R. A. Frost, M. F. Stoyle) and no fewer than thirty visited Ogston Reservoir briefly on 23 November 1975 (T. A. Gibson, M. F. Stoyle, B. T. Wheeldon).

Ruddy Duck
Oxyura jamaicensis
Rare winter visitor and breeder.

Small numbers of this North American species escaped from the Wildfowl Trust in Gloucestershire from the 1950s onwards, and have subsequently succeeded in establishing feral populations in several English counties. The bird has found some of the West Midland waters to its particular liking and no doubt most of our records originate from that area. The first county record was of two males shot on the River Trent at Drakelow on 12 January 1963 (T. W. Tanton). There were single birds on one date only in 1965, 66, 69 and 1971. One was present at Ogston Reservoir from December 1972 to February 1973. There was one other record in 1973, none in 1974 but several in 1975–7 with up to eight together (at Staunton Harold Reservoir in January 1977). The bird is probably in the process of becoming a regular visitor, especially in winter. There are records for all months except March. Away from the sites already mentioned Ruddy Ducks have also occurred at Sudbury, Kedleston, Drakelow Wildfowl Reserve, Egginton, Willington and Clay Mills gravel pits and Church Wilne and Errwood Reservoirs.

In 1975 Miss K. M. Hollick saw a female with a half-grown duckling at Osmaston in September, the first breeding record for Derbyshire. A pair was at the same lakes in 1976 but breeding was not proven.

Red-breasted Merganser

Mergus serrator

Rare winter visitor, passage migrant and breeder.

A few were shot on the Trent and Derwent, and on the lakes at Sutton Scarsdale last century (Whitlock, *VCH*). 1940 saw the first county record this century. Since then these sawbills have been seen in Derbyshire in seventeen years, including every year since 1971. Prior to 1966 all dated records were between December and March. There were April records in 1966 and 1968 and a September sighting in 1969. In 1971–3 Mergansers summered in north-west Derbyshire and breeding was proved in the last of those years when D. Alsop and G. Howe saw a female with ducklings in the Goyt valley. No doubt this was connected with the species' colonisation of north-west England since 1950 (see Parslow, 1973).

Meanwhile occurrences elsewhere have become more frequent and not merely confined to winter, with sightings at lowland reservoirs in May and June, and up to six together have been recorded on passage. December and March have attracted most sightings, and only August is without any record. Additional localities where Mergansers have occurred include the reservoirs at Church Wilne, Ogston, Staunton Harold, Barbrook, Linacre and Ladybower, Belph, Allestree Lake, Shipley Lake, and the gravel pits at Egginton, Clay Mills and Swarkestone.

Goosander

Mergus merganser

Scarce winter visitor. Rare in summer.

This sawbill has always been much more numerous than the Red-breasted Merganser in Derbyshire. According to Whitlock it was seen quite frequently on the River Trent, especially in bad weather, and was known to occur at other sites. This is still the basic pattern today except that now the little-disturbed Staunton Harold Reservoir is the premier site, and has a regular wintering flock, which peaked at forty-nine in March 1974. Small numbers are still regular on the Trent and lower Dove, especially in the Newton Solney area: in hard weather numbers on the rivers increase and there were flocks of 125 in January 1952 and 117 in January 1963.

Away from the Trent Valley area Goosanders are more erratic in their occurrences but are quite regular at Ogston and the Derwent Reservoirs, and sometimes small numbers are seen on the River Derwent in central and north Derbyshire. However the bird never stays long at waters deficient in fish.

12 September (1976) appears to be the earliest genuine arrival date, and the species is tending to arrive earlier with, for example, as many as sixteen together on 16 October 1976. The largest numbers may be seen at any time between December and March, with an average maximum of only twenty-eight for the last five seasons for which figures are available (from 1969–70 to 1973–4). Small groups may remain well into April, whilst May records are occasional, and birds considered sick or injured summered in 1963, 1974 and 1975.

Smew

Mergus albellus

Rare winter visitor.

The occurrence of Smew in Derbyshire depends largely upon the incidence of cold weather when a few birds may be driven on to the unfrozen Trent and other waters in the south of the county. Numbers are invariably small, with peak counts of six at Repton in March 1947, about twenty-four at King's Mills in March 1955 and at least nine, chiefly around Newton Solney, between January and March 1963.

Records away from the Trent area are exceptional; one was shot at Staveley in 1774 and singles were at Osmaston in 1855 (Whitlock) and 1965. One was at Ednaston in 1966 and three at Ogston Reservoir in 1964, with singles there in 1963 and 1966. One was seen at Belper in January 1977.

Records span the period 17 November (1968) to 23 March (1963) with most in the first-mentioned month. There has probably been little change in status since Whitlock's day.

Shelduck
Tadorna tadorna
Scarce passage migrant. Has bred.

Shelduck are quite regular migrants in Derbyshire, having occurred at almost every substantial water including reservoirs, gravel pits, sewage farms and floods, and they have visited much smaller ones, such as a tiny dam in the Via Gellia and Ashbourne Hall Pond. They have been reported at all times of year but probably most occur in late summer when J. E. Robson (*pers comm*) says flocks of up to fifty fly east over Glossop. Doubtless these are birds on moult migration from Cheshire to the Knechtsand, Germany. Although Barbrook Reservoir has also had late summer flocks of up to thirty-five there are few other records to suggest that this well-known movement involves Derbyshire. It seems likely that the birds pass further north or else fly so high on reaching the Peakland hills that they cross the county undetected. Sometimes there are large numbers late in the year, such as the fifty at Staunton Harold Reservoir in November 1970 and thirty-one at Drakelow in November 1974. More usually Shelduck occur in single figure numbers. Whitlock said they were occasional migrants.

In 1966 E. T. Lamb found a pair with ducklings on the Trent at Twyford, the first county breeding record. In 1975 a pair remained at Elvaston Quarry for much of the spring but there was no evidence of breeding.

Ruddy Shelduck
Tadorna ferruginea
Rare vagrant or escape.

One was killed at Weston on Trent on 18 April 1913 (J. Drury). Two drakes were at Drakelow Wildfowl Reserve on 11–19 May 1975 (T. Cockburn, J. R. Collison *et al*). Lord Scarsdale saw two at Kedleston on 14 May 1975 but the record has not been submitted to the *British Birds* Rarities Committee. Probably all records relate to escapes.

Egyptian Goose
Alopochen aegyptiaca
Rare visitor.

Several were seen in the Trent Valley last century (Whitlock, *VCH*) One was at Yeldersley in March 1903 and one was shot near Staveley in 1906. Two were on Ashbourne Hall pond in March 1939. In the spring of 1966 four were at Westhouses and one at Ogston Reservoir, and since 1970 there have been several sightings of odd birds from ornamental waters in south Derbyshire, and from Drakelow Wildfowl Reserve, Shipley Lake and Sutton Scarsdale. Jourdain considered all the old records to be of feral or escaped birds as no doubt are all the subsequent ones. Most are seen in spring but there are records for most months of the year.

Greylag Goose
Anser anser
Rare vagrant or resident.

Derbyshire records of genuinely wild Greylags are few and far between. Sir Oswald Mosley found them plentiful on the Dove around 1810 but there were few other records last century (Whitlock). This century the only records certainly relating to wild birds were of forty-three over Taddington on 25 April 1946, and eighty-seven at Hurst Reservoir, Glossop, on 14 March 1976.

In 1957 and in every year since 1961 there have been sightings of Greylags in very small numbers (up to nine together), usually accompanying Canada Geese: most are thus seen in southern Derbyshire, some have stayed for several months, and are probably best classified as wandering residents. These birds are almost certainly releases of the Wildfowlers' Association, or their progeny.

White-fronted Goose
Anser albifrons
Rare winter visitor.

Prior to 1789 White-fronted Geese were seen on the Trent and at Sinfin Moor and J. J. Briggs later stated that individuals visited the Trent in bad weather. Over a century later, C. M. Swaine identified a flock of sixty-five moving east over Glossop in January 1946. *In litt* to F. G. Hollands, he thought that most of the flocks of geese passing south to south-east over Glossop were White-fronts, with perhaps a few Pinkfeet. However no such flocks have subsequently been recorded from that locality.

In fact, since 1946 most of the twenty-five or so records have involved grounded birds, with only two flocks seen in flight. Most White-fronted Geese now visiting Derbyshire do so in parties of one to eight and are seen on lakes, gravel pits and in river valleys. Some of them have accompanied Canada Geese and were perhaps escaped birds. The period of observation is 8 October 1972 to 4 May 1975, embracing all intermediate months.

Lesser White-fronted Goose
Anser erythropus
Rare vagrant.

An adult joined a party of Canada Geese at Swarkestone gravel pits for six minutes on 8 June 1976 (Mr and Mrs P. H. Johnson). The date strongly suggests that this was an escaped bird, though the *British Birds* Rarities Committee accepted the record, the ninety-seventh for Britain.

Bean Goose
Anser fabalis
Rare vagrant.

According to J. J. Briggs, writing in 1849–50 Bean Geese were occasionally seen on the Trent. Three were killed on the river in December 1890 (Whitlock). In 1977 one was seen at Kedleston from 27 January to 13 February (Mrs O. Billings, B. C. Potter) and another was at Drakelow Wildfowl Reserve from 19–27 April (T. Cockburn *et al*).

Pink-footed Goose
Anser brachyrhynchus
Scarce winter visitor.

It seems that Pinkfeet regularly transfer from their wintering grounds on the Lancashire mosses to the Wash in Lincolnshire and Norfolk and vice-versa. North Derbyshire lies on this flight path and several skeins of geese are seen over the area each winter, usually moving south-east or north-west, though occasionally in other directions. Most, if not all, of these flocks are undoubtedly of Pinkfeet. Movement may be seen at any time between October and March, though there are reliable April and August records and a probable July sighting. Very occasionally a flock will alight on farmland to feed or on water to rest. In 1953 a flock of up to seventeen stayed at Barbrook from October to December. Although most are seen in the north, Pinkfeet flocks are occasionally seen in southern Derbyshire.

Single Pinkfeet are sometimes seen with Canada Geese and are most likely escapes. Sometimes such birds have remained throughout the year.

It is uncertain whether any great change in status has taken place since Whitlock's day. He said that flocks occasionally flew over the upper reaches of the Trent but this may merely reflect the lack of observers elsewhere in Derbyshire at that time.

Snow Goose
Anser caerulescens
Feral vagrant.

An adult blue phase Lesser Snow Goose *A. c. caerulescens* at Drakelow from 29 June–2 July 1967 was captured during a round-up of Canada Geese and taken to Stafford Zoo (T. Cockburn, DOS Bulletin No 134). All other reports were of light-phase birds. One was at Locko Park in October 1971, and in May 1975 what may well have been the same individual in each case was seen at Queen's Park and Birdholme (both in Chesterfield) and Egginton. Another was at Swarkestone gravel pits in May 1976 and between September and November 1977 one visited Kedleston and Drakelow Wildfowl Reserve. All of these were presumed to be escapes.

Brent Goose
Branta bernicla
Rare vagrant.

Although there is only one recent sighting, of a dark-bellied bird at Ogston Reservoir on 14 March 1964 (D. B. Cutts, R. G. Hawley), there are several older records. Briggs stated that it was occasional on the Trent (Whitlock) and Jourdain (*VCH*) added a record of two on the Derwent near Derby around 1890. One was shot near Rocester in January 1903 (*The Zoologist*, 1903) and one caught in an exhausted state at Winshill in January 1912 or 1913. From Newton Solney Repton School Field Club reported six on 11 February and ten on 23 February 1947.

Barnacle Goose
Branta leucopsis
Rare vagrant. Not uncommon escape.

A few were recorded by Whitlock and four or five visited Ashbourne Hall pond about 1880 (*VCH*). Since then only two records are thought to refer to wild birds: a skein of twenty-five flying south-east over Glossop on 20 October, 1940 (Swaine, 1944), and five on ploughland at Sutton Scarsdale on 20–22 March 1969. Since 1958 up to four Barnacle Geese have been recorded in many years and in all months, usually consorting with Canada Geese on ornamental lakes, and doubtless all originate from waterfowl collections.

Canada Goose
Branta canadensis
Fairly common resident.

Whitlock said that the Canada Goose had been extensively introduced to many of Derbyshire's waters (around 1820–30 according to Jourdain), large flocks existing at Kedleston and Chatsworth with lesser numbers in several other places.

The Kedleston flock still thrives and held most of the 900 assessed by the Wildfowl Trust as the 1967–9 Derbyshire population (Ogilvie, 1969) though no fewer than 1,400 were seen there in September 1976. Other parklands in southern Derbyshire, such as Locko and Markeaton, are often visited by herds of these geese, presumed to be wanderers from Kedleston. In winter, especially in cold weather, flocks visit the Trent and nearby gravel pits, and up to 550 have been seen at Drakelow Wildfowl Reserve. Few are seen elsewhere in the county in winter. The five National Wildfowl Counts of 1969–70 to 1973–4 gave an average winter maximum of 1,034 making it second only to Mallard in overall abundance: largest numbers occurred between September and December.

In addition to Kedleston, many other parks and lakes and gravel pits in the south have nesting birds. North of a line through Ashbourne and Belper, however, the Canada Goose is uncommon. The Chatsworth colony has long been extinct and only very small numbers have bred erratically at Pebley Pond, Idridgehay, Alderwasley, Birdholme, Chesterfield, Combs Reservoir, Litton Mills and Bradford Hollow. In the BTO Atlas enquiry the bird was found in fourteen squares, with breeding proven in ten of them.

In 1956 about 220 birds were transported from Kedleston to the Wildfowl Trust in Gloucestershire, many quickly returning. One likewise taken to Anglesey came back to Kedleston, but another, taken to Westmorland was later found dead in Hampshire! Some of the Canada Geese caught at Drakelow had originated from the Birmingham area, whilst one ringed as a chick at Drakelow in 1972 was found amongst the regular moulting flock on the Beauly Firth, Invernessshire in July 1973. Another ringed at this latter site at the same time was caught at Kedleston in June 1975. There is a well-established interchange of birds between Kedleston and the Nottinghamshire Dukeries.

Mute Swan
Cygnus olor
Fairly common resident.

Mute Swans occur widely in Derbyshire but frequent mainly lowland waters, including reservoirs, lakes, canals, rivers and gravel pits. The BTO Atlas investigation of 1968–72 showed breeding in nineteen ten kilometre squares, and the bird was noted as present in a further three. It was absent from five squares, all of them containing a large proportion of high ground. In fact few Mute Swans are found in the Peak and the bird is rare on upland waters, Lakes, ponds and 'flashes' in central and eastern Derbyshire may support a breeding pair but most nest in the south, especially in the valley of the River Trent, where there is a greater abundance of suitable aquatic habitat. Numbers are probably reasonably stable at present.

In the five winters 1969–70 to 1973–4 the average county maximum of the National Wildfowl Counts was 136, a large percentage always being in the Trent Valley. The largest individual flocks reported were of seventy-eight at Swarkestone gravel pits in October 1971 and the same number at Sawley Bridge in January 1958.

Many Mute Swans have been colour-ringed in the West Midlands by Dr C. D. T. Minton and helpers and results were published in *Wildfowl* 19 and *Wildfowl* 22. Many of these birds have been subsequently found in the Derbyshire Trent Valley; birds ringed at Burton on Trent have moved further north to Westhouses, Ogston Reservoir, Staveley and Renishaw, whilst one marked in the Tamworth area was seen at Williamthorpe. One ringed at Clumber Park, Nottinghamshire in January 1961 was found in Pleasley Vale in May 1971.

Whooper Swan
Cygnus cygnus
Rare winter visitor.

Whitlock knew of several Derbyshire records of Whooper Swans, in contrast with only two of Bewick's Swans, and earlier writers said they were annual visitors to the Trent valley. From 1900–54 the larger swan continued to be more regular, and every year since 1957 has produced a few records. Meanwhile, however, Bewick's Swans have become much more regular and numerous.

Whoopers may occur on any sheet of water, such as lakes, reservoirs, the larger rivers and floodwater. Occasionally a small party stays for a few weeks. Any part of the county may be visited by Whoopers but none appears to have been seen in south-western Derbyshire since 1950. The largest flocks were of sixty at Barbrook Reservoir in 1934–5 (Smith, 1974) and fifty over Fernilee Reservoir in December 1957 (Bell, 1962).

Records span the period 5 October (1977) to 27 April (1963) with most in November, December (especially) and January.

Bewick's Swan
Cygnus bewickii
Scarce winter visitor and passage migrant.

Last century these small Siberian swans visited the county in 1845, 1864 (Whitlock) and 1895 (*VCH*), and there were only five records in the first half of this century, in 1904, 1907, 1925, 1927 and 1948. A herd of seventy-six at Combs Reservoir in March 1954 heralded their more regular appearance and 1957 has been the only subsequent year with no records. Several flocks of over fifty have been seen in recent years with the largest 100 at Combs, again, in March 1956. These large flocks usually occur on spring passage, their flight directions suggesting that they have come from wintering grounds in Gloucestershire and Somerset. As further support for this idea two birds marked by the Wildfowl Trust at Slimbridge have been seen in the Trent Valley.

Bewick's Swans have now occurred at many Derbyshire localities, particularly in the valley of the Trent where there are many pastures and sometimes shallow floods suitable for feeding. Many are seen only in flight or when grounded for a short time but small numbers winter on the Trent and occasionally at reservoirs and lakes. One remained from January until 8 August 1970 at Swarkestone; although it could fly it was considered sick. Otherwise extreme dates are 2 October (1977) and 11 May (1969) (DOS Bulletin No 155). September is the only month for which no records exist.

Griffon Vulture
Gyps fulvus
Rare vagrant.

On 4 June 1927 Dr H. H. Hollick, Miss Kathleen Hollick and E. A. Sadler saw two Griffon Vultures over Ashbourne while watching for the return of homing pigeons. This constituted the second British record. None has occurred since.

Golden Eagle

Aquila chrysaetus

Vagrant. Formerly bred.

A nest with a single youngster and an addled egg was found at Derwent Woodlands in 1668. One end of the two yard square nest lay on a rock and the other on two birches. This is quoted in Pilkington (1789) and is the only certain breeding record for the county. In 1720 one was taken on Kinder Scout and eagles at Hardwick in 1759 and 1782 may have been of this species. A definite Golden Eagle was shot near Cromford in 1823, and what may have been one was at Matlock in 1843 (Whitlock, *VCH*). A Golden Eagle was reported by E. H. Peat at Derwent in April 1952 following a probable sighting in December 1948.

Buzzard

Buteo buteo

Rare resident. Scarce passage migrant and winter visitor.

Whitlock considered that the Buzzard bred commonly in the Peak District before the destruction of the forest there. According to Pilkington it was one of the common raptors, along with Kite, Kestrel, and Sparrowhawk. The forest denudation, he concluded, drove this species to the woods of south Derbyshire, where it was still common at the beginning of the nineteenth century: for example Sir Oswald Mosley could recall seeing 'upwards of twenty at one time sailing along with outstretched wings over Egginton Heath and Etwall Common'. But by the end of the century the bird was all but extinct.

This century, despite some hundreds of records of Buzzards in Derbyshire, there are remarkably few records of nesting; in fact this certainly occurred only in 1922, in the myxomatosis years of the 1950s (probably at three sites), in 1964–5, and 1975. Although much apparently suitable habitat exists in the Peak with its woods, moors and agricultural land, human interference is thought to limit the birds' breeding success.

Migrant or vagrant Buzzards have occurred in many parts of the county. They usually occur singly though there are records of up to seven together. Most are seen in the Peak but sometimes lowland areas may be tenanted for several weeks. An analysis of the records suggests that a small population winters, with a small movement in March and April, and a more pronounced one from August to October, especially in September. The origin of these birds is unknown.

Rough-legged Buzzard

Buteo lagopus

Rare winter visitor.

Rough-legged Buzzards are now much rarer in Derbyshire than in the nineteenth century. Whitlock wrote of their regularity every time an immigration to Britain took place. John Wolley of Matlock saw at least a dozen in the winter of 1839–40. This century there have been but nine records: from Big Moor in March 1903 (Storrs-Fox diaries); at Ashford in the Water in February 1907; from Curbar in the early months of 1920; at Derwent in April 1923 (C. H. Wells, *in litt*); with two observed 'near Sheffield' in November 1949. The only recent records are from Lumsdale, Matlock on 2 February 1975, one seen occasionally between 12 October and December 1975 in the Upper Derwent area, and one at Leash Fen on 10 October 1976.

Sparrowhawk

Accipiter nisus

Scarce resident and possibly winter visitor.

Whitlock and Jourdain found the Sparrowhawk well-scattered throughout the county but nowhere common. According to Coward (1910) it was the commonest bird of prey in Longdendale. Despite human persecution the bird maintained its numbers early this century, showing a marked increase during the war when gamekeepers were active elsewhere: in 1943, for example, Repton School Field Club found ten nests in their area. However during the late 1950s the population collapsed. An expert on the species, Dr Ian Newton, who formerly lived at New Whittington, knew of about ten regular sites in north-east Derbyshire until 1958. All were vacated between 1958–60 (*pers comm*). Numbers remained extremely low for several years thereafter, with only one nest reported in the county in 1966–7.

This decline was attributed to poisoning by pesticides; with their use now subject to stricter control, numbers have since revived with six nests found in 1971 and at least eighteen in 1976, but the bird remains below its former level, at least on low ground. Though the Sparrowhawk is still occasionally destroyed by gamekeepers this is no longer considered a serious threat.

Whilst not rare in the lowlands, Sparrowhawks prefer higher ground and are not surprisingly most numerous in the gritstone area of the Peak, the area which one might expect to be most free from pesticide usage. Conifers and mixed woodlands, especially those containing tall Larches are preferred, though purely deciduous woods are occasionally used. The bird hunts both in woodland and over open country including farmland and moorland, and is sometimes sighted over urban areas. Our birds seem to be largely resident, but there is some evidence to suggest that additional birds from outside the county may winter with us.

Birds ringed as chicks in Derbyshire have been recovered in Cheshire, and Staffordshire, both within twenty miles of their birthplace.

Goshawk
Accipiter gentilis
Rare resident.

The Goshawk was mentioned in Glover's list and one was shot at Ashover, presumably last century (Whitlock). One was seen at Bakewell in 1893 (*VCH*).

Goshawks now breed in some of Derbyshire's woodlands and, though very small, the population is increasing. Breeding has been confirmed since at least 1966, and may have occurred for several years before that. There is evidence to suggest that at least part of the population may be of birds (or their offsprings) released in the area by falconers. All recent nests have been in the northern half of the county but in the mid

1950s a female with a brood patch was found on a gamekeeper's gibbet on an estate in southern Derbyshire (T. W. Tivey, *pers comm*), strongly suggesting breeding there. Though most are sedentary, birds are sometimes seen well away from known breeding areas.

These birds are sensitive to disturbance and bird-watchers should take every care not to prejudice their chances of breeding successfully.

Red Kite
Milvus milvus
Rare vagrant.

Writing in 1789, Pilkington regarded the Kite as one of the commoner raptors and Glover in 1829 said it was 'the best known and most ignoble of the falcon tribe'. When Briggs wrote his Birds of Melbourne notes in 1849–50 there were still a few Kites to be seen 'sailing over our grass fields at a considerable height, and in a steady and graceful manner'. One was seen near Branston in 1855 but in 1863 Sir Oswald Mosley spoke of its complete disappearance. Whitlock postulated that the Kite's Derbyshire headquarters were 'in the wooded portions of the Peak, the common Buzzard taking its place in the lower parts of the county'. Three appear to have been obtained locally late in the nineteenth century.

Since 1900 only six have been seen: perhaps the same bird at Matlock and Somersal Herbert in the summer of 1913; at Hell Bank, Beeley, on 11 December 1961; one which departed north-east from Egginton on 8 April 1969; in Coombs Dale from 22 August–1 September 1971 (SNHS Newsletter); at Hayfield on 17–18 December 1971; and finally at Elmton on 24–25 August 1975.

White-tailed Eagle
Haliaeetus albicilla
Rare winter visitor.

'The White-tailed Eagle is a not uncommon winter visitor to the Derbyshire moors.' So said Jourdain (*VCH*), who was able to give details of eight individuals and thought two more records of unspecified eagles likely to refer to this species. This century an immature was at Derwent from 20 December 1920 to 8 February 1921 when it was killed by Lord Fitzallan's gamekeeper. Another gamekeeper, E. H. Peat, who later submitted many useful ornithological records, was presented with a pair of binoculars by the RSPB for his efforts to protect this bird. An immature frequented the Derwent area from 9–17 March 1939. In addition, eagles seen in the Kinder area in 1933 and Derwent again, in 1940, would most likely have been White-tailed Eagles.

Honey Buzzard
Pernis apivorus
Rare passage migrant or vagrant.

There are eleven records. One was shot at Aston on Trent prior to 1789 and one obtained at Renishaw in 1843 (Whitlock). The next four were also shot: at Allestree in June 1904; at Osmaston in September 1908; at Clay Cross in October 1920; and near Melbourne about August 1936. A decomposed bird was found below wires at Buxton on 5 June 1958. At Hassop one flew west on 12 September 1970; one was over Birdholme on 5 July 1971 and a very pale bird was at Ogston Reservoir on 27 August 1971. More recently one was seen near Owler Bar on 2 August 1977.

Marsh Harrier
Circus aeruginosus
Rare passage migrant or vagrant.

In 1789 Pilkington stated that Marsh Harriers had been seen at Foston and Croxall. One was seen near Strines in the summer of 1891 and one shot near Bradfield in 1895 (Whitlock, *VCH*). One was seen twice in the Dove Valley in November 1916. From 1949 to 1951, an unusually long stay, one frequented the Whitwell district (Walker diaries). One was mobbed by Herons in the Dove Valley near Calwich on 25 July 1955 and possibly the same bird was at Osmaston on 27 November that year (Miss K. M. Hollick, *pers comm*). On 1 May 1966 two flew west from Derbyshire into Cheshire over Goyt's Moss (T. Hedley Bell, *pers*

comm). One quartered cornfields at Whaley, near Bolsover, on 14 August 1966 and an immature was on Eyam Moor on 28 May 1967. The most recent records, all in 1977, concern a male on Beeley Moor on 28 April, a female on Ramsley Moor two days later, and one on Brampton East Moor on 15 May.

Hen Harrier
Circus cyaneus
Rare winter visitor and passage migrant. Formerly bred.

In 1863 Sir Oswald Mosley wrote that, 'The Common Harrier, before the enclosure of our wastes and forests, merited that epithet but it is now become uncommon among us.' Both Whitlock and Jourdain agreed that there was enough evidence to show that at one time the bird was common and widely distributed throughout Derbyshire. The last definite nest seems to have been one with eggs at Drakelow in 1870 (Whitlock, *VCH*).

Hen Harriers have continued to visit the county between late autumn and early spring and, even considering the much greater number of observers, have greatly increased in recent years. 1963 was the last year when the species was not recorded. Gritstone moorland and adjacent upland farming is the favoured habitat. Only very rarely are Hen Harriers seen in lowland areas. The 'East Moors' between Ringinglow and Matlock provide the bulk of the records, though Hen Harriers have been seen frequently in the Derwent and to a lesser extent, the Goyt regions. The numbers passing through in late autumn are usually greater than those which actually winter. Up to four have occurred together and in some winters at least six individuals have been identified on the East Moors.

There are at least two August records and in some years Hen Harriers have been seen as late as May. Display has been noted. Despite rumours to the contrary, breeding is so far unconfirmed, but is a future possibility.

Montagu's Harrier
Circus pygargus

Rare passage migrant. Formerly summer visitor.

The first county record was of one shot in the Big Moor area in late April 1903 and recorded by W. Storrs-Fox in *The Zoologist* (1903). There were six definite records and two of 'harriers', probably this species, between 1940 and 1956, a period when numbers breeding in Britain were much higher than today (see Parslow, 1973). In 1953 a male and two females frequented Ringinglow Bog on the county boundary but nested in Yorkshire: two broods were thought to have been reared. Though birds were again present in 1954 they did not breed (W. E. Gibbs, *pers comm*). In 1955 a pair summered at Whitwell but did not breed, and in the following year a female summered at Derwent.

Since 1957 there have been but four definite records – from Big Moor in May 1961, Eastmoor in May 1966, Ladybower in August 1971, and Lightwood Moor in June 1976. There have been other sightings of harriers which may have been Montagu's including one which summered at Whitwell in 1971 (J. Ellis, *pers comm*). Less convincing are Montagu's Harrier records claimed by E. H. Peat on the unlikely dates of 6 November (1948) and 26 March (1950).

Osprey
Pandion haliaetus
Rare passage migrant.

Though obviously more regular last century than this, Ospreys have become regular migrants through Derbyshire in the past five years, probably as a result of increased breeding numbers in Scotland. Whitlock quoting J. R. Towle of Draycott, said that 'not so long ago the appearance of an Osprey on the Trent or Derwent excited no surprise'. The Weston Cliff area of the Trent and nearby Melbourne Pool were always favourite spots. The only records in the first half of this century, however, were in 1921 and 1949. There were six occurrences in the 1950s, two in the 1960s and twenty-one between 1970 and 1977, including unpublished records from Chatsworth on 9 May 1971 (G. P. Mawson, *pers comm*) and Picory Corner in May 1974, (Trevor Marshall, *pers comm*).

Ospreys may visit any sizeable water and occasionally small pools. Derwent, with its chain of trout-stocked reservoirs, has been the most regular calling place this century. Excepting December, records exist for all months with most in May, June and July. In 1952 one stayed for three months at Derwent. Most Ospreys occur singly, though two were together at Cresswell in September 1974 and two, possibly three, at Ogston Reservoir in May 1976. There were no fewer than five records in June 1977 and future breeding in the county is not unthinkable.

Hobby
Falco subbuteo
Rare passage migrant. Former breeder.

Now but migrants, Hobbies have occasionally bred in Derbyshire. Briggs claimed that they rarely bred near Melbourne; nesting may have taken place in the Peak District in 1891 (Whitlock) and a nest was found near Buxton in 1894 (*VCH*). Hobbies nested at Tansley in 1902 (per F. Price), Newton Park in 1926 and almost certainly in the Goyt Valley, which then formed the Derbyshire–Cheshire boundary in 1938 (H. G. Atlee, *British Birds*, 1948). Others were seen or shot in summer in the late nineteenth and twentieth centuries. These superb falcons have recently been seen in midsummer in marginally suitable nesting habitats and the possibility of their breeding again should not be overlooked.

Since 1955 approximately thirty-one have been seen at widely scattered localities on passage between 3 May (1977) and 16 September (1974), with most in July and August. Four were found on Beeley Moor on 21 July 1977, some of them staying into August. There is a most surprising record of one seen at close quarters at Ashbourne in January, 1936, though it may merely have been an escape.

Peregrine
Falco peregrinus
Rare passage migrant or vagrant. Former breeder.

Not until 1919 did Peregrines certainly

breed in Derbyshire but Whitlock's statement that 'it is difficult to doubt that eyries formerly existed in the lofty limestone cliffs of the Peak' is beyond argument. In 1919 one or both of the pair was shot. Although not fully documented it seems likely from observations by C. H. Wells and personal comments from the late E. H. Peat, that the species attempted to nest every year in the Peak until 1954 or 1955; at least three sites were involved. Only rarely were they successful because of human persecution. There are signs that in recent years Peregrines have summered in Derbyshire and a return is not impossible.

Outside the breeding season, Whitlock said that they were not uncommon visitors to the Trent valley and the High Peak, some of them (as today) escapes wearing falconers' equipment. Peregrines are now rare visitors which may turn up almost anywhere in the county. Records concern sites as unlikely as Chesterfield Market Place, Bolsover Castle, and a cooling tower at Drakelow Power Station. On rare occasions a Peregrine has wintered in an urban area. The pattern of occurrences suggests a small passage in September and March. Immatures are identified more frequently than adults.

Merlin
Falco columbarius
Rare summer visitor. Scarce winter visitor.

Merlins have bred for a long time on the Peak District moors but have seemingly always had problems to contend with. Whitlock considered this dashing little falcon once common but subject to a high degree of persecution by game preservers; for the same reason Jourdain predicted its disappearance. This has not happened but our Merlins hold on only by the most tenuous of threads.

32   *A Merlin with young in an old Carrion Crow nest on Kinder Scout. This species' population is at a dangerously low level. (H. A. Hems)*

Destruction at the hands of gamekeepers has continued this century and many birds are known to have been shot and many nests destroyed. Populations appear to have fluctuated: C. M. Swaine said that in the Glossop area there were three or four pairs in some years, but none in others. In 1922 C. H. Wells found five nests in the Peak District, and in 1955 there were three or four pairs in the Derwent area alone. Shortly after this a major decline set in and by the early 1960s they were rare with no definite breeding records in 1961–9. Since 1970 nests have been found in most years, largely as a result of especial interest by a few ornithologists, but the current population is almost certainly under five pairs.

Although gamekeepers may still occasionally destroy this species, the main reasons for its virtual disappearance seem likely to concern pesticide poisoning (which would occur mainly in winter when Merlins move to lower ground) and disturbance from hikers and climbers. Most recent nests have been in secluded areas. These falcons prefer small valley sides, usually with a good look-out in at least one direction. Most nest on the ground but sometimes old Carrion Crow and Magpie nests in trees are used.

From September to April occasional Merlins may be seen anywhere in the county, often hunting finches in their typically swift, exhilarating flight. The East Moors are a popular wintering ground, and five were seen on Leash Fen on 13 January 1974.

While some of our wintering birds may come from abroad (perhaps from Iceland) ringing recoveries so far have concerned only British birds. Merlins found in the county between August and October had been ringed as nestlings in Northumberland, Lancashire, Cheshire and Yorkshire.

Red-footed Falcon
Falco vespertinus
Rare vagrant.

A male was shot on moorland in the Peak District in early May 1939 (per R. G. Abercrombie). In 1969, Mr and Mrs R. A. Frost saw a female at Great Hucklow on 14 June and on 21–22 June a male frequented Egginton sewage farm (A. B. Wassell, C. N. Whipple *et al*). Two visiting ornithologists from Cheshire, Mr and Mrs Dean, saw a female at Chelmorton on 28 May 1973. An immature visited Church Wilne Reservoir on 6 and 9 July 1975 (T. A. Gibson, R. W. Key, K. J. Lyon), and a male was at Upper Derwent on 28 May 1977 (D. Gosney, D. Herringshaw, M. E. Taylor).

Kestrel
Falco tinnunculus
Fairly common resident and partial migrant.

As in Whitlock's time the Kestrel is by far the most numerous and widespread of the county's diurnal raptors. The bird's characteristic hovering silhouette may be seen throughout Derbyshire over open country of all kinds, and not uncommonly over built-up areas and motorway embankments. Nesting sites include trees (in holes or the old nests of another species), buildings (even in towns), railway bridges and viaducts, electricity pylons and rock faces, whether natural or man-made (where they are surprisingly tolerant of blasting operations).

Whitlock thought the species most common in the Peakland dales, and certainly the population in the hills is much higher than that on low ground. In Dovedale in July 1916 twelve were seen so close that they 'could almost have been covered by a large table cloth'. One observer recorded thirty-two in five and a half hours' birdwatching in the Peak District on 21 August 1972, mainly over steep west-facing slopes which are very much used when the wind has a westerly component.

In 1956 a report of decreased numbers in the Trent Valley was the first indication of a quite sudden drop in numbers, which remained low until the mid 1960s. In 1964 the results of a census organised by the BTO caused A. B. Wassell to estimate the county population at thirty-five to forty-five pairs — a fraction of today's level: however the estimate was probably very pessimistic. Poisoning by persistent organochlorine pesticides was adjudged the reason for the decline. The major threat now to the species' welfare comes neither from pesticides nor gamekeepers, but from those (inspired by a recent film) who would take and attempt to rear nestlings.

There are many ringing recoveries. Birds ringed as chicks in Derbyshire have been found in several English counties as far as Durham, Sussex (twice), Berkshire, and Wiltshire, whilst ringed birds found in the county had come from Lancashire, Yorkshire and Northumberland. One ringed at Hathersage in July 1954 was found dead three months later at Croix du Perche in France and, similarly, another travelled from Longendale to Villepinte. One ringed in Lappmark, Sweden in July 1959 was trapped at Swadlincote in October of the same year.

Red Grouse
Lagopus lagopus
Common resident.

Whitlock and Jourdain considered Red Grouse common residents on our moors south to the vicinity of Matlock. This status applies today, but they are not nearly as numerous as they were. Yalden (1972), who has studied certain Peak District birds and mammals in depth, revealed the extent of the decline: for example eight selected Peakland moors on which 25,019 grouse were shot in 1935–6 yielded bags totalling only 3,226 in 1957–8. Increased competition for heather food with the greatly increased number of hill sheep was, he concluded, the main factor for the decline, though fewer gamekeepers and poorer moor management would contribute. Poor spring weather may have an adverse temporary effect – for example in 1955 a great number of nests were destroyed by a two feet depth of snow on 17 May.

Yalden showed that the main grouse population which he estimates (*pers comm*) at five thousand six hundred spring pairs is on the Kinder and Bleaklow plateaux, around Longdendale, and in the Derwent–Bamford region. There are other populations in the Combs Moss–Goyt Valley–Axe Edge area, and on the East Moors. Isolated populations survive on several other small moors, including some overlying Carboniferous Limestone. The preferred habitat is Ling moorland, especially where the plant is systematically burned. Some are found in quite damp situations. Afforestation usually causes Red Grouse to leave within a few years.

Grouse used to be seen occasionally on low ground in severe weather, having occurred in the Erewash valley, and at Kirk Ireton, Culland and elsewhere. This now happens only exceptionally: the only recent bird some way out of its range (at Ogston Reservoir in October 1976) was probably disorientated by fog. From May to October 1956 one or two were seen in south-east Derbyshire between Little Eaton and Morley but did not persist. In winter, especially in colder weather, grouse pack together, sometimes over 100-strong. The largest records concern 300 at Bamford in October 1971 and 200 at Woodhead in December 1974, though it is likely that earlier figures exceeded these.

Black Grouse
Lyrurus tetrix
Rare resident.

This species is dangerously close to extinction as a Derbyshire breeding bird, with numbers at a very low level and confined to two or three sites. Whilst the rate of decrease has accelerated in the past decade, it is clear that for a very long time our Black Grouse have been declining. In 1789 Pilkington wrote that 'formerly these birds appeared in great numbers in the Peak but now are very seldom seen'. In 1893 Whitlock reported that they still bred in four areas and Bryden (1907) stated that thirteen were shot on the Chatsworth Estate in the 1903–4 season. Numbers may have shown some recovery in the 1930s: W. E. Gibbs estimated a breeding population of twelve to twenty-five pairs between Owler Bar and Baslow in 1930 (Smith, 1974) and there was an increase at Derwent in the late 1930s, perhaps connected with the afforestation programme there.

In the 1950s and early 1960s up to fourteen Black Grouse were reported fairly regularly from the Goyt and Derwent Valleys, and around Abney, Longshaw, and Matlock Forest. A marked decline seems to have begun in the mid 1960s when the Abney, Longshaw and Matlock populations became very small or extinct. At present this species may still be found in the Goyt and Derwent areas and possibly in one other area, with only a few birds at any site: the county total is almost certainly under fifteen pairs.

Lovenbury, Waterhouse and Yalden (*in press*) say that Black Grouse numbers on the nearby Staffordshire moors seem to be stable and consider that habitat changes are chiefly responsible for the loss of Derbyshire's birds: in particular they think the replacement of open moorland or birch woodland by 'tight' coniferous woodland the most injurious factor, while conceding that some of our moorlands still look ideal for the species.

In October 1976 a male was seen at Mapperley, close to the densely-populated lowlands of the Erewash Valley. The record is convincingly documented but so improbable that the bird is as likely to have been released as it is to have been genuinely wild.

Red-legged Partridge
Alectoris rufa
Scarce resident.

This species was introduced into England about 1770 but the first county report came from J. J. Briggs who said that a few pairs were released at Castle Donington prior to 1849, one pair breeding in the first year of liberty. Although the locality mentioned is in Leicestershire, Whitlock accepted the record for Derbyshire.

By 1893 the same author was able to report that it was by no means uncommon in the lowlands, especially in the Trent Valley. Jourdain (1905) also considered the valley the bird's stronghold though it was found locally throughout the county south of Belper, with a few pairs north to Taddington.

The next notes concerning numbers came in 1942–3 when the species had disappeared from North Wingfield and had become very scarce at nearby Clay Cross: however four records between 1944–54 referred to recolonisation of old sites or occurrences in new localities. Since then there is some evidence of local decreases but rather more of increased numbers.

Its strongholds now are the Trent Valley, still, the area south of the Trent, the Magnesian Limestone region, and the Moss Valley. In the last two decades the bird has appeared in several Peakland localities where it was formerly unknown, with breeding reported in Bradford Dale, the Goyt Valley, Matlock and Woo Dale, and its presence was reported from fourteen squares during 1968–72. The largest recorded covey was of thirty-five at Whitwell, in August 1970, and sixty were estimated in the Shirebrook area on 8 October 1977.

The species frequents arable farmland, especially on lighter soils, but may also be found on more barren sites such as colliery tips and quarries. It is known that some shooting syndicates have released this bird in certain areas, which may explain the increase and its presence in some unlikely places.

Partridge
Perdix perdix
Common resident.

Grey Partridges are quite common birds in Derbyshire, frequenting arable land, pasture and waste ground. They are thus naturally most numerous in the lowlands but may be seen on rough ground up to 1,200 feet, and occasionally higher. A pair bred on Bamford Moor in 1973 but generally Red Grouse replace Partridges on heather moors. Only one ten kilometre square lacked the species in 1968–72. On the two censussed Coal Measures farms at Barrow Hill and Tibshelf Partridges were the fifth and seventh commonest species, totalling thirteen pairs, but the Fernilee, Mapleton and Hathersage sites totalled only five pairs in all. On the Magnesian Limestone plateau R. A. Frost counted forty-two pairs in the fields bordering Scarcliffe woodlands in the spring of 1971, compared with twelve pairs of Red-legged Partridges. In winter coveys of up to seventy have been seen.

33 *Partridges are thought to have decreased less in Derbyshire than they have done nationally. (J. Russell)*

Whitlock said that the Common Partridge was generally distributed in varying abundance over the whole county, excepting the moorlands. It was most common in the south. Both he and Jourdain considered that the bird must have been more numerous in earlier times. The Reverend Francis Gisborne of Staveley killed great numbers in the eighteenth century, despite the interference of Hen Harriers and Kites with his sport. Bryden (1907) said that the annual bag on the Haddon Estate was around 600 birds, and that here and in the dales 100 brace might be secured in a day. This clearly indicates a decline this century as such numbers would be extremely unlikely now. Furthermore the Catton Game Book reveals that many more were shot in the 1930s than in the 1960s, though numbers were at their lowest in the late 1950s. However the decrease in

Derbyshire is thought to be less than that which has occurred nationally.

Quail
Coturnix coturnix
Rare summer visitor and passage migrant.

Always erratic visitors, Quail are less regular now than formerly. They were found every year in southern Derbyshire according to Whitlock, who guessed that they occasionally visited the east also. They appeared to be decreasing at that time, having formerly been common in certain areas, for example around Swarkestone.

The diminution has continued this century, though there have been years when several were recorded, as in 1947, 1964, 1970, 1974 and 1977. Breeding was proven only in 1945, 1947, 1953, 1956 and 1974. However the bird's usual habitat, cereal fields, is hardly conducive to nest searching. Slightly undulating land is preferred and the three areas most favoured by Quail are the Magnesian Limestone plateau and the Keuper region between Repton, Ticknall and Ingleby and around Grangewood. There are records this century of Quail uttering their distinctive triple calls from about twenty-five other areas, nearly all in the lowlands. At Etwall possibly six were calling in August 1974, and there were no fewer than eleven calling in the Grangewood area in the summer of 1977.

Only occasionally are Quail seen: sometimes a migrant may be flushed from stubble or grassland, and telegraph wires have claimed the lives of a few. In May 1904 an injured bird was found in a street in Derby.

This century records have fallen within the period 27 April to 5 September, with over half in June. There are eighteenth and nineteenth-century records for October, December and February (Whitlock).

Pheasant
Phasianus colchicus
Fairly common resident.

Large numbers of Pheasants, sometimes a few thousands, are reared and liberated on many of the county's sporting estates each year, to be shot in the late autumn and winter. On most estates the numbers liberated greatly outnumber those breeding in the wild. They feed both in woods and on agricultural land, and nest in woods, thickets and sometimes below rank hedgerows.

Generally Pheasants are absent from moorland though a nest was found on an open heather moor at Longstone in 1962.

Golden Pheasant
Chrysolophus pictus
Rare resident.

Small numbers of Golden Pheasants have been released on a few private estates in the county. Whether they have nested in the wild in Derbyshire is uncertain. A male in a small shrubbery at Shardlow in the winter of 1976–7 seems likely to have been an escape, as does another at Drakelow in April 1975 (since the species is kept in captivity only a

few miles away). In December 1977 a male was seen on Hoo Moor.

The British Ornithologists' Union has accepted the Golden Pheasant as a full British species on the grounds that it is breeding freely in Britain in a wild state.

Water Rail
Rallus aquaticus
Scarce winter visitor and passage migrant. Rare breeder.

From September or October to March or early April, Water Rails are scarce but quite widespread visitors to the county, frequenting sewage farms, Reed and Reedmace beds, sluggish streams, the marshy edges of lakes and ponds, and similar wet sites. They occur in small numbers, the largest counts being of seven at Hilton gravel pits in December 1966 and six at Killamarsh in October 1971. However counting such secretive birds is not easy and although Water Rails not infrequently feed in the open, most betray their presence by their unearthly screaming calls.

Whitlock knew of breeding records from Melbourne and Longdendale, and Sudbury and Kirk Ireton are further localities mentioned in Jourdain's diaries. The only recent instances of proven nesting came from Hilton gravel pits in 1969, Killamarsh in several years between 1970–6, and Mapperley in 1976. Water Rails may nest elsewhere in Derbyshire but, even considering their secretive natures and the difficulties of searching their aquatic habitats, they must be regarded as rare breeding birds.

Spotted Crake
Porzana porzana
Rare passage migrant.

Last century Spotted Crakes were probably regular breeders in the valleys of the lower Dove, Trent and Erewash, according to Whitlock and Jourdain. Nests were reported from Repton and near Derby. One killed on the Lathkill in October 1897 was probably migrating.

This century there have been very few records and no evidence of breeding. Birds

34　*Water Rails have bred at three sites recently, but are better known as winter visitors.*
(J. Russell)

were killed at Little Eaton in 1900 (Jourdain diaries) and near Derby on 27 October 1903 (*The Zoologist*). The next was found in an exhausted state at Willington number one gravel pit on 23 August 1963. Two more have occurred in the same region: at Egginton sewage farm on 1–9 October 1965 and at Egginton number four gravel pit on 27 August 1966 when T. A. Gibson liberated a bird trapped in a floating tin can. One was watched by a number of observers at Killamarsh during 18–22 September 1971. In 1977 at Drakelow Wildfowl Reserve one was calling in June and there were up to four in August and September, but breeding was not suspected.

Baillon's Crake
Porzana pusilla
Rare vagrant.

Whitlock records one killed within three miles of Derby in November 1821.

Corncrake
Crex crex
Rare summer visitor.

In Derbyshire, in common with most lowland areas of Britain, Corncrakes have become rare breeding birds. Whitlock stated that the bird was distributed throughout the county in suitable habitats with its headquarters in the valleys of the Trent, Dove and Erewash where it was said to abound. It was less common in the north, though numerous in the Wye and Hope valleys. By 1911 a decline was under way though Corncrakes were still common in some localities and more generally in certain years. Five were calling in one Kniveton field in May 1917 and they were plentiful around Hazelwood in 1937. By 1940 only small numbers remained in Derbyshire and all occurrences were apparently being recorded in *DAJ*.

Since then the decline has continued and nowadays records average about one a year:

most are heard in the upland fields of the Peak District where the farming is not so intensive and the crops cut later. The only records of confirmed breeding since 1950 came in 1952, 1956, 1962 and in the late 1960s from Walton, Burbage, Rodsley and the Baslow area (P. Tooley, *pers comm*).

Since 1965 'song' has also been heard at Ogston, Ashford, Palterton, Barlow, Grangewood, Staveley, Carr Vale, Buxton, the Goyt Valley, Drakelow, Taxal, Idridgehay, Killamarsh, Shirland, Birdholme and Clay Cross. The national decrease has been attributed by Parslow (1967) to changed agricultural methods, especially the introduction of mechanical hay cutters.

Records involve all months between 3 April (1946) and 28 November (1953) with a winter sighting of one on 3 January (1920).

Moorhen
Gallinula chloropus
Common resident.
The Moorhen is found on waterways throughout the county, from narrow streams and ditches to the largest rivers, though it is absent from rocky, swift-flowing streams. It also occurs in some numbers on sewage farms, lake margins and the smallest of ponds (provided there is cover into which it may retreat) and may penetrate into towns, but is absent from most of our exposed upland reservoirs.

The 1974–5 Waterways Bird Survey gave some idea of its abundance. There was an average of eighteen territories on six kilometres of the River Wye, thirty-seven on nineteen kilometres of the Derwent (from Bamford to Beeley) and twenty-eight on only five kilometres of the River Noe between Hope and Bamford. R. A. Frost found five nests with eggs on a 350 metre stretch of a very small stream at Belph on 28 May 1971. Generally the species nests in aquatic vegetation but not uncommonly does so in trees and bushes, sometimes in the old nest of another species. More unusual sites have included the glovecompartment of a car partly submerged in a

35   *Moorhen: a common breeding bird of wetlands throughout the county. (Derick Scott)*

gravel pit and the inside of a dustbin wedged in river silt. The bird has a long breeding season and broods have very occasionally been seen in winter.

Though the Moorhen may stay in its breeding territory all year, small gatherings may be found at favoured sites, sometimes in loose flocks of fifty or more. 154 were counted at Westhouses 'flash' in September 1967.

The Moorhen's status seems unlikely to have greatly changed since the time of the last Derbyshire avifauna, except for mortalities caused by severe winters, such as that of 1962–3 which caused heavy losses; this was thought to be the only bird which suffered much more in Derbyshire than it did nationally.

One ringed at Killamarsh in March 1962 was found near Leeds a year later, and a Moorhen skeleton bearing a ring at Whitwell in April 1976 had been ringed the previous May in Jutland, Denmark.

Coot
Fulica atra
Common resident and winter visitor.

Around the turn of the century the Coot was quite an uncommon species, breeding locally on southern ponds and lakes such as Bradley, Osmaston and Sudbury, at Sutton Scarsdale and apparently on the Longdendale reservoirs (Whitlock, *VCH*).

From then until 1944 nothing was recorded of the bird's breeding status. There may have been a small increase during that period but that there has been a great increase in breeding numbers in the past thirty years or so is beyond dispute. The Coot is now a common bird in the county, breeding on almost any water larger than a couple of acres in size though barren waters, such as some of the upland reservoirs, are shunned. Slow-flowing rivers may hold small populations, and the species is not uncommon in some of the limestone dales, with, for example an average of nine territories on six kilometres of the Wye in 1974–5. The main reason for the Coot's increase must be the creation of new aquatic habitats such as res-

ervoirs, 'flashes' and gravel pits, but the fact that the species has increased on long-existing waters indicates that other factors are involved.

Numbers in winter greatly exceed those breeding, even accounting for the species' tendency to congregate on certain favoured waters at that season. Even in late summer some large concentrations have been recorded – for example there were 450 at Staunton Harold Reservoir in July 1973. An increase is usually more obvious from September onwards, large numbers remaining until the following February or March, especially in the vicinity of the Trent Valley, and it is likely that some of these additional birds are Continental immigrants. 1,133 at Staunton Harold in November 1972 is much the largest flock yet recorded in the county.

Little Bustard
Otis tetrax
Rare vagrant.

A female was shot on Etwall Common in 1797 (Whitlock) and another female was killed by a farmer at Middleton Top, near Youlgreave, on 14 May 1901 (*VCH*).

Oystercatcher
Haematopus ostralegus
Rare passage migrant. Rare summer visitor.

Whitlock knew of a few southern Derbyshire records in the eighteenth and nineteenth centuries, and regarded Oystercatchers as accidental visitors. After 1904 there were no more records until 1944 and 1949, with nine in the 1950s and many since. Records have been submitted annually since 1959, from many wetland areas. Some have been seen flying over open countryside, and migrants are occasionally heard at night. Thirty were seen over Hathersage on 22 September 1967 (DOS Bulletin no. 136) with seven the second largest gathering.

A small passage takes place in March and April, and autumn passage is mainly from July to September with about a third of all records falling in August. Though there are few for November and December, Oystercatchers have been recorded in Derbyshire in all months of the year.

Since 1969 this species has prospected in the Trent valley frequenting gravel pits and riverside beaches. Breeding was proved in 1972 when a pair with a chick was seen at Egginton number seven gravel pit (T. G. Smith, *pers comm*) and 1973 when a nest with eggs was found at Clay Mills by R. A. Frost. Both attempts were considered unsuccessful.

Lapwing
Vanellus vanellus
Common resident, passage migrant and winter visitor.

Whitlock and Jourdain considered the Lapwing a very common resident from low-lying meadows up to the moorland edge, the former saying that it was probably most common in the Peak. After breeding it occurred in large flocks.

While this would still describe the bird's status today there is no doubt that these fine waders have declined considerably. This was generally noticed around 1950 and since then most, but not all, reports of changed numbers refer to decreases. In particular this has affected Lapwings on farmland in the lowlands where numbers are now generally low. For example, the combined 400 acres of the farms studied at Barrow Hill and Tibshelf averaged only seven pairs a year. An interesting survey by P. Shooter of four square miles of land south-east of Clay Cross revealed 121 pairs in 1950 but only 79 by 1958. The increased amount of arable land and increased drainage seem the most likely causes of the decline.

At present Lapwings are most numerous on the borders of the moors where some of the upland fields have damp patches and clumps of rushes. If the vegetation is short

36 *Lapwing. Numbers in the lowlands have shown a decline since about 1950 though upland populations are thought to be more stable. (Derick Scott)*

nests may be found on moorland up to 1,700 feet. There were twenty-six pairs on the 200 acre hill farm at Fernilee in 1972, and near Bakewell a large, newly-ploughed, ninety acre field held thirty-nine pairs in 1976.

Our Lapwings return to territory by March. After the breeding season, sometimes as early as late May, they form small flocks. Westerly movement perhaps of Continental birds, is often seen in June and July. Meanwhile, numbers in the lowlands build up to large flocks, sometimes of thousands by late autumn, and P. I. Vickers estimated 13,000 in the Erewash Valley between Ilkeston and Alfreton on 23 November 1961 (DOS Bulletin no 74). If the weather is reasonably mild such flocks winter, but snow or heavy frost causes movements between south and west, though the birds quickly return when the weather improves. The last flocks, largely composed of presumed immigrants, are seen in March.

Birds ringed as chicks in Derbyshire have been subsequently recovered in Counties Limerick, Westmeath and Wexford in Eire, and in the 1962–3 winter in southern France and northern Spain. An adult ringed at Glossop in March 1969 was found in the Ukraine in August 1970. One ringed at Kotala, Finland in June 1963 was found dead at Pilsley (near Alfreton) in 1971.

Ringed Plover
Charadrius hiaticula
Scarce passage migrant.

Whitlock found Ringed Plovers to be annual migrants through Derbyshire especially in April and May and to a lesser degree in August and September. This is still the basic pattern of Ringed Plover migration in the county. However this species has now been seen in all months of the year, though winter sightings are rare. May is the chief month for spring passage, and flocks of up to thirty-one have been seen then. Autumn passage, from July to October, usually peaks in August. Thirty-six at Ogston Reservoir in August 1970 is the largest flock yet recorded in Derbyshire. Though autumn records are more widely dispersed the larger numbers usually occur in spring.

Most large wetlands in the county have Ringed Plover records. Clay Mills and Drakelow gravel pits, Barbrook and Ogston Reservoirs, and Egginton sewage farm have been the most regular calling places.

Whitlock is unconvincing about a possible breeding record in 1889. Territorial behaviour and display have been noticed in some recent spring birds, however, and it may be that Ringed Plovers will soon breed regularly in Derbyshire as they do in some adjacent counties.

Little Ringed Plover
Charadrius dubius
Scarce summer visitor and passage migrant.

Little Ringed Plovers first bred in Britain in 1938, when a pair nested in Hertfordshire, and subsequently spread to several other counties. In 1950 a pair appeared near the River Trent at Repton and by careful observation by Repton School Field Club, breeding was proved. The river ran high in 1951 and none were seen. The next record was of passage birds in 1955, but breeding was confirmed at two sites in 1956 and has been regular since in the vicinity of the Trent Valley. In 1958 breeding was proven for the first time in north-east Derbyshire (per F. Price) while the first breeding record for the Peak District was in 1970. The total population rose to an estimated thirty-one to thirty-four pairs in 1970 with a similar number in 1977, but fewer in the intervening years.

Most breed either in gravel pits or on colliery waste areas. Other sites have included limestone quarries (up to 1,300 feet in the Peak District), reservoir shores, clay pits and opencast coal sites.

Records span the period 9 March (1975) to 22 October (1977). Sometimes breeding birds have not settled into their territories until late May. Autumn passage is from July to October, with biggest numbers generally in the first month. Parties of up to a dozen are not rare and there are larger counts of up to twenty-nine (at Drakelow Wildfowl Reserve in July 1973).

A fully-grown Little Ringed Plover ringed

37   *Little Ringed Plover. A small breeding population inhabits gravel pits, quarries, colliery waste areas and similar sites. (Derick Scott)*

at King's Lynn, Norfolk, in August 1970 was controlled at Drakelow in July 1972.

Kentish Plover
Charadrius alexandrinus
Rare vagrant.

One was seen at Ogston Reservoir on 18 September 1959 (Dr I. Newton, *pers comm*) and an immature was at Westhouses 'flash' on 23 July 1968 (R. A. Frost).

Killdeer
Charadrius vociferus
Rare vagrant.

One frequented the open fields of Egginton sewage farm from 29 February–22 March 1964 and, though elusive at times, was seen by a large number of observers (R. H. Appleby, C. N. Whipple *et al*). This was only the sixteenth British and Irish record.

Grey Plover
Pluvialis squatarola
Rare passage migrant.

Whitlock, examining skins in Derby Museum, found a Grey Plover which had been shot at Egginton sewage farm in 1890 and considered to be a Golden Plover. There were other reports for 1893 and 1917, but no more until 1946 since when they have been more frequent. Records are annual since 1967, though they are still uncommon migrants, occurring only in small numbers. Nine over Ramsley Reservoir on 28 September 1972 was the largest party. About seventy individuals have occurred in all months except July, with most occurrences in September, October, March and May.

Grey Plovers have been recorded in Derbyshire at Egginton, Old Whittington and Spondon sewage farms, Barbrook, Ramsley, Ogston, Staunton Harold and

Church Wilne Reservoirs, Elvaston, Clay Mills, Willington, Egginton and Drakelow gravel pits, Shardlow, Derby, Ashbourne, Beeley Moor, Breadsall Moor, Westhouses, and Staveley.

Golden Plover
Pluvialis apricaria
Locally fairly common summer visitor.

flocks. This is still basically the situation today, though we know more now of the bird's breeding status as a result of work by Yalden (1974). He estimated that the Derbyshire element of a maximal 432 pairs in the Peak District National Park was 195 pairs: including Tintwistle RDC (transferred from Cheshire to Derbyshire in 1974) the figure is about 250 pairs.

38   *A Golden Plover photographed on Ladyclough Moor. The southern race, of which this is an extremely pale example, breeds on the high gritstone moors of the Peak. (H. A. Hems)*

Fairly common winter visitor and passage migrant.

Whitlock stated that Golden Plovers bred not uncommonly on all high moorlands in the county, though they were nowhere very numerous. They were widespread winter visitors, sometimes in large

Yalden found Golden Plover more widespread and two to three times more numerous than Dunlin. Though centred on Bleaklow they also breed elsewhere in north-west Derbyshire and on the East Moors, from 1,100 feet to the highest tops. Most nest on Cotton-grass moorland with lesser numbers on Crowberry–Bilberry heaths and burnt areas of Ling. Apart from peripheral decreases, the population was considered relatively stable. Our breeding birds, of the southern race *P.a. apricaria*, take up territory from February onwards with most departing in July.

Golden Plover may be found in non-breeding areas from July to early May. They initially arrive in very small numbers but three-figure flocks are sometimes seen in August, and following further arrivals in September and October (especially) gatherings of some hundreds are sometimes seen. If mild weather prevails these flocks may stay all winter but severely cold conditions cause southward movement, as with Lapwings. By March, when most of the local breeding stock has returned to the hills, large flocks may be seen in the lowlands. From then to late April numbers may increase and these springtime gatherings are usually the largest of all: on occasions over 2,000 have occurred at Egginton sewage farm and well over 1,000 on the Magnesian Limestone plateau. Most, if not all, of these are of the beautiful northern race *C.a. altifrons* which breeds in Iceland and northern Europe. The proportion of southern to northern race birds in the autumn and winter flocks, when the races are indistinguishable, is unknown.

Dotterel
Eudromias morinellus
Rare passage migrant.

According to Whitlock and Jourdain, Dotterel were regular spring migrants in the Peak District in flocks of up to forty. Sometimes birds remained for up to two months, causing conjecture that they might be breeding, but no evidence of this was ever found. Only odd stragglers were seen in the lower parts of the county. As late as 1910 Coward, while reporting a considerable decrease in the preceding fifty years, said that trips of Dotterel were still seen almost every spring in the neighbourhood of Crowden and Woodhead. Thereafter the decrease obviously accelerated since, apart from seven at Dore Moor

in 1916, no more were reported until the 1930s when two were apparently shot in the Moscar area (Herringshaw and Gosney, 1977).

Since the war there have been nine sightings. Two were at Alport Stone on the early date of 18 April, 1946. Three haunted Big Moor in September 1951 and one was seen east of Derwent Dale in May 1953. There were single birds on Bleaklow and at Minninglow in May 1972, two at both Derwent and Melbourne in May 1976, four at an undisclosed locality in October 1976, and three on East Moor in August, 1977.

Turnstone
Arenaria interpres
Rare passage migrant.

This species was first recorded in the county when three were killed by telegraph wires at Longcliffe on 1 June 1906. The next record came in 1943, and Turnstones were seen in four more years before 1957 since when they have transpired to be annual passage migrants. Most are seen singly and any record of more than three is unusual. Exceptional gatherings were of fifteen at Ogston Reservoir in August 1970 and ten at Church Wilne Reservoir in August 1975. Only in January have they not been recorded in Derbyshire though February, October and November have only single records. August has had most sightings, followed by May.

Turnstones are recorded mainly at well-watched waters such as Ogston, Barbrook, Staunton Harold and Church Wilne Reservoirs, Egginton sewage farm, the Trent valley gravel pits and the Trent itself. Other records have come from subsidence lakes in the east, Kedleston Park and a fluorspar tailings dam at Middleton Moor.

Snipe
Gallinago gallinago
Fairly common resident or summer visitor. Common passage migrant and winter visitor.

Whitlock said that many pairs of Snipe bred in various parts of the county, and that the bird's stronghold was in the High Peak, Jourdain adding that few bred in the south.

There is very little published information on subsequent status changes but the number nesting in the lowlands has certainly declined and continues to do so as farming becomes more efficient and marshlands are drained. In these areas the Snipe is now distinctly scarce, and is usually found only in marshes and boggy ground. However the bird maintains its numbers on the gritstone moorlands where there are rushy valleys and bogs, probably to 1,800 feet or so. In these areas in early spring up to a dozen are sometimes seen displaying simultaneously. Good populations are also found in unimproved pastures bordering moorland. There was a pair at the Fernilee hill farm site in 1972, and an average of three territories in the damp field at Broadhurst Edge, but less than a pair at all the other Common Birds Census sites.

In winter the distributional pattern is reversed with large numbers at several lowland localities but few in the Peak District. At this time the Snipe frequents such sites as marshes, reed beds, 'flashes', sewage farms, and the like, and wisps of up to sixty are not uncommon. In the 1960s as many as 500 were recorded at Willington number two gravel pit where a bed of young willows was used as a diurnal gathering ground, the birds arriving early in the mornings (C. N. Whipple, *pers comm*). Autumn passage is evident from July to November and spring movement in March and early April. Numbers at these times are usually considerably higher than those in winter.

Snipe ringed at Willington in autumn or winter have been recovered in France in February (twice), Portugal in December, Denmark in September, Poland in August, and the USSR in September. Birds ringed at Killamarsh in winter have been reported three times from the USSR (in July, August, and September) and from Norway in September. A Drakelow-ringed bird was also recovered in the USSR. One trapped at New Mills in March was caught in Spain in a subsequent January. In Britain, Derbyshire-ringed Snipe have travelled as far as Shropshire, Huntingdonshire and Cornwall.

Great Snipe
Gallinago media
Rare vagrant.

Briggs, Mosley, and Brown all give rather vague references to the occurrences of Great Snipe in their areas. Joseph Whitaker of Rainworth had two from Derbyshire in his collection (Whitlock). These latter birds are now in Mansfield Museum. *VCH* states that one was killed at Bolsover on 12 October 1892 and several were shot in the county in January 1902. Since then three have occurred. A male was shot at Egginton sewage farm on 11 August 1928 (Jourdain diaries) and one on Spondon sewage farm on 11 September 1933 (F. Williamson). One was seen in a marshy field by the River Dove at Ashbourne on 8 December 1941 (Miss K. M. Hollick).

Jack Snipe
Lymnocryptes minimus
Scarce winter visitor and passage migrant.

Jack Snipe are inconspicuous but not uncommon winter visitors and migrants to marshy places throughout Derbyshire. Unlike Common Snipe they do not readily fly and a walk through the marsh is necessary to flush them. Most occur at marshes, sewage farms, subsidence 'flashes' and gravel pits. Thus most are seen in the lowlands with Peak District records rather few. In severe weather Jack Snipe may sometimes be seen in the open, feeding at water margins.

Although 15 August (1965) is the earliest arrival date the species usually arrives in the county from late September to November. Since the largest counts are frequently made in October and November a proportion of our birds must be migrants bound elsewhere. Several remain all winter in the same haunts, numbers increasing as spring migrants pass through from late February into April. There are a few May records, 5th (1973) being the latest. Eighteen is the largest recorded gathering (at Willington, November 1962 and Staveley, October 1973). Any count of eight or more is noteworthy.

There seems to have been no change in status since the days of Whitlock and

Jourdain.

One ringed at Killamarsh in December 1968 was found at Kalingrad, USSR, in October, 1969.

Woodcock
Scolopax rusticola
Scarce resident and winter visitor.

'Though the Woodcock is best known as a migratory bird in Derbyshire a few pairs remain to breed in various localities.' These were Whitlock's words in 1893. Hayfield, Ashford in the Water, Derby and Melbourne were breeding areas known to Jourdain, who wrote in *VCH* of 'a pair or two' breeding annually, with no sign of any increase.

Even as late as 1931 a breeding record from the Chesterfield district in *DAJ* was appended, 'Definite breeding records from Derbyshire are few and far between.' However there were reports from certain districts of remarkable increases later in the 1930s, continuing to at least 1945. The population is probably stabilised now. Howe (1972) estimated the upper Goyt Valley population at ten pairs. In 1952 G. T. Walker considered that about twenty pairs bred in Whitwell Wood and J. Ellis thinks the 1970s population of the wood not much lower. The bird is present in most if not all of the larger woods in northern Derbyshire but more local in the south, and was found in twenty-two of the twenty-seven Atlas squares. Deciduous, mixed or coniferous woodland is accepted, especially in those areas with boggy ground nearby for feeding. An interesting nesting site at Pebley in 1972 was a small hole in a quarry bank, while in 1967 a pair bred successfully in the school grounds at Taxal (DOS Bulletin no 134).

This secretive species would be easy to overlook but for its unique 'roding' flights over its breeding area at dawn and dusk. These begin in February and continue to midsummer.

After the breeding season the species is little seen until October or November when Continental Woodcock arrive in the county to stay until the following spring. Numbers vary: in 'good' winters some woods may hold up to thirty or so individuals, and at this season the bird is sometimes seen in more open country such as farmland hedgerows and small thickets. An interesting record, obviously relating to immigrants, was of a flock of thirty flying over Stanage on 1 November 1892 (Whitlock).

One ringed as a chick at Whitwell in April 1976 was killed at Plesidy, France, in November of the same year.

Curlew
Numenius arquata
Fairly common summer visitor. Scarce passage migrant and winter visitor.

Whitlock stated that Curlews were found all over our high moors northwards from Castleton, though nowhere in any great numbers. Jourdain added that they bred on East Moor as well as in the High Peak, and made the interesting comment that they were often driven up to twenty miles on the first day of the Grouse shooting season.

Since then Derbyshire's Curlews have had fluctuating fortunes. The late 1920s saw a considerable extension of their breeding range, to the areas around Parwich, Newhaven and the Dove valley between Doveridge and Sudbury. The spread continued: by 1931 the species was well-established around Wolfscote Dale, and in 1938 was described as numerous on the hills around Elton and Winster. In the latter year Curlews bred for the first time in the extreme south, near Burton on Trent. Four years later several pairs were nesting in the Trent valley and everywhere they appear to have thrived until the 1950s, when they were common almost throughout the Peak and established in many lowland areas. In 1953 some nests of the forty pairs breeding on East Moor were only thirty yards apart.

In the early 1960s numbers on the gritstone moors were thought to be declining, and this trend continued throughout that decade and into the early 1970s with, more recently, signs of a slight resurgence. Eight pairs were found on the 200 acre Fernilee hill farm site in 1972. While still present in low-

39   *Curlews have been subject to fluctuating fortunes this century. (H. A. Hems)*

land areas, Curlews seem to have declined there too. Anne Shaw, on behalf of DOS, is currently organising a distribution survey.

On moorland, where the wide, flatter stretches are preferred, nests have been found up to 2,000 feet. Elsewhere Curlews breed in pastures, hay meadows and on rough grassland. Territories are usually claimed from late February onwards with most occupied by early April, though cold weather may cause delays and flocking. Most have left the breeding grounds by late August, though occasional laggards may be found until November.

Not infrequently parties are seen on migration over non-breeding areas. Numbers are usually small but E. Walker (*pers comm*) saw 130 over Belper on 1 March 1974. On autumn passage gatherings of sixty have been counted at Drakelow and Egginton sewage farm but present numbers are much smaller. Occasionally birds are seen in winter, most often in the Trent valley.

One ringed as a chick near Bamford in 1971 was shot at Pembrey, Carmarthenshire, in July 1972.

Whimbrel
Numenius phaeopus
Rare passage migrant.

'A regular visitor to the county, in small numbers, during the periods of migration – they seldom alight, though as a rule they do not fly high.' This is how Whitlock described the Whimbrel's status and his words apply today.

Nearly all of the Whimbrel seen in Derbyshire draw attention to themselves by their arresting flight calls which may be heard in any part of the county. Several have been heard nocturnally and it is likely that a considerable amount of passage takes place in darkness. The few grounded birds have been recorded at water margins, on farmland, and especially on the fields of Egginton sewage farm where occasional groups have stayed a few days.

Whimbrels have been recorded in Derbyshire between 22 March (1938) and 6 October (1968). August sees the heaviest movement, followed by May, September and April; June records are rare. The largest flocks have occurred in autumn with about fifty over Shardlow on 16 September 1924 and 'an even larger flock' there at the end of the same month. Thirty-eight flew southwest over Hackenthorpe on 31 July 1967 (Smith, 1974) and twenty flew west over Gleadless on 25 August 1963.

Most of the autumn birds fly between south and west; those in spring are usually moving north to north-west.

Black-tailed Godwit
Limosa limosa
Rare passage migrant.

Whitlock discussed the views of five authorities in accepting the Black-tailed Godwit as a Derbyshire bird. None of the records was completely acceptable to Jourdain, however, and a female shot at Egginton sewage farm on 25 August 1928 must be regarded as the first (per F. G. Hollands). There are twenty-eight subsequent records. Black-tailed Godwits are now fairly regular passage migrants. Most have occurred in the vicinity of the Trent Valley, especially at Egginton sewage farm, but also at Aston, Weston, Willington, Shardlow, Hoon, Drakelow, Newton Solney and Elvaston. Elsewhere in Derbyshire this species has been reported from Borrowash, Ogston Reservoir, Westhouses, Staveley, and the Doe Lea Valley. A maximum of six have occurred together (at Drakelow in May, 1975). Of all twenty-nine records, six have been in August, five in April, May and September, and four in March and July, with extreme dates of 5 March (1972) and 18 September (1974).

Bar-tailed Godwit
Limosa lapponica
Rare passage migrant.

There were three records last century from the Trent valley and Baslow (Whitlock, *VCH*). This century Bar-tailed Godwits have been recorded in eleven of the years between 1953 and 1977, from Barbrook, Ogston and Church Wilne Reservoirs, the gravel pits at Egginton, Elvaston, Drakelow and Swarkestone, Langley Mill, Long Eaton, Staveley, Sutton Scarsdale, Williamthorpe, Buxton, Breaston and the Rivers Dove and Trent. No more than three have been seen together, and almost all have been in the grey-brown immature or winter plumage. Of the twenty-nine dated records there are eight for April, seven for May and September, three for October, and two each for March (the earlier 24th, 1974) and November (the later, 22nd, 1969).

Green Sandpiper
Tringa ochropus
Fairly common passage migrant. Scarce winter visitor.

Green Sandpipers were not rare as passage migrants in the days of Whitlock and Jourdain, chiefly in autumn and winter, and sometimes in spring. Most of these birds frequented rivers and streams. Green Sandpipers are still observed in this habitat but most are now seen at gravel pits and sewage farms, with lesser numbers at reservoirs and other sites. These shy waders prefer smaller enclosed areas rather than the open shores of larger waters.

Several are seen in winter each year, especially in the Trent Valley where they may move around from one site to another. Relatively few are seen in April and May. Return passage takes place from late June onwards, reaching maximum numbers for the year in August and September, though October and November occurrences are not uncommon. Green Sandpipers are seen at many sites every year with the Willington and Egginton sewage farms, which have attracted up to twenty at a time, especially favoured.

Wood Sandpiper
Tringa glareola
Rare passage migrant.

One was shot at Breadsall in August 1885 (Whitlock). Two were recorded in the 1940s, five in the 1950s and a few each year from 1962. Numbers are always small, six at Willington sewage farm in the autumn of 1965 being the largest gathering. Wood Sandpipers have been seen only in the period 1 May (1965) to 29 October (1966) with a little over half of all records in August. There are several May, July and September records but only two each for June and October.

Sewage farms, reservoirs, gravel pits and subsidence 'flashes' form the usual habitats for this migrant. Most of the well-watched wetland sites in the south and east have produced Wood Sandpipers: more unusual localities have included Mercaston, Markeaton, Linton, and Barbrook and Ramsley Reservoirs.

Common Sandpiper
Tringa hypoleucos
Scarce summer visitor. Fairly common passage migrant. Rare winter visitor.

Common Sandpipers are not rare breeding birds along the rivers and large streams of the Peak District, spending their time on the banks and on boulders in midstream. Several pairs also breed by reservoirs though where these are popular with hikers and picknickers the bird often nests some way from the water, sometimes in woodland. The BTO Atlas recorded breeding in eleven squares with birds present or probably breeding in seven others. The current population is probably in the order of seventy to a hundred pairs, a considerable proportion of which breeds in the valleys of the Goyt (with about twelve pairs according to Howe, 1972), Ashop and Derwent. On the last river the Waterways Bird Survey of 1974–5 found an average of eight territories on the nineteen kilometres between Bamford and Beeley. Relatively few breed along limestone streams, however.

These sandpipers have also bred in the lowlands on several occasions. In 1903 a pair

40   *The Common Sandpiper nests mainly by rivers and reservoirs in the Peak District. (H. A. Hems)*

nested in a wheat field a quarter of a mile from water at Osmaston (*The Zoologist*). Breeding was recorded at Williamthorpe in 1933, Ogston Reservoir in 1964 and 1976, at Drakelow in at least three years since 1966, and at Egginton gravel pits and Spondon in 1976.

Whitlock said that they nested in several localities in the Peak, with a few by the upper reaches of the River Trent. There has probably been no great change since those days, though numbers have certainly declined slightly in parts of the Peak in the past two decades.

As passage migrants Common Sandpipers are quite common at a variety of waters, especially in autumn. Spring movements are recorded from early April to late May. The more noticeable return movement is from June onwards with the heaviest passage in late July and August. Thirty at Drakelow in August 1965 is the largest recorded gathering.

Since the early 1950s these waders have tended to remain later into the autumn and since 1958 one or two have overwintered in most years, most of them by the River Trent and adjacent gravel pits, with others at Ogston Reservoir and Shipley Lake.

An adult ringed at Glossop in July 1968 was found dead in 1973, probably in October, at Le Grandbourg, Creuse, France.

Redshank
Tringa totanus
Scarce summer visitor and winter visitor. Fairly common passage migrant.

The Redshank established itself as a Derbyshire breeding bird towards the end of the nineteenth century, and by 1893 was breeding at many places along the Trent (Whitlock). The bird bred in the Dove Valley from 1896 onwards and in 1902 nested near Staveley (Jourdain). In 1910 *DAJ* stated that 'The increase in the breeding distribution of the Redshank in south Derbyshire has been one of the most remarkable features of the bird life of the last half century.' The spread continued and by the 1930s the species was breeding on some of the county's high moorland regions and even 'the barren country round Peak Forest'. (*DAJ*, 1933.)

By the 1940s the increase had slowed or halted and there may have been a decline in the 1950s. However, the 1962–3 winter caused a great collapse which, as with the Green Woodpecker, has never been made good, though continuing wetland drainage has undoubtedly been contributory. Today the bird's breeding population is probably in the order of thirty to fifty pairs, most of which are found at subsidence 'flashes', gravel pits, and water meadows in the south and east. The small population on damp stretches of Peakland moors is showing signs of a welcome increase, with, for example, five pairs at one site in 1976. Birds return to their territories from late February or March onwards. The BTO Atlas enquiry of 1968–72 showed the Redshank's presence in thirteen squares.

As a spring and autumn passage migrant the bird is widespread but rarely numerous, and any flock of six or more is noteworthy. Up to twenty have been seen at Egginton sewage farm (April and August, 1956 and June 1957), and Barlborough (January 1975), and there were thirty at Rowthorne in February 1977. Small numbers winter in the southern and eastern lowlands, with Peak District records rare at that season.

One ringed at Staveley in May 1968 was recovered on the River Severn in Gloucestershire in January 1970 while one ringed as a chick at Whitwell in June 1972 was caught on The Wash in Norfolk in August, 1975.

Spotted Redshank
Tringa erythropus
Rare passage migrant. Exceptional in winter.

There is an undated nineteenth-century Spotted Redshank record from the Dove (Whitlock). One was shot in 1924, there were three records in the 1940s and five in the 1950s. Since 1961, however, they have been recorded annually. Although there have been sightings in all months of the year, Spotted Redshanks are mainly autumnal passage migrants with approximately three quarters of all the records falling in August and September. Spring migrants, usually in April and May, have become more regular in recent years. On two, possibly three, occasions a bird has overwintered in the Trent valley, and October and November records are increasing. Up to five have been seen together in the Trent Valley and at Westhouses.

Most of the well-watched wetland sites in the east and south of Derbyshire have produced records and in the Peak District this species has occurred at Barbrook and Ramsley Reservoirs, and Middleton Moor.

Greenshank
Tringa nebularia
Fairly common passage migrant. Exceptional in winter.

Whitlock mentioned records from the Trent valley area, Ilkeston and Overton Hall and considered Greenshanks occasional visitors. Increased observation has shown that these large noisy waders are regular spring and autumn passage migrants.

Spring migrants are occasionally seen in March but usually occur from late April until early June. Most are seen only briefly. Autumn migration is more leisurely, from late June or July until October, with odd stragglers in November. The main movement is generally in late August and early September. Parties of up to six are not unusual, with a spring maximum of nine in June 1963 and an autumn peak of nineteen near Burton in August 1976 (DOS Bulletin No 233). In 1968–9 one wintered in the Trent Valley and one was seen at Brailsford in February 1976.

Although mostly recorded in the lowlands of the east and south, Greenshanks have visited widely-scattered sites including Ladybower and Fernilee Reservoirs, Bradley, Thorpe, and Brassington.

Knot
Calidris canutus
Rare passage migrant.

Mosley and Brown recorded Knots occasionally and four individuals were shot in southern Derbyshire in 1891 (Whitlock). This century approximately eighty-five birds were recorded between 1930 and 1977. Most occur singly: larger numbers have included six at Staunton Harold Reservoir in June 1966 (T. G. Smith, *pers comm*) and five at Egginton sewage farm in May 1946. Other localities yielding Knot records this century are Egginton, Willington, Elvaston, Clay Mills and Drakelow gravel pits, Ogston and Church Wilne Reservoirs, Westhouses, Beighton, Chinley, Bakewell, Middleton Moor, Williamthorpe, Shipley Lake, and Old Whittington sewage farm. About five visited the Trent and lower Dove in the severe weather early in 1963.

There are records for all months except December. The peak months have been September, August, January and March. Only rarely are summer-plumaged birds seen in Derbyshire.

Purple Sandpiper
Calidris maritima
Rare passage migrant or vagrant.

There are ten records, of which the first two come from Egginton sewage farm where one was killed 'many years ago' and two late in 1890. One was also shot on the River Doe Lea near Sutton Scarsdale in March 1891 (Whitlock). Subsequently single birds have been observed at Ramsley Reservoir on 30 October 1955, and at nearby Barbrook Reservoir on 22 August 1965 and 5 October 1974. Peak Dale quarries was an unlikely locality for one on 16 September 1972. One was at Staunton Harold Reservoir on 22–23 September 1974, one at the Derbyshire side of Attenborough gravel pits on 4 November 1976, and finally one at Ogston Reservoir on 13–14 November 1977.

Little Stint
Calidris minuta
Rare passage migrant.

Whitlock saw the first, near the Erewash mouth on 21 September 1890. There were subsequent sightings or shootings in 1905, 1908, 1922, 1933, 1940, 1952 and 1953. Excepting 1971 this attractive tiny wader has occurred annually since 1957 in varying numbers – for example, there were only two in 1957 and one in 1968 but at least thirteen in 1965 and 1973 and nineteen or more in 1967. Over 150 individuals have been recorded in Derbyshire. Well over half have occurred in September, with several records in August and October, and a very few in March, April, May and July. The earliest date is 8 March (1964) and the latest 21 October (1972 and 1973).

The largest gathering was twelve at Clay Mills gravel pits in September 1967; small parties of one to five are more usual. Most autumn birds are immature, adults being uncommon.

Little Stints have occurred at Egginton sewage farm, Williamthorpe, Barbrook, Ogston and Staunton Harold Reservoirs, Hilton, Clay Mills, Elvaston, Drakelow and Egginton gravel pits, Westhouses, Beighton, Whitwell, and Middleton Moor.

Temminck's Stint
Calidris temminckii
Rare passage migrant.

There are five records, all quite recent. One was at Westhouses on 25 September 1967 (R. A. Frost) and two at Breaston on 25–26 May 1969 (R. A. Frost *et al*). At Drakelow Wildfowl Reserve single birds stayed during 25–28 May 1971 and 16–18 May 1974 (T. Cockburn *et al*). An adult remained at Ogston Reservoir from 16–21 August 1975 (M. F. Stoyle, E. Walker *et al*).

Pectoral Sandpiper
Calidris melanotos
Rare vagrant.

One frequented Egginton gravel pits and sewage farm from 12–24 August 1962 (R. A. Frost *et al*). Another was at Shipley Lake on 1 September 1975 (A. Warren, P. Wright). Two different birds occurred in 1976: at Drakelow Wildfowl Reserve on 25 September (J. C. Eyre-Dickinson, M. J. Giles) and Elvaston Quarry on 26 September (D. Kent, R. W. Key).

Dunlin
Calidris alpina
Scarce summer visitor. Fairly common pass-

age migrant and winter visitor.

Although in 1893 Whitlock suspected that Dunlin bred in or near Derbyshire, this was first proven by Arthur Whitaker in the mid 1930s, though there had been records of birds seen in summer in suitable breeding terrain in some intervening years. There followed several rather vague and sometimes conflicting reports of their true numbers but the position has been clarified by Yalden (1974). He found that out of a maximal Peak District National Park population of 195 pairs, some sixty-seven would be in Derbyshire: including Tintwistle RDC, which was transferred to the county in 1974, the figure becomes ninety-three pairs. Dunlin breed in much the same areas as Golden Plover in roughly one third to half the latter's numbers. Yalden thought that the paucity of past Dunlin breeding records was mainly the result of its being overlooked: however, excellent ornithologists like Gibbs and Whitaker rarely found the species, implying a genuine increase in numbers this century.

Dunlin arrive on their breeding grounds rather later than Golden Plover – from April usually, with most gone by August. There are occasional records from breeding sites as early as February and as late as November. Yalden (*loc cit*) found Dunlin breeding from 1,300 feet to the hill tops. Cotton-grass moorland is favoured, especially in areas containing small pools. The Bleaklow complex is the main Derbyshire breeding area with much smaller numbers in sites like Axe Edge and Ringinglow Bog.

At Derbyshire's reservoirs, lakes, gravel pits, sewage farms and riversides, Dunlin are not uncommon passage migrants. They may occur in any month but are usually most numerous on autumn migration between July and November, when flocks of up to thirty have been seen. However the largest gatherings of all have occurred in spring. 140 were near Castleton on 29 March 1977; and on 25 April 1969, there were at least ninety at Staunton Harold Reservoir and sixty-five at Clay Mills gravel pits. There are usually a few somewhere in the lowlands in winter and hard weather often brings in small parties, presumably from the coast: in the 1962–3 winter up to sixty-two were seen on the River Trent. There are signs that Dunlin are becoming more regular winter visitors to the county.

Curlew Sandpiper
Calidris ferruginea
Rare passage migrant.

Curlew Sandpipers were first recorded in Derbyshire by H. Tomlinson in 1905, at Egginton sewage farm, almost inevitably. The pattern for several other species of migrant waders is then repeated with no more records for a long time (in this case 1952) followed by an era of more intense watching which has proved them to be more regular than previously thought. Curlew Sandpipers have occurred in seventeen years since 1952, though their appearances are still irregular. In some years, as in 1967, parties of up to sixteen have been seen; in others none are reported. Most are immature birds: adults are uncommon and those in summer plumage rare.

Apart from two spring records in May 1958 and April 1963 all have occurred between 13 July and 10 October, with September providing about three-quarters of all records. Curlew Sandpipers have been reported from Egginton, Spondon and Willington sewage farms, Barbrook and Ogston Reservoirs, Egginton, Willington, Clay Mills, Elvaston and Drakelow gravel pits and Westhouses.

Sanderling
Calidris alba
Rare passage migrant.

Whitlock recorded three shot at Walton on Trent on an unknown date. There are many records from 1943 onwards and Sanderlings have occurred annually since 1960, especially in spring. Just over half of all the records have been in May, with the remainder largely in April, July, August and September, and a very few in all months except March.

Usually small numbers are involved. The largest group was of twenty-five at Breaston in May 1969 and Drakelow Wildfowl Reserve has been host to parties of nine and ten.

Drakelow is now the most regular calling place in the county for Sanderlings. Other sites where they have been seen include the reservoirs at Barbrook, Ramsley, Ogston, Staunton Harold and Church Wilne, Derby, Shardlow, various Trent Valley gravel pits, Egginton sewage farm, Westhouses, Williamthorpe, Staveley, Sutton Scarsdale, Beighton, Whitwell, and Middleton Moor.

Ruff
Philomachus pugnax
Scarce passage migrant. Rare in winter.

Though recorded at many sites in Derbyshire Ruffs have been seen most often at Egginton sewage farm where the wet fields have formed an ideal habitat for them. Now that the sewage farm's size is diminished, fewer are seen, though the bulk of the county's Ruffs still use the Trent valley as a migration route. Other sites which have yielded Ruff records are Butterley, Barbrook, and Ogston Reservoirs, the 'flashes' at Sutton Scarsdale, Beighton, Westhouses, Langley Mill, Brinsley and Staveley, Spondon sewage farm and Clowne. Whitlock knew of only a few Trent valley records.

Occasionally Ruffs are seen in winter though only rarely has over-wintering been proven. Spring passage usually takes place from March to May and involves only a few birds, with a maximum of ten at Willington sewage farm in April 1965. Autumn passage takes place from late June or July until October or November. Numbers are greater than in spring, with twenty at Egginton sewage farm in August 1964, the largest Derbyshire gathering.

Avocet
Recurvirostra avosetta
Rare passage migrant or vagrant.

Whitlock and Jourdain give details of four nineteenth-century records from the Dove and Trent Valleys. R. H. Appleby and C. E. Brown found five on Egginton sewage farm on 6 September 1956, one remaining to 9th. Eight flew south-east near Shardlow on

3 April 1960. One was seen at Clay Mills gravel pits on 30–31 May 1969 and Elvaston Quarry held two from 11–15 May 1975 and one on 9 May 1976. Two were at Egginton sewage farm on 1–3 June 1977.

Grey Phalarope
Phalaropus fulicarius
Rare vagrant.

About eighteen have occurred including five since 1968, at Barbrook and Church Wilne Reservoirs and Egginton number four gravel pit. Of all the dated records five were first recorded in October and four in September. There are also records for August, November and December. Most if not all are gale victims and are seen only briefly but in September 1935 one remained for a fortnight on Cromford Canal. Although all the recent birds have occurred on larger waters, other Grey Phalaropes have been seen on a pond near Winster, and a small dam in Sheffield.

Wilson's Phalarope
Phalaropus tricolor
Rare vagrant.

An adult female visited Ogston Reservoir on 23–24 June 1965 (R. A. Frost, M. F. Stoyle *et al*). This was the eighteenth British and Irish record.

Stone Curlew
Burhinus oedicnemus
Rare vagrant.

In 1829, Glover stated that Stone Curlews bred on our moors and Whitlock thought this may have been possible since a few pairs bred in Nottinghamshire at that time. Jourdain (*VCH*) was more sceptical, and as there appear to be no instances of Stone Curlews breeding on upland moors elsewhere Glover's statement must be regarded as unproven.

One was shot near Ashover in 1890 (Whitlock) and one killed in October 1922 almost certainly came from Shardlow. D. C. Hulme gave a convincing description of one flying east over Findern on 7 November 1954. On 2 September 1961 one flushed from a rubbish tip at Woodhouse, Yorkshire flew to Beighton, Derbyshire, (F. N. Barker, R. G. Hawley) and one was seen in tussocky grassland on Big Moor on 22 May 1971 (R. A. Frost, M. F. Stoyle *et al*).

Great Skua
Stercorarius skua
Rare vagrant.

Four of the five county records have occurred since 1971. One was at Church Wilne Reservoir on 26 September 1971 (R. W. Key, T. G. Smith). Two flew south over the Goyt valley on 27 May 1972 (per G. Howe). One at Ogston Reservoir on 12–13 April 1974 was seen to kill and eat a Coot (J. R. Calladine, S. Jackson *et al*). One was at Egginton number seven gravel pit on 2 September 1974 (J. C. Barker). The earlier record was of an exhausted bird standing on a road near Sheldon on 14 October 1934, following a violent north-westerly gale in the night (W. Shipton).

Pomarine Skua
Stercorarius pomarinus
Rare vagrant.

An immature was killed on moorland near Strines in early October 1898 (*VCH*). Strines is just in Yorkshire but as Chislett (1952) does not include it, presumably the record was for Derbyshire. Whitlock admitted a record of one obtained near Burnaston in September 1854 but Jourdain regarded it as unproven and in view of this only the later record is acceptable. K. Bollington saw an adult flying over Drakelow Wildfowl Reserve on 20 September 1977.

Arctic Skua
Stercorarius parasiticus
Rare vagrant.

Whitlock knew of two undated birds killed near Burton and one found at Mickleover in 1879 or 80. The next records came in 1948 when C. B. Chambers saw nine over Ashover on 25 March and two at Hardwick on 25 May. There were two records in the 1950s, three (all at Ogston Reservoir) in the 1960s and nine in 1970–6; three was the largest group. No fewer than ten of the sixteen dated records have been in September, with three in August and singles in March, May and July. Many, but not all, appear to have occurred as a result of gales.

Other Derbyshire sites where Arctic Skuas have been identified are Derwent, Ramsley, Staunton Harold, Church Wilne and Barbrook Reservoirs, Leash Fen, Drakelow and Buxton.

Long-tailed Skua
Stercorarius longicaudus
Rare vagrant.

One was picked up in an emaciated condition on the Derwent at Derby at the end of October 1922. Whitlock thought the evidence 'very slender' for Mosley's claim of its occurrence near Burton.

Great Black-backed Gull
Larus marinus
Regular visitor, fairly common in winter, scarce in summer.

The winter incursions of Great Black-backed Gulls into Derbyshire are a recent phenomenon. Whitlock and Jourdain found these rapacious gulls occasional visitors, with never more than five together. This pattern of affairs continued in the first half of this century. Even as late as 1964 there had been no record of more than single figures. Thirteen in 1965 and fifteen in 1966 were the largest gatherings in those years but in 1967 flocks of sixty and seventy occurred. Since then numbers have rapidly increased and several hundred now visit the county each winter, frequenting farmland and other open ground, and rubbish dumps in particular. At roost, counts of 100–250 have been made at Church Wilne, Staunton Harold, and Ogston Reservoirs.

Great Black-backs are quite common from November to April, with the largest numbers between December and February. They remain scarce however, between May and October, with only single figures recorded in these months.

A bird ringed on Great Ainov Island in the Murmansk region of the USSR was found dead at Shirland in spring, 1967.

Lesser Black-backed Gull
Larus fuscus
Common summer visitor, passage migrant and winter visitor.

Whitlock thought that Lesser Black-backs were migrants in the Trent Valley but were only storm-driven to other parts of the county, and Jourdain echoed this. Few records were received in the first half of this century. However an increase was noted from 1951 onwards and by the mid 1950s flocks of some hundreds, now quite commonplace, were being noted in the east (especially at rubbish tips and opencast coal sites) and south. M. J. Rayner said in 'The Lesser Black-backed Gull in Derbyshire' (*Bird Study*, 1963) that those summering were mainly sub-adults and immatures. He found evidence of southward movement from July to September and a heavy west north-west spring passage over Duffield. This still holds good today.

A major change since Rayner's time is the great increase in numbers wintering and in January 1975 as many as 1,800 were counted at Ogston Reservoir, though this was rather exceptional. A few hundred is more normal, both here and at roosts in south Derbyshire.

Largest counts are made at the various roosts. Drakelow Wildfowl Reserve supported 5,000 birds in August 1972, whilst the maxima for Staunton Harold and Church Wilne Reservoirs are 2,500 and 1,850 respectively. The autumnal roost at Barbrook has held up to 1,200 birds.

Scandinavian Lesser Black-backed Gulls, *L. f. fuscus*, recognisable from the British race, *graellsii*, by their very dark upperparts may be seen at any time of year but are mainly autumn migrants. Up to twenty-five per night have been counted at the Barbrook Reservoir gull roost.

Birds ringed as chicks at Walney Island, Lancashire, have been recovered at Beighton and Drakelow, and likewise one from Anglesey was found at Church Wilne Reservoir twelve years later.

Herring Gull
Larus argentatus

Common winter visitor. Scarce in summer except in north-west.

Now a familiar wintertime sight at rubbish dumps throughout Derbyshire Herring Gulls, too, have increased remarkably in the last two decades. Whitlock reported that they were commoner than other large gulls and flocks regularly moved north over the Trent valley in spring. In November 1905 a flock of 150 plus gulls, believed mainly of this species, was seen in the Dove valley; yet between 1906 and 1952 no double-figure flocks were seen. Numbers began to increase around 1953 and in 1958 a gathering of 210 was reported. By 1961 maximum flocks reported had topped 500. Gulls began to roost on Ogston in 1963 and this reservoir has provided the largest Derbyshire counts, 2,800 roosting in January 1969 (Frost et al, 1969) Meanwhile gulls started to use the Staunton Harold and Church Wilne Reservoirs shortly after flooding and numbers at the two have reached 900 and 1,300. Doubtless the creation of safe roosting places such as these has enabled gulls fully to exploit inland environments.

While most are seen in lowland regions Herring Gulls are common in the Peak District in winter and counts of over 500 have been made. However while large numbers in the lowlands are usually found from November to March or April, counts in the north-west of Derbyshire may still exceed three figures in summer.

A bird ringed on the Isle of Man in July 1958 was killed at Ilkeston in the following February. One ringed at Beighton in February 1963 was found in Aberdeenshire in May 1965, and an adult caught near Swadlincote in January 1974 was found dead in Norway in July 1975.

Herring Gulls with yellow legs or dark mantles, indicating a northern race, have been seen on occasions.

Common Gull

Larus canus
Fairly common winter visitor and passage migrant.

Whitlock found Common Gulls to be frequent visitors, passing through in small parties. This is still the case today, though with our large reservoirs providing roosting places Common Gulls also winter in the county.

The species prefers limestone grassland for feeding and is most numerous on the Carboniferous Limestone of the Buxton area where flocks of up to 200 have been recorded. Most of the birds wintering in this area probably roost on the Manchester reservoirs. The Magnesian Limestone area of north-east Derbyshire is also favoured by Common Gulls, though to a lesser degree.

Though small numbers may be found anywhere else in the county the largest counts usually come from reservoir roosts. Up to 100 have been seen at both Ogston and Church Wilne. Even in winter numbers vary from day to day, and a considerable amount of movement may take place in mid-winter. Late March and April usually sees a passage between east and north when adults move back to their breeding grounds. Small numbers may be seen in May and June with a return passage, less concentrated than that of spring, from July to October.

Glaucous Gull

Larus hyperboreus
Rare winter visitor.

Whitlock had little doubt that Glaucous Gulls sometimes occurred in the county as he often saw light-coloured immature gulls which he could not certainly identify. Additionally two were shot just inside the Nottinghamshire boundary in 1872. However the first definite sighting came as late as 28 January 1968 when D. H. Bloom and R. A. Frost saw a third winter bird at Ogston Reservoir. Each subsequent year has produced sightings, both at the same reservoir and elsewhere. Recordings embrace all months in the period 8 October (1974) to 22 April (1969) with most seen in March, February, January and December, and least in November. Of a grand total of over eighty individuals, just over half have been first winter birds. About twenty-two adults have been seen; third year birds are rare.

The well-watched Ogston Reservoir has

supplied many records. Others have come from Church Wilne, Staunton Harold, Barbrook and Ladybower Reservoirs, Willington and Elvaston gravel quarries, Drakelow Wildfowl Reserve, Monsal Dale, Staveley, Belper, Sawley, Shipley and Castle Gresley.

Iceland Gull
Larus glaucoides
Rare winter visitor.

R. A. Frost saw a second winter bird at Beighton on 25 November 1966, the first Derbyshire record. This heralded a spate of records, as with the Glaucous Gull, though not to the same extent and Iceland Gulls remain rarer than their larger relatives. About forty have since occurred, in all years save 1967 and 1971. No third winter birds have been identified: some seventeen were adults, with first and second winter birds in almost equal numbers.

Records have fallen within the period 21 November (1974) to 13 April (1969) with over half in February and March, and with surprisingly few January sightings. The sites where these gulls have been recorded are generally the same as those for Glaucous Gull – Ogston, Staunton Harold and Church Wilne Reservoirs, Sawley, Drakelow Wildfowl Reserve, Elvaston Quarry, and Arkwright.

Mediterranean Gull
Larus melanocephalus
Rare vagrant.

R. A. Frost saw one in second summer plumage at Westhouses on 18 July 1965, probably the first to be recorded in the Midlands.

Little Gull
Larus minutus
Rare passage migrant.

At least three were seen or killed on the Trent last century (Whitlock, *VCH*). Subsequent records came as late as 1962 when single birds visited Barbrook and Ogston Reservoirs in August. None was seen in 1963 but there are records annually since 1964, and numbers have generally increased, though four is the largest group reported.

Approximately seventy have been seen since 1962 with most arriving in August, September and May in that order. There are records for all other months between April (earliest 8th, 1976) and October (latest 28th, 1970) with an isolated January report in 1851. An immature summered in the Trent Valley in 1973. Most Derbyshire Little Gulls are immatures, though adults are not rare.

Little Gulls have occurred mainly at Ogston, Barbrook, Staunton Harold and Church Wilne Reservoirs. A few records have come from the River Trent and associated gravel pits, Butterley and Combs Reservoirs, Middleton Moor and Palterton.

Black-headed Gull
Larus ridibundus
Rare breeder. Common non-breeding resident, passage migrant and winter visitor.

Although at the present time the lagoons of Derby sewage works, which hold an annual population of twenty to forty pairs, form the only regular Derbyshire nesting site for this small gull, the position was very different earlier this century. The first record of breeding in the county was in 1918 at Leash Fen, and this site held over 100 pairs in some years until 1944 when military operations caused the birds to desert. Between 1920 and 1944 gulleries were also recorded on Big Moor (maximum fifty-six pairs), near Hathersage (up to 200 pairs), Egginton sewage farm (200 to 300 pairs) and Celanese Lakes, Spondon (200 pairs) with much smaller numbers elsewhere. Willington number two gravel pit was occupied from 1956–61; in the final year 100 pairs were present but they were very unsuccessful and the site was abandoned. Since 1955 small numbers have nested erratically at the gravel pits at Drakelow, Clay Mills and Swarkestone, at Egginton sewage farm, Ringinglow Bog, and in Longdendale.

Conversely, as a non-breeding visitor, the Black-headed Gull has increased enormously. Whitlock found it the commonest gull, to be observed in many parts of the county, and he had himself seen flocks of up to forty. Numbers continued to increase and flocks became much more regular. Even as recently as 1955, however, the largest gathering of the year was of 300. Now four-figure counts are common-place at roosting sites. Up to 14,000 have been seen at Church Wilne Reservoir, 7,000 at Drakelow Wildfowl Reserve, 5,200 at Ogston Reservoir, and 3,500 at Staunton Harold Reservoir. That all of these sites are of relatively new creation indicates why the species has been able to spend so much of its time in Derbyshire. The bird feeds on farmland, water bodies and rubbish tips, and the largest numbers occur in winter, but flocks are commonly seen at any time between July and March with smaller numbers from April to June.

There have been several foreign recoveries of this gull, chiefly of those ringed by the Sorby Natural History Society. There are four recoveries involving both Sweden and Denmark, three from Finland, two from Norway and one from Russia.

Sabine's Gull
Larus sabini
Rare vagrant.

The Zoologist (1903) records a young bird shot at Chaddesden about 26 August 1894.

Kittiwake
Rissa tridactyla
Rare passage migrant and vagrant.

There has been a major change in status this century. Whitlock described Kittiwakes as second only to Black-headed Gulls in their Derbyshire appearances, the two species often consorting. They were 'pretty regular' in the Trent valley, being visible almost any day in March and April. At other times of year, and in other areas, Kittiwakes were storm-blown vagrants. Jourdain largely agreed, stating that they were met with even more frequently than Black-headed Gulls on the upper Trent.

The next reported occurrence, almost incredibly, was forty-one years after the publication of *VCH*, in 1946. Whether Kittiwakes were seen in the intervening years and considered too insignificant to record is unknown. The four records in the 1950s were all of dead or dying birds. However over fifty were recorded in the 1960s and the years 1970–77 produced around ninety individuals. Most visit Derbyshire singly but there are several records of up to four, and two of surprisingly large flocks of twenty at Derwent Reservoir in March 1962, and twenty-two at Ogston Reservoir in April 1977.

There are sightings for all months with most in April and March and fewest in June and October. Some of the spring birds have occurred in calm weather and have accompanied Common Gulls. It seems from this, plus the fact that adults outnumber immatures, and flight directions that, at least in spring, Kittiwakes are migrants rather than vagrants.

Since 1945 Kittiwakes have been recorded at all the large lowland reservoirs, Barbrook and Derwent reservoirs, Ashbourne, Sawley, Shardlow, Swadlincote, Drakelow, Egginton, Elvaston, Clay Mills, Matlock, Sutton Scarsdale, Ladycross Moor, Big Moor, Monsal Dale, Belper, Loscoe Dam, Brinsley, Mapperley and Shipley Lake.

Black Tern
Chlidonias niger
Scarce passage migrant.

Whitlock knew the Black Tern only as a spring visitor and stated that it was 'pretty regular' when easterly winds blew during its migration periods. Nowadays these graceful birds are regular both in spring and autumn but are usually most numerous in spring, when they are still very much connected with easterly airflows: in autumn their presence often seems to be associated with frontal systems.

In spring small parties are seen every May, when roughly a third of all records have occurred. They rarely linger at any water. About a quarter have occurred in both August and September, while there are several June and July records, and a few for April and October, with extreme dates of 18 April (1964) and 13 October (1957). The largest flocks occurred on 30 May 1966 when twenty-eight were at Ogston Reservoir and twenty-five at Staunton Harold Reservoir. Twenty-two visited Barbrook Reservoir on 22 July 1969.

The usual reservoirs, lakes and gravel pits produce the bulk of our Black Tern records, though a few have visited quite small waters such as Bradley Dam, and Yeldersley and Ednaston ponds.

White-winged Black Tern
Chlidonias leucopterus
Rare passage migrant or vagrant.

An immature was at Staunton Harold Reservoir on 23–24 August 1968 (R. A. Frost, M. J. Giles, J. H. Horobin) and an adult visited Ogston Reservoir on 30 August 1976 (T. Sexey, K. Smith, M. E. Taylor).

Whiskered Tern
Chlidonias hybrida
Rare vagrant.

One was shot on the Trent near Barrow in the autumn of 1883 (Whitlock).

Caspian Tern
Hydroprogne caspia
Rare vagrant.

One was seen at Egginton number seven gravel pit on 3 June 1968 (R. H. Appleby, T. G. Smith, C. N. Whipple). Another flew over Drakelow Wildfowl Reserve on 10 October 1976 (T. Cockburn). The former was approximately the sixty-seventh record for Britain and Ireland and the latter the 120th.

Common Tern
Sterna hirundo
Rare summer visitor. Scarce passage migrant.

Common Terns, as in Whitlock's day, are quite regular at migration times though they do not generally occur in such large flocks as Arctic Terns. They have been recorded in all months between the extreme dates of 26 March (1964) and 28 October (1967), most frequently in May, August and September. In January 1940 one was seen on the Derwent at Rowsley. Some of those recorded in late summer are in family parties, with migrant adults feeding their young. Most

records come from the lowlands of the south and east, and Peak District sightings are rather uncommon. The reservoirs and gravel pits supply most records: some have been observed flying over open country or urban areas and there is one record of a Common Tern with gulls in a field well away from water.

They occur quite commonly in small groups, with twenty-five at Ogston in May 1970 the largest assembly of migrants. One at Church Gresley in April 1947 suffered an unlikely fate when it was killed by a Sparrowhawk.

Common Terns first nested in Derbyshire in 1956 at Clay Mills and Swarkestone gravel pits (Miss B. Y. Aldred, R. H. Appleby). In most years since 1966 pairs have held territory at several Trent Valley pits (only those with small islands are accepted), with nesting proven in eight of the years. Five pairs held territory in 1976, and about ten pairs in 1977, seven of them at Elvaston.

Arctic Tern
Sterna paradisaea
Scarce passage migrant.

Although generally less regular than Common Terns, Arctic Terns have occurred in larger flocks and many are recorded in some years – for example, 1967, 1972 and 1974. Similar influxes obviously occurred last century, as Whitlock says Arctic Terns were 'very numerous' in May 1842. However he knew of few other records. One was seen in 1938 and birds were found dead in three places on 26 April 1947, following a severe gale. The next sightings came in 1961 and 1962, and records have been annual since 1964. Arctic Terns have been seen in all months between the extreme dates of 10 April (1966) and 12 November (1967), the greatest numbers occurring in spring. Small parties are regular and the largest flocks were of about 100 in May 1972 and thirty-eight in April 1974, both at Ogston Reservoir. By contrast the largest autumn record is of only nine (September, 1967).

Arctic Terns may be seen on any water

body in the county but are chiefly seen at the larger reservoirs. Most occur at times of strong winds and or wet weather.

One ringed as a chick in Lolland, Denmark, in June 1969 was found dead at Butterley Reservoir in April 1974.

Roseate Tern
Sterna dougallii
Rare vagrant.

The first Derbyshire sighting was of four at Staunton Harold Reservoir on 18 June 1965 (S. Pimm, B. C. Potter) and probably the same four were at nearby Swarkestone gravel pits four days later (P. Hall, S. Pimm, J. Middleton). One was with other terns at Clay Mills gravel pits on 14 May 1967 (J. C. Barker, P. Hall) and similarly at Ogston Reservoir on 15 May 1968 (M. F. Stoyle). Three authorities made reference to the occurrence of this tern in Derbyshire but none was acceptable to Whitlock or Jourdain.

Little Tern
Sterna albifrons
Rare passage migrant.

Whitlock quoted five eighteenth and nineteenth-century records from the neighbourhood of the Trent and Sinfin. Since 1944 about forty have been recorded, usually singly but occasionally in twos with three together in May 1977. Most are seen very fleetingly, though one roosted overnight at Drakelow gravel pits on 1 July 1974. There have been thirteen May records, seven in September, and one to four in April, June, July and August. Extreme dates are 9 April (1948) and 29 September (1944).

Little Terns have occurred at Combs, Butterley, Mapperley, Barbrook, Ogston, Church Wilne and Staunton Harold Reservoirs, Melbourne Pool, Calwich, Sawley, Marlpool, Shipley Lake and Swarkestone, Clay Mills, Willington and Drakelow gravel pits.

Records unpublished by DOS are of singles at Staunton Harold Reservoir on 22 May 1966 and Swarkestone gravel pits on 21 May 1972 (T. G. Smith, *pers comm*) and

Pebley Pond on 17 September 1967 (SNHS Newsletter).

Sandwich Tern
Sterna sandvicensis
Rare passage migrant.

Whitlock saw one on the River Trent in May 1888: he was disinclined to accept Briggs' statement that they were regular around Melbourne in spring. Remarkably, no more records followed Whitlock's until 1967 since when there have been twenty records, some in each year except 1975. Apart from groups of six and three which flew north-west over Ogston Reservoir on 28 July 1969 all records have been of four birds or fewer. Seven records have come from Ogston Reservoir, five from Staunton Harold Reservoir, two each from Clay Mills, and Drakelow gravel pits, and Church Wilne Reservoir, and one from Elvaston Quarry, and Staveley where two were seen flying over open countryside. Of all the records eight were in May, seven in September, with two each in July and August, and one in April and June. Extreme dates are 30 April (1976) and 29 September (1968).

Razorbill
Alca torda
Rare vagrant.

The only record concerns an adult which stayed at Staunton Harold Reservoir from 18 October – 13 November 1970 (R. W. Key, T. G. Smith *et al*).

Little Auk
Plautus alle
Rare vagrant.

About five were reported from the south of the county last century (Whitlock, *VCH*) and in this century about twenty-five have occurred in widely-scattered localities, about half of them between 25 January and 18 February 1912. Usually Little Auks in Derbyshire are picked up dead or dying in sites often unconnected with water and not uncommonly in urban areas. The most recent record is of one (ultimately killed by Carrion Crows) at Staunton Harold Reservoir on 25–27 December 1976. No doubt most occur as a result of severely cold weather or coastal gales, or a combination of the two.

Surprisingly there are records for all months between the two extreme dates of 21 September (1968) and 24 April (1918).

Puffin
Fratercula arctica
Rare vagrant.

One was shot near Derby before 1789 (Whitlock). For 1945 there is an astonishing record of forty to fifty on Melbourne Pool in severe weather in mid-January: one is reported to have entered a house. It appears however that the birds were not seen by an ornithologist and the record cannot be accepted. Doubts also arise over the next report, of a juvenile at Markham Colliery in July 1952. Since the bird could not fly it was thought to have been brought from the coast by humans.

The last four records are more authentic and concern Puffins picked up sick or dead. These come from Chesterfield on an unspecified date in 1954 (*Birds of the Chesterfield Area 1870–1970*), Fernilee Reservoir on 7 July 1963 (A. C. Burgess, J. Sorenson), Old Whittington on 26 October 1969 (per *The Derbyshire Times*), and Monsal Dale on 20 October 1970 (T. B. Carter).

Pallas's Sandgrouse
Syrrhaptes paradoxus
Rare vagrant.

Two were shot 'on our northern borders' in 1863. In May 1888 one was found dead at Breaston and others were said to have been seen, and one shot but not preserved (Whitlock). Two were shot at Parwich in June 1888: both Whitlock and Jourdain (*VCH*) give the date as July 1889 but this was corrected in *The Zoologist* (1909). Jourdain thought he saw three near Ashbourne in May 1900 but later withdrew the record.

Stockdove
Columba oenas
Fairly common resident.

Whitlock and Jourdain were of the opinion that Stockdoves were fairly common throughout the county, the latter thinking that the availability of nesting sites governed their distribution. In 1932 numbers around Buxton were reported to be increasing, but the first major change of status seems to have happened in the late 1950s and early 1960s when a fairly general decrease in numbers was noticed. This was attributed to poisoning by pesticides, and like other affected species, Stockdove numbers increased again as greater control was placed over pesticide usage. However, some old sites remain unoccupied and Howe (1972) stated that numbers in the Goyt Valley were still lower than formerly. On the other hand numbers in north-east Derbyshire have increased markedly in recent years: and although three observers described Stockdoves as rare in the Peak District in 1958, they are now quite common in places – notably in the limestone quarries around Buxton. Only one ten kilometre square was without this species according to the BTO Atlas findings. At Mapleton there were no territories in 1963–5, one in 1966 and four or five by 1972.

Our birds nest in a variety of sites – chiefly in holes or among epicormic shoots of trees in woods and parks, or isolated specimens in hedges and fields. Many nest in crevices in cliff faces. Nests have been found in buildings and walls, even in towns, under grass tufts and in rabbit burrows. Like the Wood Pigeon, this species may have a long breeding season with young recorded in the nest in late October.

Farmland, of a variety of types, forms the chief feeding habitat for Stockdoves. Outside the breeding season feeding flocks of a hundred or more may be seen in favoured areas. The largest recorded gatherings have been seen at roosts with up to 400 at Carr Wood, Ogston, and some 550 at Renishaw in the 1971–2 winter.

Feral Pigeon
Columba livia
Fairly common resident.

This species is rarely recorded by ornithologists and yet it is found not only in towns but rurally too, even in remote sites like Kinder Downfall, and it should be more fully reported. Many breed on buildings and other structures such as bridges and old colliery chimneys and in Peakland cliffs, as reported by Whitlock who queried whether our white-rumped pigeons were genuine Rock Doves.

The BTO Atlas received reports of confirmed breeding in six ten kilometre squares, probably breeding from two, and presence in a further six, though possibly some field-workers did not bother to look for or report this bird.

Woodpigeon
Columba palumbus
Abundant resident.

This is a very numerous bird which breeds throughout the county, frequenting all kinds of woodland, tall hedgerows, parkland, large suburban gardens and even in scattered trees on moorlands. There has probably been an increase since the turn of the century when Whitlock and Jourdain described the bird as common in all wooded parts. As the species is not included in the BTO Common Birds Census, however, no quantitative infor-mation on breeding numbers can be given; however it is very much more numerous than any other pigeon or dove, and is a prominent member of the woodland community. Like the Stockdove this species has a long breeding season, with eggs recorded as late as October. Although severe winters cause some mortality recovery is very swift.

The Woodpigeon feeds to some degree in woodland but finds much more of its food on farmland. Large flocks (sometimes of hundreds) often occur, especially in stubble and root fields. Sometimes there appear to be minor invasions of Wood Pigeons though it is not known whether these have come from outside the county or are merely local birds congregating at an abundant food supply. However, the largest yearly totals usually concern flocks roosting in woodland. There were some 4,000 at Pleasley Park in December 1974 and up to 2,000 have been reported from other woodlands.

Turtle Dove
Streptopelia turtur
Fairly common summer visitor.

The Turtle Dove was not included in the

41   *Wood Pigeons may breed wherever there are trees, and they form large winter flocks on farmland. (J. Russell)*

42 *Turtle Doves breed in hedgerows, thickets and woodlands, feeding largely in nearby cereal fields. (J. Russell)*

lists of Pilkington or Glover and the keen-eyed J. J. Briggs of Melbourne apparently met with only a solitary pair in his many years of birdwatching. In 1893 Whitlock described the bird as common and to be seen 'any day in the summer months on the fallows in all the lower portions of the county'. Twenty years prior to that it had been unknown. In 1905 *VCH* said that it was fairly numerous in the Trent valley and locally distributed over the whole of south and north-east Derbyshire. It was first noted at Curbar in 1890 when it was still extending its range northward.

There was little further comment on numbers until the period 1949–54 when several observers detected a decline, but in the late 1950s the trend was reversed. Numbers vary annually and at present there are no pointers to any long-term change. Any losses caused by increasing urbanisation have probably

been offset by the conversion of pasture to arable farming.

The Magnesian Limestone plateau is now the Turtle Dove's county headquarters, the mixture of cereal fields, spinneys and larger woodlands admirably suiting its needs. Flocks of thirty or more are frequently seen in late summer. Elsewhere the species is widely scattered on low ground. In 1962 seventeen pairs bred in Melbourne and Stanton by Bridge parishes. However in the Peak the Turtle Dove remains distinctly local. Most breed in woodlands or tall hedges bordering arable land. This dove's gentle song is perhaps the most soporific of all summer sounds.

The main arrival period is in early and mid May though there are April records in most years. The earliest of all was on 14 April (1972). September sees the main departure with occasional laggards in October, as late as 19th (1976).

One ringed as a chick at Dronfield in May 1952 was recovered in the following May at Utrera, Spain.

Collared Dove
Streptopelia decaocto
Common resident.

This species first bred in Britain in Norfolk in 1955 and subsequently spread to most parts of the land. *The Derbyshire Bird Report* states that the first Derbyshire sightings were in 1962 but B. C. Potter and J. J. Wood now consider (*pers comm*) that this dove was present at Brailsford in the autumn of 1961. In 1962 one or two were seen at Youlgreave and numbers increased in 1963 when the species was proved to breed in Derbyshire for the first time, at Spondon (see Hudson, *British Birds*, 1965): and in that year birds were seen in five other localities, notably at Shardlow where a flock of twenty-three was present by November. In the following year records came from seventeen localities with breeding proven at four sites, including Staveley in the north of the county.

Since then the increase has continued, the bird still finding vacant niches to fill, and the BTO Atlas reported its presence in all except three squares. Now the species is well-established in many towns and villages especially those with plenty of trees, conifers being favoured for nesting and roosting sites. Many breed in roadside trees, and some in woods away from settlements. They often congregate in large flocks where there is an abundant food supply – for example around flour mills, certain farms and at pheasant feeds. The north-east usually has the largest flocks, especially around Whitwell where up to 280 have been counted. At Buxton, where the bird first bred in 1969, there was a flock of 200 roosting in the Pavilion Gardens by 1975. Attractive though it is, there is no doubt that to some parties the Collared Dove is becoming a pest.

Occasionally records thought to concern passage birds are submitted, usually involving west to south-west headings during the autumn months.

Cuckoo
Cuculus canorus
Fairly common summer visitor.

Whitlock found Cuckoos very common in all parts of Derbyshire especially in certain

43   *Dunnock feeding a fledgling Cuckoo. Dunnocks, Meadow Pipits and Pied Wagtails are the commonest foster parents in Derbyshire. (Derick Scott)*

Peakland areas. There is little documentary evidence but it seems likely that Cuckoos have slowly declined this century, except perhaps on high ground. However the male Cuckoo's song is still a frequent sound in our woodland and farmland regions, and even more so on moorland, especially that with scattered trees. Numbers vary from summer to summer; recent 'good' years were 1964, and 1971 when nine males and three females were recorded in Derwent Dale on 13 May, with six males and three females in Scarcliffe Park on 14 May. Cuckoos were found in every ten kilometre square in the county by BTO Atlas workers. The only record of a rufous phase female came from Alport Moor in June 1966.

In the uplands most Cuckoos' eggs are laid in Meadow Pipits' nests: in the lowlands those of Dunnocks and Pied Wagtails are most favoured. In 1902 six eggs were found in a Reed Warbler colony near Newton Solney and likewise seven at Sawley in 1950. Other fosterers recorded in Derbyshire include Tree Pipit, Grasshopper Warbler, Whinchat, Linnet, Greenfinch, Sedge Warbler, Reed Bunting, Yellowhammer, Blackbird and Song Thrush.

Most arrive in late April and early May. Adults apparently leave in July, though juveniles may be seen until September. Extreme dates are 24 March and 7 October, both in 1977.

A Cuckoo ringed as a chick at Totley in July 1960 was recovered near Stowmarket, Sussex, a month later.

Barn Owl
Tyto alba
Scarce resident.

Whitlock stated that Barn Owls were 'pretty commonly diffused throughout the county,' and more numerous than Tawny Owls in southern Derbyshire. Jourdain said that they were found in most parts of the county, though generally less numerous than Tawny Owls. Both authors condemned its persecution at the hands of shooters. Whit-

44   *Though easily overlooked, Barn Owls have decreased in recent years. (J. Russell)*

lock considered this treatment was causing Barn Owls to decrease.

Barn Owls were rarely reported this century until the 1940s when they were said to disappear from certain localities: by the 1950s they had become scarce. For example in 1956 E. H. Peat reported their absence from the Derwent area where formerly up to five pairs nested. Although a few nests are found each year, these owls are still rather scarce birds today, being thinly but widely scattered in the county though in certain districts they may be more numerous – B. C. Potter knows five or six pairs within a mile radius of his home at Culland. The BTO Atlas suggested their absence in eight squares, mainly in the west. It is strongly suspected that pesticides are largely responsible for the decline, though lack of suitable nesting sites and road accidents may also be contributory. When the quiet diesel trains were first introduced, several were killed on the county's railway network. Nest sites have included the traditional barns and other buildings, hollow trees, the eaves of railway bridges, caves and holes in rock faces. A pair in north-east Derbyshire nests regularly in the roof of a church hall, ignoring such events as whist drives and 'pop' concerts a few feet below. They hunt over open country, especially farmland.

Barn Owls conduct their affairs discreetly and are perhaps best known to many as a shape in the car headlights. However corpses, owing to their size and colour, are often found and thus this species shows a high ringing recovery rate. Few of those recovered have travelled far, however, the greatest distance being about forty-eight miles.

Eagle Owl
Bubo bubo
Rare vagrant.

One, recorded as a 'Great Horned Owl,' was shot near Shardlow in 1828 (Whitlock).

Snowy Owl
Nyctea scandiaca
Rare vagrant.

Whitlock quotes two records. One was shot near Ashover in 1825, and one which visited Melbourne in May 1841, 'departed in a few days after baffling the endeavours of several persons to shoot it'.

Little Owl
Athene noctua
Fairly common resident.

Until the late nineteenth century, when they were successfully introduced in Northamptonshire, Little Owls were rare vagrants to Britain. An unsuccessful attempt to introduce them to Yorkshire in 1841 may thus have some bearing on the first Derbyshire record, near Derby in 1843 (Whitlock). One was shot at Hartshorne in 1888 (Roworth, 1974) but only after 1906 did records become more frequent. The first nest was found at Sinfin Moor in 1909 and thereafter numbers increased quickly. By 1918 Little Owls were breeding in the Peak District, and by 1932 they were said to be common around Buxton, though the species was not observed in the Glossop area until 1938. By this time Little Owls were seemingly quite common and were well-distributed throughout most of the county.

In 1955, however, the species was reported as rare in the Buxton district and in 1958 opencast coal mining methods were causing the destruction of a number of breeding sites in the east of the county. In 1959 in the Matlock–Tansley–Ashover area there was approximately a pair to each square mile. In 1965 Little Owls were considered to be increasing at Staveley; R. A. Frost located some ten pairs in the parish, whilst in 1969 the Grangewood–Rosliston area population was apparently thriving. On the other hand B. C. Potter has noticed a decline in numbers in parts of the Sandstone belt and considers that this may be connected with a change from dairy to arable farming, and several other observers have noticed the abandonment of old nesting sites. The BTO Atlas Survey (1968–1972) showed Little Owls present in all but two ten kilometre squares in Derbyshire.

However Little Owls may still be found

45 *Little Owls are still quite common in many parts but are thought to be declining.*
(Derick Scott)

throughout Derbyshire in a variety of habitats: woodland edges, lowland farmland (especially that with large hedgerow timber) the 'stone wall country' of the Peak District, industrial wasteland, and moorland with quarries and crags. Roworth (1971) found the greatest concentrations along the eastern edge of the county where agriculture and industry intermix, and also in the Trent Valley.

Tawny Owl
Strix aluco
Fairly common resident.

Now much the commonest owl in Derbyshire, the Tawny was 'fairly diffused throughout the county,' according to Whitlock, but was outnumbered in the south by the Barn Owl. Jourdain thought it probably the commonest owl overall, especially in hilly, broken country, but less numerous in the south-eastern plains.

The number of Tawny Owls has certainly increased since this was written, and the in-

crease seems to have been first noticed in the 1940s (when Barn Owl numbers were declining). By 1945 Arthur Whitaker reported that the Tawny Owl had in recent years become the commonest owl in the Dore and Totley region. In 1964 B. C. Potter found at least ten pairs in the parish of Brailsford, and four at Kedleston, whilst ten were heard calling in Cordwell Valley in August of the same year and fourteen at Shipley Country Park in October 1976. In 1957 each Rookery in the Clay Cross area was found to have a pair of Tawny Owls' nesting in a previous year's nest. There is some evidence to suggest that even now numbers continue to increase. Despite their success, Tawny Owls are not uncommonly killed by road traffic and are still shot, perhaps with some justification, by gamekeepers.

At least part of the success of Tawny Owls may perhaps be explained by their adaptation to a variety of woodland habitat – they may be found in pure deciduous or coniferous woodland, and are perhaps at their most dense in mixed woods. Very small belts of trees and churchyards may harbour breeding Tawny Owls, even well inside urban areas. Most nest in holes in trees, though the old nests of other birds are commonly used. Ground nesting has been reported on occasions, and there are instances of breeding on rock ledges and in rabbit burrows. Where the woodland lacks suitable breeding sites, the provision of nesting boxes may help to swell the population: at Whitwell Wood the number of breeding pairs has thus risen from two to seven pairs, (J. Ellis, *pers comm*).

Long-eared Owl
Asio otus
Rare resident, passage migrant and winter visitor.

Records of Long-eared Owls in Derbyshire are strongly indicative of a long-term decline in numbers. Whitlock thought that a few pairs bred in Peakland woods and elsewhere, and that the bird had previously been much more numerous. In 1912 three occupied nests were found by W. Storrs-Fox in one afternoon between Middleton and Arbor Low. Around 1924 J. Armitage reported that many plantations and woods around Buxton had breeding Long-eared Owls but many had disappeared by 1940. That a pair bred at Repton Shrubs in 1945 is noteworthy as it appears to mark the last breeding record for the south of the county.

Since the formation of the DOS in 1955 several members have taken a special interest in this shy owl, and at present about a dozen breeding pairs are known, all in northern Derbyshire. It seems likely, however, that the species is still present in the southern part of the county; breeding can most easily be established by listening at late dusk in June for the piercing hunger cries of the young birds. The majority of our breeding population nests in coniferous woodland, with a few pairs in hawthorn and elder scrub. Most breeding woods are remote from settlement on open moorland or farmland, or in quiet dales. Whilst the increase in coniferous woodland has created certain new nesting

sites other pairs have disappeared for no apparent reason.

In 1905 a nest with four young was found on the ground amongst Bilberry at Baslow (Storrs-Fox diaries). All other nest sites reported have been in old nests of other species, especially Magpie and Carrion Crow.

Whitlock said that Long-eared Owls were best known as autumn visitors to Derbyshire and presumably this applies to the immigration of Continental birds. This century few Long-eared Owls have been recorded away from known breeding sites but in the 1975–6 winter two roosts of five and twelve birds were found. These must have been composed of Continental immigrants, since most of our breeding birds appear to be resident.

One ringed as a nestling in north-east Derbyshire in May, 1973 was found dead at Kneesall, Nottinghamshire, a year later, and one ringed in Longdendale in June 1975 became injured at Ossett, Yorkshire, the following January.

Short-eared Owl
Asio flammeus
Rare breeder. Uncommon passage migrant and winter visitor.

Whitlock stated that a few pairs of Short-eared Owls bred on the Peakland moors but only twelve years later Jourdain considered them extremely scarce owing to persecution, though formerly a regular breeder. Since 1905 breeding has been definitely established in only eleven years, though in a few other years there have been sightings suggesting breeding. Only in the early 1940s did it seem that Short-eared Owls might be gaining a foothold as regular breeding birds. In 1942 there were at least eight territorial pairs, six of them at Derwent. By 1945 they had disappeared from the latter area, though they have occasionally bred there since. Short-eared Owls have also nested at Combs Moss, in the Goyt Valley region and on the East Moors. As Derbyshire is at the edge of the Short-eared Owl's breeding range, nesting probably occurs only when the number of small mammals, especially Short-tailed Voles, is relatively high.

Passage birds, probably of Continental origin, may be seen at any time between August and early May, although in some years Short-eared Owls have wintered in Derbyshire. They may be seen on moorland or upland pasture, but are more common on low ground where there is rough grassland or marshland. One or two together is usual but in the 1974–5 winter, which produced an exceptional glut of records, a flock of up to nine wintered at a gravel pit at Elvaston. An analysis of their pellets by G. P. Mawson revealed that they fed mainly on passerine birds.

Nightjar
Caprimulgus europaeus
Rare summer visitor.

Whitlock described the Nightjar as a regular spring visitor to Derbyshire, more common in the High Peak than elsewhere. It was said to be common near Glossop and on the moors on the Sheffield side of the county. *VCH* added that it was a scarce and irregular visitor to the south and south-east. Although there have been local increases this century, perhaps as a result of felling or new afforestation, the general trend has been one of decline, which seems to have accelerated since about 1940. Nightjars are now rare, the population almost certainly being under twenty pairs. Most are found in the Beeley Moor–Matlock Forest region where up to twelve pairs bred in the early 1970s. There are signs that this population is declining as the young coniferous plantations mature. Elsewhere there are a very few pairs in other woodland areas and below gritstone edges. A pair bred near Glossop in 1968 but prolonged searching since then has failed to reveal any (J. E. Robson, *pers comm*). There have been no records from southern Derbyshire since 1972 and breeding is not thought to have taken place there since the early 1960s. Though it is possible that Nightjars are overlooked, the species seems likely to become extinct as a Derbyshire breeding bird before the end of the century. Even information

gleaned for the BTO Atlas enquiry, which revealed the bird's presence in ten squares, is now out of date.

Although changing habitats cause variations in numbers, there are many old Nightjar sites now unoccupied, so clearly this is not the cause of the decline. More likely reasons are human disturbance (especially in the Peak District) and perhaps climatic factors.

A very early arrival record, on 6 April (1904) is quoted in *The Handbook*. Generally Nightjars arrive in May, and apparently depart in August. Passage birds are occasionally reported, from various localities, such as the one shot in error at Meynell Langley on 20 October 1949, the latest date reported.

A juvenile ringed near Curbar in August 1975 was killed by a car in Widnes, Lancashire a week later.

Swift
Apus apus
Common summer visitor and passage migrant.

Although there were records for 5 April in 1944 and 47, Swifts generally arrive in Derbyshire towards the end of April and in the first half of May, when they rapidly build up to full numbers. Until August they are a familiar sight over all parts of the county, on fine days even above the highest hill tops many miles from any breeding areas. At certain favoured reservoirs and more particularly at Egginton sewage farm flocks of up to 1,000 have been noted. The largest concentrations at our wetland localities usually occur in wet or windy weather. Southward movement is often noticeable in August. September records are quite common, and there are a few for October, one on 21 November (1976) and even 21 December (1888) (*The Handbook*).

It is unlikely that the status of Swifts has changed to any great degree, at least this century. Whitlock said they were numerous spring visitors to all parts of the county. Jourdain (*VCH*) said most nests were placed under eaves or in thatch. Most still breed under eaves and in crevices in taller buildings and structures such as factories, mills, and railway viaducts. *VCH* also stated that small numbers of Swifts bred in natural rock crevices in the Carboniferous Limestone and in 1932 E. Grindey stated that they were 'evidently breeding in crevices' at Raven's Tor on the Staffordshire side of the Dove valley. It would be interesting to know whether our Swifts still use these natural sites.

Extensive ringing of this species in Derby-

In 1893 Whitlock wrote of the persecution meted out to Derbyshire's Kingfishers by fishing interests. Either they were shot, or caught in 'the deadly hanging net, a most fatal trap for this beautiful species'. However they appear to have been plentiful enough if Whitlock's own record of 'quite a dozen pairs . . . during a long row up the Trent nearly to Burton' in May 1888 is reliable.

Jourdain spoke in 1905 of a recent increase which he connected with protection

46   *The Kingfisher's distribution is limited only by river pollution and, more temporarily, severe winters. (H. A. Hems)*

shire and its adjoining counties has produced many local recoveries, involving Lancashire, Yorkshire, Staffordshire, Lincolnshire, and Leicestershire, with a September recovery from Morocco, a November recovery from Zaire, and a December report from Southern Rhodesia.

Kingfisher
Alcedo atthis
Fairly common resident.

measures introduced by the county council. Before that one man had trapped as many as twenty-two in a single year on the River Dove.

There are no further references to human persecution. The two current factors limiting this beautiful bird's numbers are severe winter weather and river pollution. Very cold weather, when streams and rivers freeze, causes heavy mortality though numbers are made good within a few years: by 1969 Kingfishers had fully recovered from the great frosts of 1963. The species avoids grossly polluted waterways though it may use their banks for nesting if a feeding pond or lake is nearby.

At present Kingfishers are reasonably common on all suitable rivers and streams throughout Derbyshire. They are often seen at gravel pits, reservoirs and other water bodies. Their presence was noted in twenty-three of the twenty-seven squares assessed for the BTO Atlas. Evidence of their density was provided by the 1975 Waterways Bird Survey which revealed seven territories in forty kilometres of generally upland streams and rivers.

One ringed as a chick at Whitwell in June 1974 was found dead in the following June at Pitsmoor, Sheffield.

Bee-eater

Merops apiaster
Rare vagrant.

In 1879 singles were shot near Mapperley on 4 May and 10 June (Whitlock).

Roller

Coracias garrulus
Rare vagrant.

One was seen by the Derwent between Duffield and Derby on 3 May 1856 (Whitlock).

Hoopoe

Upupa epops
Rare vagrant.

Whitlock knew of two undated records from Swadlincote and the River Dove. Between 1885 and 1900 Hoopoes were recorded at Sutton Scarsdale (*Birds of the Chesterfield Area 1870–1970*), Stanton by Bridge and twice at Ashbourne (*VCH*, Jourdain diaries). This century has produced thirteen more Hoopoe records, all of singles, from Chesterfield, Ashbourne, Haddon Hall, Breadsall, Little Eaton, Bolsover, Old Brampton, Woodville, Scarcliffe, Drakelow (twice), Padley and Egginton. Four have first occurred in both April and May, two in

June and October and singles in March, August, and September, with extreme dates of 28 March (1952) and 6 October (1911).

Green Woodpecker

Picus viridis
Scarce resident.

Whitlock described the Green Woodpecker as by far the most common of its family in Derbyshire, met with throughout the county save on the moors, and not at all uncommon in many localities. We can but guess what happened to the species until the 1940s, but in that decade and the next it clearly spread and increased greatly: it was said to be 'flourishing exceedingly' at Shottle in 1953. In that year F. Morris, writing of the Darley Dale area, reported, 'Forty years ago it was very common and the Great Spotted Woodpecker unknown: by the late 1930s the Great Spotted Woodpecker was very common and the Green becoming rare: now I think the reverse is taking place.' Dr Ian Newton, formerly of New Whittington, described the bird as (*pers comm*) 'Very common in the 1950s, now almost (or completely) gone from my area. It was almost everywhere where old trees grew – woods, hedgerows, parks etc. and you would hear it on every outing. I remember about ten sites within a very small radius in 1953–4.'

The latter comment was written in 1973, ten years after the 1962–3 winter which decimated the Derbyshire Green Woodpecker population. Although the bird has recovered elsewhere it has never made good its losses here and though it increases very slowly, it remains uncommon in most areas, except in the Central Gritstone region (especially around Grindleford) and the Carboniferous Limestone dales where there are reasonable numbers. In the Moss Valley there were considered to be thirteen pairs in 1977. The bird frequents woodland (especially mature deciduous), interspersed with open ground, parkland and sometimes open country with isolated trees. Breeding was confirmed in only six of the seventeen squares where it was recorded by the BTO Atlas enquiry.

An adult ringed at Fernilee in July 1961 was killed forty-three miles to the south at Stretton, Staffordshire, in January 1963.

Great Spotted Woodpecker
Dendrocopos major
Fairly common resident.

The Great Spotted Woodpecker was much less numerous than the Green in 1893, according to Whitlock who described it as local but 'fairly common where it occurs'. It was said to be most common in the south but occurred also in the north-east and the High Peak.

Numbers steadily increased this century so that by the 1940s it was undoubtedly the most common of the three woodpeckers, as it is today. No doubt one of the chief reasons why this is the most successful of its family is its greater adaptibility to a wider range of woodland. Though preferring deciduous woodland, the bird is often found in pure conifers, and may breed in quite small woods. However, the only Common Bird Census area where the species was regularly recorded was Shiningcliff where there was a pair a year on average. In 1943 Arthur Whitaker found five pairs feeding young simultaneously in a fifty acre wood in north-east Derbyshire. Atlas work proved the species' presence in twenty-five ten kilometre squares. However there have been some signs of a decline in recent years, suggested reasons for which include habitat destruction, the increased number of Grey Squirrels, and displacement from its nesting holes by the Starling.

In 1952 one was seen at the Friary Hotel in urban Derby on 24 October. There have been other autumn and winter records of birds found well away from known breeding areas – even on open moorland on rare occasions. Some of these wanderers are probably of Continental origin but this is unproven. Bird table feeding was first recorded in 1952 and is not uncommon now in several areas.

Lesser Spotted Woodpecker
Dendrocopos minor
Scarce resident.

Lesser Spotteds are the least demonstrative of all the woodpeckers. They generally frequent the upper branches of trees and are relatively quiet except in spring when they drum and utter their repetitive calls. As a result they are amongst our most overlooked birds. They are thinly scattered throughout Derbyshire in most well-wooded areas, including the Peak District, but are certainly most numerous in southern districts. The BTO Atlas project found them in eleven squares, though nesting was confirmed only in four. Parkland and deciduous woodland, especially oak, constitute the preferred habitats. Sometimes they visit hedgerow trees.

These woodpeckers appear to be largely resident with little evidence of wandering. However Miss K. M. Hollick has recorded them regularly in alders bordering Bradley Brook since 1934, where they are seen only in early spring, but not at other times of year.

It is unlikely that there has been much change in the species' status during the past century or so. Both Whitlock and Jourdain thought them overlooked and most frequent in the south of the county.

Wryneck
Jynx torquilla
Rare passage migrant.

Jourdain and Whitlock agreed that Wrynecks were local summer visitors to woods and parks in south, south-west and north-east Derbyshire, with one or two pairs nesting in the upper Derwent Valley. Although *The Handbook* described Wrynecks as very scarce summer visitors to Derbyshire no twentieth-century records have been found prior to 27 August 1966, when one was seen at Tibshelf (W. S. Jacklin *pers comm*). Since then increased observation has suggested that Wrynecks pass regularly through the county given certain weather conditions. Of the fourteen individuals recorded recently, all have occurred between 25 August and 25 September at Palterton, Abney, Hilton gravel pits (twice), Clay Mills, Long Eaton, Egginton, Errwood, Brailsford, Bolsover, Netherseal, Derby, Sutton Scarsdale and Tibshelf.

Woodlark
Lullula arborea
Rare passage migrant. Former breeder.

In the middle of the nineteenth century it appears that the Woodlark was 'pretty common in certain parts of Derbyshire' according to Mr Neville Wood of Foston. By the time J. J. Briggs (1850) and Sir Oswald Mosley and Edwin Brown (1863) appeared in print it was much less common and the only recent dated record known to Jourdain (*VCH*) was in 1881 when a nest was said to have been found in the Burton district.

There are seven records this century. A clutch of five eggs was taken by G. T. Walker from Whitwell Wood on 10 June 1910 (J. Ellis, *pers comm*). A male sang in Longshaw on 26 April 1958 but did not stay. T. G. Smith (*pers comm*) saw one at Egginton sewage farm on 13 January 1968, a time of cold weather. Two were at Matlock Forest on 3 December 1969 and one flew over Ogston Reservoir with migrant Skylarks on 8 October 1971. The last record is of a single bird at Drum Hill, Breadsall, on 24 April 1976. The BTO Atlas reveals the presence of this species in the Glossop area; apparently the record relates to 1972.

Skylark
Alauda arvensis
Common resident and passage migrant.

Whitlock thought the Skylark one of the most numerous birds in the county, abounding in the Trent valley and breeding up to the edge of the moors. Jourdain described it as most numerous in the southern plain and found everywhere but the moors.

The species remains numerous everywhere today and even on the highest hills is certainly quite a common member of the moorland avifauna especially on grass moors and not rarely in Ling also, although numbers on some moors may be declining. Elsewhere the bird is numerous on arable land and rough grazing. It was the commonest species on the Coal Measures farms averaging twenty-three pairs at Barrow Hill and twenty-five at Tibshelf, and on the similar sized farmland plot at Fernilee (200 acres),

where forty pairs were found in 1972. However on the farmland areas at Hathersage and Mapleton, where the fields are much smaller, it was scarcer, averaging only a pair a year at the former and sixteen pairs at Mapleton. It was the commonest species in one eleven-acre field by Broadhurst Edge Wood, with an average of eleven pairs.

Whitlock noted that many migratory Skylarks reached us in autumn, sometimes swarming in the turnip fields. An increase is often discernible from September onwards and in that month, but more so in October, a much visual movement takes place, usually on a heading between south and north-west. For example 305 flew west over Barbrook in one hour on 10 October 1957.

In winter Skylarks tend to flock, especially in cold weather. On 2 January 1971 1,000 were counted on Egginton sewage farm. Any flock of 200 or more is noteworthy. Cold weather movement is often seen and is sometimes quite spectacular – for example 767 flew south south-west in thirty minutes over Staveley on 25 December 1970. In mild weather song flights are recorded from early January onwards and high moorland territories are occupied by mid-March.

Shore Lark
Eremophila alpestris
Rare passage migrant or vagrant.

Three flew west-north-west at Abney on 18 October 1971 (R. A. Frost). One was at Church Wilne Reservoir on 26 October 1973 (J. R. Calladine, A. R. Clarke, T. Sexey) and one flew east over Willington gravel pits on 12 October 1975 (R. A. Frost).

Swallow
Hirundo rustica
Common summer visitor and passage migrant.

Whitlock thought that Swallows were extremely common and Jourdain made a similar statement. This is still the case today, though it is generally thought that in recent years numbers have been smaller, perhaps because of the same factors which have reduced the Whitethroat population. Swallows may be found breeding in a wide variety of habitats from the edge of urbanisation up to the moors. They are common around villages and farmsteads, often congregating over lakes, reservoirs, and rivers. Many nest in barns and under bridges and less common sites have included rock faces and caves in the north-east and the Peak, underground manholes and the top of an electric lampshade. The various Common Birds Censuses show an average of fifteen pairs at Mapleton, four at Hathersage and Tibshelf and two at Barrow Hill.

A very early arrival date was 11 February (1957). There are occasional late March records but most arrive from early April into May. Sometimes large numbers gather at reservoirs, mainly in wet or windy weather, and the biggest such count was 1,200 at Ogston Reservoir in May 1967. Departure seems to commence in August and by mid or late October most are gone, though November records are not rare and there are four December records, the latest on 26th (1968) (S. Jackson, *pers comm*).

In spring and to a much greater extent in autumn, Swallows often roost communally in Reed and Reedmace beds, often in four figure numbers with counts of 10,000 at Willington number two gravel pit in 1965, and 6,000 at Old Whittington and 5,000 at Williamthorpe in 1977. Unusually 1,500 roosted in heather and bracken at Tansley Moor on 15 September 1967. Visual passage is often recorded in September and October, sometimes involving hundreds of birds an hour.

Birds ringed in Derbyshire have been recovered in Morocco (twice in April, once in May), Spain in October, France in November, Transvaal in February, and the Orange Free State in May and December. There are many recoveries involving several other British counties, including Suffolk, Flintshire, Wiltshire, Essex, Gloucestershire, Cumberland and Stirlingshire.

House Martin
Delichon urbica
Common summer visitor and passage migrant.

Whitlock and Jourdain said that House Martins were common birds in Derbyshire though more local than Swallows. This is still the situation today. House Martins breed quite commonly on a variety of buildings throughout the county. Many breed on natural cliffs and quarry faces in the Carboniferous Limestone area of Derbyshire, especially in the valley of the Wye and around Stoney Middleton. An incomplete survey of rock-nesting birds in 1975 revealed 159 pairs. In 1906 breeding was reported on beams inside open sheds at an inn at Thorpe. In 1968–9 A. P. E. Cain-Black conducted a survey of this species in Derbyshire and published preliminary results in DOS Bulletin No 220. Among his findings were that over sixty per cent were within 400 metres of the nearest permanent water supply; and as in Whitlock's day many House Martins' nests were taken over by House Sparrows.

Most arrive from mid April onwards, well into May. There are very few March records, the earliest on 21st (1947). Departure takes place from August onwards, but numbers in late September may still be considerable and flocks of up to 150 have occurred in October. Passage flocks of up to 800 are recorded, usually from reservoirs. Young are sometimes found in the nest in the latter half of October and the latest recorded date concerns a pair which remained until 27 November (1836) to rear a brood in Derby.

A young bird ringed at Kirkbridge, Cumberland in June 1951 was recovered at Chesterfield three months later and an adult ringed at Sinfin, Derby in May 1965 was recovered at Bodenham, Herefordshire in July of the same year.

Sand Martin
Riparia riparia
Fairly common summer visitor and passage migrant.

Since 1969 the numbers of Sand Martins reaching Derbyshire have been much smaller, apparently as a result of the drought in West Africa which is considered to have caused the decline in Whitethroats and other species. Before then numbers were more static. Whitlock called the bird abundant, its headquarters being in the river valleys of the south. Jourdain said it was common wherever suitable breeding places existed, with the largest colonies in the valleys of the Trent and the lower Dove and Derwent, with few in the Peak. Certainly this still describes the basic distribution of Sand Martins today.

Most nest in river banks, including those of rocky Peakland streams, and at sand pits and gravel pits nearby. Other breeding sites have included drainage pipes in river banks at Chesterfield, the interstices of a stone wall, the faces of spoil-heaps, sandy roadside banks and soil two feet deep on top of a home-guard shelter. It is doubtful whether any three-figure colony exists today. The Waterways Bird Survey of 1975 found only one territory in 40 kilometres of generally upland streams.

13 March (1946, 61 and 77) is the earliest arrival date. Most come from late March into May and departure takes place from July to early October with the latest on 20 October (1954). Before 1969 spring flocks of up to 300 were not rare. In autumn gatherings are larger with three-figure flocks recorded most years in south Derbyshire, the largest counts being of 800 at Church Wilne Reservoir in July and September 1974. Sand Martins often roost with Swallows but in much smaller numbers, rarely reaching three figures. Thus a roosting flock of 6–8,000 at Elvaston Gravel pits in August 1977 was exceptional.

These hirundines have been extensively ringed in Britain. For Derbyshire there are three recoveries involving France, and many from other counties including at least seven from Sussex, three from Norfolk and others as far afield as Somerset, Hampshire, Kent and Monmouthshire.

Golden Oriole
Oriolus oriolus
Rare passage migrant or vagrant.

Jourdain and Whitlock quote five records, one of which, in 1841, refers to a pair thought to be nesting at Egginton. In 1910 a pair was seen at Cratcliffe Tor near Birchover but a boy killed the male bird.

J. Bocking saw one in north-west Derbyshire on 24 July 1951. In the book on Derbyshire in the series, 'The Little Guides' is a stated occurrence in Lathkill Dale in 1943 but without further evidence, and in view of the several errors in the same book, it cannot be accepted. One was seen and heard singing in a south Derbyshire woodland on 13 June 1976 (per T. Cockburn).

Raven
Corvus corax
Rare vagrant. Former breeder.

Pilkington said in 1789 that Ravens, along with Carrion Crows and Rooks, were common in Derbyshire. In the nineteenth century the species became uncommon in the county with breeding recorded only at Raven's Tor (Ashover), Alport Castles, Howden Chest, Lathkill Dale, and in a willow tree near Ashbourne. Garner (1844) said that they were not uncommon in Dovedale and Ravens were repeatedly seen near Edale and in Chee Dale from 1866–73. In 1905 they were still occasional on the grouse moors (Whitlock, *VCH*). Persecution was perhaps the chief reason for their decline.

It seemed likely that the Raven had gone forever but in September 1966 a pair appeared in the Bleaklow area and bred at Alport Castles in 1967–8 (R. A. Frost). However these were thought to have been released. Otherwise Ravens remain casual vagrants with recent records suggesting the presence of one errant bird in the Peak District and possibly another released bird in the extreme south of the county.

Carrion Crow
Corvus corone
Common resident.

Although regularly persecuted by sporting interests, the Carrion Crow thrives and is common or fairly common throughout the county. It nests in bushes and trees and not uncommonly on electricity pylons, on moorland and farmland or at the edge of woodland, through to the edge of surburbia. The bird is most numerous on higher ground but is still locally numerous in the south; at

Egginton sewage farm up to 400 have been counted, with over 100 in mid-summer. All of the Common Birds Census sites held the species, though none held more than five pairs a year. Three-figure roosts have been found in many parts of the county, sometimes with Rooks and Jackdaws, sometimes alone.

Whitlock said that this crow existed in most parts of the county but that its chief breeding grounds were in the Peak, in those areas where game preservation was not strictly practised. Jourdain said it was decidedly common in one or two districts, such as the Dove Valley between Thorpe and Hartington. Increased breeding numbers were reported in 1917 and 1944, both significantly being war years when little gamekeeping was practised.

That the bird continues to increase must be largely connected with the decline in game preservation. J. Armitage believed that a flock of eighty at Kingsterndale in 1938 consisted of males whose mates had been shot off nests earlier in the season, and which had been unable to find fresh partners. However, C. M. Swaine (*in litt* to F. G. Hollands) considered that persecution was not the only limiting factor as the Carrion Crow was not found in certain remote valleys or parks where it would not have been shot.

There are a few ringing recoveries, involving movements of up to twenty-five miles. Whitlock thought that many foreign Carrion Crows wintered in Derbyshire; this may have been correct at the time but is unlikely now.

Hooded Crow
Corvus corone cornix
Rare winter visitor and passage migrant. Rare breeder.

Around the turn of the century Hooded Crows were regular, if local, winter visitors to Derbyshire. Whitlock and Jourdain described them as numerous on the lower Trent and not uncommon around Sutton Scarsdale and on some of the Peakland moors. Hoodies were still numerous on the East Moors in the 1920s and E. H. Peat (*in litt* to F. G. Hollands) said that to shoot thirty in an evening at a roost in Longshaw was not uncommon at that time. Whitaker (1929) said that Hooded Crows could be seen almost daily during the colder months of the year. A marked decline obviously began shortly afterwards, only ten being recorded from 1934–49, and only one in the 1950s. About ten occurred in the 1960s but the years 1970–77 have produced about twenty-four Hooded Crows, including one record of three together. An unusually concentrated passage involving six individuals was witnessed between 11–16 October 1975. 11 October (1975) was the earliest recorded date with 5 May (1973) (*Sheffield Bird Report*) the latest, excepting a Hoodie × Carrion hybrid on 6 June (1969).

In 1915 a pair of Hooded Crows nested in Dovedale on the Staffordshire side of the river (E. Grindey). In 1959–60 a female Hooded Crow paired with a male Carrion Crow at Hardwick. Three of their total of six progeny had Hoodie markings (C. B. Chambers, E. H. Peat, P. Shooter).

Rook
Corvus frugilegus
Common resident.

There have been four important surveys of Rook breeding numbers in Derbyshire. In 1929 Roebuck (*British Birds*, 1933) estimated 240 colonies containing 10,620 nests. In 1944 A. Roebuck and L. M. Waud (unpublished) found 371 colonies with 16,114 nests. Unfortunately it is not certain that equal coverage was obtained on these two counts. P. D. R. Lomas conducted an almost complete survey in 1965–6 and published his findings in *Bird Study* (1968). This census revealed 440 Rookeries holding 12,630 nests, a decline of almost 3,500 on 1944. The decline was most marked in the Sandstone Belt and Southern Gritstone regions, whereas numbers in the High Peak region showed a considerable increase. Lomas considered that numbers increased from 1944 to 1958 but decreased thereafter, especially in grain-growing areas. In 1970 Lomas compared two areas near Ashbourne with the 1966 situation and found a further decrease in grain-growing areas but a maintenance of the limestone grassland population. In 1975 T. Cockburn organised the Derbyshire element of a national census and reported 9,713 nests at 320 Rookeries – a decrease of nearly 3,000 nests compared with 1965–6. In north-west Derbyshire, Derek Alsop (*pers comm*) recorded a fifty per cent decrease in the number of nests between 1970 and 75. Clearly our Rooks, though still common, are declining at an alarming rate, and further fieldwork is being undertaken in an attempt to discover the cause.

Both Whitlock and Jourdain (*VCH*) considered them extremely common birds. In 1931 a rookery on the Staffordshire side of Dovedale held 800 nests, whereas the largest colonies in 1966 and 1975 were of 217 and 279.

Rooks roost communally in winter, often with Jackdaws and sometimes with Carrion Crows. There are a number of such roosts in the county, some holding several thousand birds. It is probable that immigrants winter with us, as suggested by Whitlock, but proof is lacking.

One ringed at Great Budworth, Cheshire, in January 1939 was recovered at Ashover in April, 1948.

Jackdaw
Corvus monedula
Common resident.

The Jackdaw nests virtually throughout Derbyshire, and was reported from all but one ten kilometre square during the BTO Atlas investigation of 1968–72. It feeds on open ground, especially farmland, and nests in cavities in trees, rocks and buildings, often colonially. Thus it may be found in suitable woodland, parkland (especially where there are old oaks), cliffs and quarry faces, and in built-up areas, though, of the Common Birds Census areas only Mapleton had a regular breeding population which averaged nine pairs a year. The largest colonies now are probably in the Carboniferous Limestone region, on those natural rock faces not overrun with climbers, and in quarries. It is likely that the bird has increased in view of the enormous new expanses of the last-mentioned habitat, though this is undocu-

mented. Whitlock said that it was extremely common in many parts, and abounded in some of the Peak District dales.

In winter the species often roosts in large flocks with Rooks, and sometimes with Carrion Crows as well. Four figure gatherings have been reported from several places, with up to 3,000 utilising a pine wood at Holmesfield in recent years. There is no evidence that our birds are anything but sedentary.

Magpie
Pica pica
Common resident.

In 1893 Whitlock considered that the Magpie was declining, though it was still not uncommon in some areas. Jourdain said it was uncommon only in those districts where game was strictly preserved including the grouse moors, whilst it was often very numerous where undisturbed. There was no indication of any change until the late 1940s and 1950s when an increase was recorded, most likely as the result of diminished persecution, Numbers are probably still increasing today and the Magpie is present throughout the county in a variety of habitats including moorland with scattered trees, farmland of all types, thickets, the edges of woodlands, and now not uncommonly in residential areas. It seems most common in those pastoral areas with big hedgerows and scattered spinneys. In the Common Birds Census areas there were five pairs at Hilton gravel pits, an average of four at Mapleton, three at Barrow Hill, two at Broadhurst Edge Wood, Hathersage and Tibshelf, and one at Fernilee, but none at Shiningcliff Wood.

The Magpie is gregarious and there have been at least two records of no fewer than forty birds in a single tree, and 100 were seen in a stubble field at Grindleford in January 1964. Birds often roost communally, usually in flocks of up to sixty or so, but there were 100 at Hathersage in 1967 (Smith, 1974).

Unlike the Carrion Crow the species has not adapted to nesting on electricity pylons, though a pair regularly attempted to do so during the 1950s. In *VCH* Jourdain recorded that a wild female paired with an escaped wild male Jackdaw at Fenny Bentley in 1899, building a nest but laying no eggs.

There are a few ringing recoveries, none of them involving a movement of more than ten miles.

Jay
Garrulus glandarius
Fairly common resident.

Whitlock and Jourdain differed in their opinion of the Jay's Derbyshire status. Whitlock said that while it was formerly common, only a few lingered in wooded districts by 1893. However, in 1905 Jourdain described the bird as fairly numerous wherever woods existed. Since then numbers have most likely increased, especially from the early 1940s to the mid 1950s, most probably as a result of diminished persecution from sporting estates. In the early 1940s H. J. Wain reported nests in hedgerows and gardens, considered to be the result of felling of firwoods. In 1960 about twelve pairs were seen at Fernilee where previously the bird was considered rare, though Howe (1972) gave the upper Goyt Valley population as five pairs. Although nowhere really common the bird is found in most sizeable woods, especially those of oak or at least partially of conifers. The Jay was found by BTO Atlas workers in all but one ten kilometre square in Derbyshire, whilst Common Birds Census results show two pairs a year at Shiningcliff Wood and single pairs at Hathersage and Broadhurst Edge Wood: elsewhere it was irregular or absent.

In autumn the Jay collects and buries acorns and in some years, such as 1971 when the acorn crop was poor, the species is found in unusual localities or flies very high as if on passage. R. A. Frost saw thirty on a two mile walk along Cromford Canal in October 1971. In 1975 one was seen at 1,600 feet on moorland. Small groups of up to ten may be seen in winter.

Amongst several ringing recoveries the only one of note involves a movement of twenty miles from New Mills, where it was ringed in August 1973, to Arley Hall, Cheshire, where it was found six months later.

47   *A Jay photographed at its nest in Whitwell Wood. (J. Russell)*

Great Tit
Parus major
Common resident.

Whitlock considered the Great Tit the second most numerous of its family, after the Blue Tit, but Jourdain thought this the commoner bird. However the Great Tit is certainly the less numerous today, and this is borne out by Common Birds Census results which show an average total of forty-four territories in the eight areas, compared with eighty-three territories of the Blue Tit. This was the fifth commonest species at Shiningcliff Wood with an average of ten pairs in fifty-six acres of woodland, and twelfth at Mapleton with sixteen pairs in 294 acres of farmland.

These two tits frequent much the same kinds of breeding habitat such as a variety of woodland, parks and gardens, and hedges with trees. However the Great Tit is less common in high-altitude woodlands, though it was proved to breed in every ten kilometre square in Derbyshire during 1968–72.

Outside the breeding season the species often flocks together sometimes with other species of tits, and in some seasons congregates particularly in areas of beech trees. However there have been no published records of more than seventy together (at Shipley in November 1976).

The more interesting ringing recoveries include one which travelled from the Goyt Valley to Wrexham, Flintshire, and one which moved from Ancaster, Lincolnshire, to Staveley.

Blue Tit
Parus caeruleus
Common resident.

The Blue Tit breeds throughout Derbyshire, wherever it can find suitable nesting sites, and in the Peak District is found almost to the tree limit. In woodland it is probably most numerous in mature oaks and because of a lack of nesting sites least common in pure conifers, though the provision of nestboxes has helped to redress the balance in some areas. In the Shiningcliff Woods census area (largely Oak, Birch and Sycamore) it was fourth in overall abundance with sixteen pairs a year, while it was sixth at Broadhurst Edge Wood with eight territories in nineteen acres of oak-birch woodland.

On farmland its numbers were less dense, though Mapleton averaged twenty pairs in its 294 acres making this the ninth most numerous bird there, equal with the Tree Sparrow. The less-timbered sites at Barrow Hill and Tibshelf totalled only five pairs a year, while Fernilee, Hathersage and Hilton gravel pits held eight pairs each. Many nest in built-up areas and Kitchen (1976) found at least four pairs in fourteen acres of suburbs at Somercotes.

Outside the breeding season the Blue Tit forms larger flocks than the other species of tit, sometimes reaching triple figures, with 250 at Chatsworth on 26 August 1977 the largest reported gathering. Some are prone to wandering and there are ringing recoveries involving counties as distant as Berkshire. Sometimes movement may be witnessed, as on 15 October 1957 when D. R. Wilson saw parties of five, eleven and four flying south-west over treeless moorland by Barbrook Reservoir.

Coal Tit
Parus ater
Fairly common resident.

The Coal Tit differs from the other members of its family in its preference for coniferous woodland. It is often among the commonest birds in the county's pine and larch woods, but also breeds in mixed and occasionally in broad-leaved woodlands, and while most concentrated in the Peak District is found throughout Derbyshire wherever suitable habitat exists. Whitlock stated that they bred in the wooded dales and plantations of the Peak, and were quite common in some areas, inferring that the bird did not nest in the lowlands; Jourdain added that it was rare as a breeding bird in the Trent and lower Dove Valleys. However, only two southern squares lacked the species in 1968–72, indicating a genuine spread which must have been facilitated by the afforestation of coniferous trees.

T. A. Gibson found an average of five territories a year in his Common Birds Census area at Shiningcliff Wood though there was little coniferous habitat. At Mapleton a pair first bred in 1966, and by 1969 the population was four pairs, though it had fallen to three by 1972.

After the breeding season, the Coal Tit forms flocks, sometimes with other species of tits. Groups of twenty or so are not uncommon and gatherings of seventy have been reported from Derwent more than once. Whilst the bird may stay in woodlands all year it is often seen in other sites such as hedgerows and gardens from September until early spring. Whitlock noticed this dispersal and said that there was often a considerable immigration in the Trent Valley in October.

Marsh Tit
Parus palustris
Fairly common resident.

Whitlock wrote his comments on the Marsh Tit without knowing of the existence of the Willow Tit, only identified as a distinct species about the turn of the century. He referred to the bird's attempt to excavate its own nest hole, a habit of the Willow Tit. In 1905 Jourdain said that the 'Marsh Tit' was absent from the north but occurred in small numbers in the southern lowlands, especially in old pollarded willows. The latter habitat would be more typical of the Willow Tit.

Though the two species still frequently confuse the inexperienced observer there is no doubt that overall the Marsh Tit is the scarcer. It prefers more mature deciduous woodland, and is probably most numerous in the dales of the Carboniferous Limestone region, where S. S. Blythe and D. T. Wilks (*in litt* to F. G. Hollands) thought it had increased, at least around Buxton. The BTO Atlas scheme found the bird present in twenty squares, six fewer than the Willow Tit. At Mapleton the population averaged a pair a year. At the other Common Birds Census sites it was absent or averaged less than one pair.

In winter though the Marsh Tit bands together in its own groups or with other tits, numbers are never large and urban and suburban areas are not commonly visited. One was seen at Barbrook Reservoir, on treeless moorland, in June 1975.

Willow Tit
Parus montanus
Fairly common resident.

This bird was not differentiated from the Marsh Tit until about 1900 and accordingly receives no mention in Whitlock (1893) nor more surprisingly, in *VCH* (1905). The first mention of the Willow Tit came in the *DAJ* for 1910 when it was said to breed in old willow trees by the brook-sides in the Burton on Trent district. Nests of this species were found at Willington in 1913, Holmewood from 1921 onwards and Dovedale from 1930. In 1937 *DAJ* stated that the bird was known to breed only in north and south-west Derbyshire. Gradually, however, records became more frequent and in 1954 eight pairs were found in a Darley Dale wood.

It is now known that the Willow Tit is considerably more widespread than the Marsh Tit and whilst their habitats may occasionally overlap, the present species is more typical of damp woodlands, scrub and tall hedgerows. It was found in all but one square by BTO Atlas workers. It is uncommon on high ground, however, and in the limestone dales is confined to thorny scrub and patches of elder. In the Common Birds Census areas it was absent only from Mapleton and Broadhurst Edge Wood, though averaging less than a pair a year at Hathersage. All of the five other sites held one pair a year on average.

The Willow Tit does not occur in such large gatherings as do most of the other species of tits, and usually is found with larger numbers of other species. Birds penetrate into suburban gardens quite regularly.

Long-tailed Tit
Aegithalos caudatus
Fairly common resident.

The Long-tailed Tit is found breeding in hedgerows, thickets, shrubberies, woodland and areas of scrub almost throughout the

48   *Willow Tits are quite common in damp woodlands, scrub, and tall hedgerows. (J. Russell)*

county; it was absent from only four of the twenty-seven squares assessed for the BTO Atlas scheme. It remains more numerous on low ground than in the hills. Jourdain said that it was scarce above 600 feet and thinly-distributed below that altitude: Whitlock had made similar comments.

There is no evidence of any great change in numbers since then. The species was present in very small numbers in the Common Birds Census areas, averaging a pair a year at Mapleton and at Hathersage but was absent or only erratically present elsewhere. During the mid 1970s numbers were higher than usual, following a sequence of mild winters. Severe winter weather causes heavy mortality but improved breeding success by the remaining population replenishes the losses within a few years.

Between autumn and spring the Long-tailed Tit forms flocks, sometimes of up to thirty or so. These may be seen almost any-where where there are trees, but the bird visits gardens less frequently than most other species of tit. Rarely birds have been seen fly-ing over open country such as moorland. One seen at Bradley on 21 November 1965 was thought to be of the Northern race, *A. c. caudatus*, but the notes submitted were inconclusive.

Nuthatch
Sitta europaea
Fairly common resident.

Whitlock said that Nuthatches were local residents in Derbyshire, apparently confined to woods and parks in the north-east, south, south-west and probably the Derwent Valley around Ambergate. However *VCH* stated that they were very local and bred only in the north-east and south of the Trent.

Very little subsequent information on distribution was published until 1937 when they were still 'noisy in old timber in the north-east,' but were thought to have become extinct in the Derby and Matlock districts. However from the early 1940s to the mid 1950s Nuthatches increased in numbers and spread to new areas in southern Derbyshire. They are still widespread in that district and quite common in some parklands.

A more dramatic spread has affected northern Derbyshire and is well analysed by Miss Hester C. Rodgers in *The Derbyshire Bird Report 1974*. In 1946 Nuthatches were reported from Chatsworth for the first time (*DAJ*) and now this is the bird's northern stronghold with several pairs breeding. Since the late 1950s and early 1960s Nuthatches have become well established elsewhere in the Derwent Valley and along the Rivers Wye and Dove and their tributaries. Since 1962 they have bred regularly in north-west Derbyshire. Miss Rodgers concluded that the population had probably become stabilised due to lack of untenanted suitable habitats. Conversely Nuthatches are now rare in the east and north-east, most probably due to habitat fragmentation.

There is some evidence that our Nuthatches wander a little outside the breeding season.

Treecreeper
Certhia familiaris
Fairly common resident.

The BTO Atlas enquiry showed this inconspicuous little bird to be present throughout the county. It is equally at home in either deciduous or coniferous woodland and will breed in small clumps of trees; in 1963 a pair nested in an isolated row of willows in marshland at Killamarsh. At least in conifers its numbers may well be limited by a lack of suitable nesting sites. Most nest in cavities and crevices in trees, or in ivy, but unusual sites in recent years have included a ground nest at the base of a pine, and a log-covered waste paper bin.

Probably little change has occurred since Whitlock reported that the species was 'fairly diffused' throughout the whole county, being common in some areas. In the early 1940s two observers reported increased numbers though this may merely have represented a recovery following the severe 1939–40 winter. Other cold winters, notably those of 1946–7 and 1962–3, have caused considerable mortality but numbers have quickly recovered. At present the population

is high following a succession of mild winters. At least twelve pairs were found in Hardwick Park in 1973 and there were nine singing in Padley Gorge in April 1975. The various Common Birds Censuses showed an average of one pair a year in the woodlands at Shiningcliff and Broadhurst Edge, and at the Mapleton site numbers increased from two pairs in 1964 to six by 1969, with an overall average of three pairs.

After breeding Treecreepers are prone to wandering, and sometimes join bands of tits and Goldcrests, when they may be seen almost anywhere where trees are present. Any record of more than four or five together is of interest. Fourteen were counted at Padley Gorge on 25 November 1973, and there is an exceptional record of seventy-five to a hundred passing through a small wood at Chatsworth in the morning of 19 August 1977.

Wren
Troglodytes troglodytes
Common resident.

'Found breeding in every part of the county. Even in the wildest parts of the moorlands its cheery little song may frequently be heard.' Jourdain's words of 1905 adequately sum up the status of the Wren over seventy years later. It is equally at home in woods, gardens, parks and on farmland and moorland. Whitlock mentioned that it nested under convenient ledges by the banks of all Peakland streams.

Only severe cold seems to affect the Wren and hard winters lead to heavy mortality. Increased breeding success causes the losses to be made good within a very few years: by 1966, for example, the Wren population had recovered from the winter of 1962–3, much the coldest of recent times. The sequence of mild winters has led to a very high population at the present time. A measure of its abundance is shown by a count of 120 singing birds heard on a ten mile walk along the River Wye from Buxton to Monsal Dale in April 1974. The average of nine pairs at Broadhurst Edge Wood made the Wren the fourth commonest species there. At both

Hathersage and Hilton gravel pits the Wren was the fifth commonest bird, with an average of eleven and sixteen pairs. At Tibshelf and Shiningcliff it was sixth (six and nine pairs) but only eighth at Mapleton (average twenty-four pairs), eleventh at Fernilee (six pairs), and lower still, with only three pairs, at Barrow Hill.

Even in winter a few may still be found in heather or among rock piles high on the Peakland hills. Some of the population may move in winter: for example there are many fewer in Scarcliffe's woods at that season than in summer. There are no ringing recoveries concerning other than purely local movements.

Dipper
Cinclus cinclus
Fairly common resident.

According to Whitlock, the Dipper was a resident on nearly all of the Peak District streams though it was nowhere really common. Jourdain said that it occurred in fair numbers on nearly all our mountain streams, breeding on the Dove as low as Doveridge, and on the Derwent down to Ambergate.

It is unlikely that there have been any great changes this century, except those wrought temporarily by severe winters and drought. The bird remains reasonably numerous on many Peakland water courses, from tumbling rocky streams to larger, more slow-flowing rivers. P. Shooter conducted an admirable investigation into the bird's Derbyshire status between 1958–68 and published his findings in *British Birds* (1970). Shooter found the county population in 1958–62 in the order of 97 to 112 pairs, some ninety per cent of which were inside the Peak District National Park. There were fifty-one pairs on the Derwent and Amber system, twenty-two on the Dove and the streams of the Ashbourne area, twenty on the Wye and tributaries, thirteen on the Goyt and Etherow and one on the Hipper at an average density of about one pair per mile. Shooter thought that the number breeding

49   *The Dipper is a familiar sight on many Peakland streams and rivers. A survey in 1958–62 revealed a county population of 97 to 112 pairs. (H. A. Hems)*

on gritstone streams varied according to the severity of the preceding winter while those of the limestone were more limited by territorial space.

It would be interesting to know the current population, since numbers are certainly higher now than in 1968 following a sequence of mild winters. The bird has recently been seen in several places where it was apparently absent at the time of Shooter's survey, and the Waterways Bird Survey suggests higher numbers in some areas.

The population is largely sedentary though some of the higher gritstone territories may be vacated in severe winter weather. Occurrences away from the hills are rare. Whitlock quoted records from Staveley and Derby; one was seen at Dronfield in December 1958 and one at Drakelow in August 1974. Possibly some of these were of the Continental race known as the Black-bellied Dipper, but the only definite record of this subspecies came from Langley Mill on 1 January 1976 (P. Bagguley).

Bearded Tit
Panurus biarmicus
Rare passage migrant or vagrant.

Jourdain referred in *VCH* to one seen between Marchington and Sudbury in the summer of 1876, and Whitlock mentioned singles shot on the Dove and on the Nottinghamshire border near Toton, though no date is given for either. Jourdain's diaries refer to three seen at Holymoorside by the botanist, E. Drabble, but the locality is very unlikely. The only recent records concern one at Hilton gravel pit on 14 and 21 April 1974 (R. H. Appleby, Mr and Mrs D. F. McPhie), three at Birdholme Wildfowl Reserve on 16 October 1977 (L. M. Plater) and one at Shipley Lake on 5 November 1977 (R. Taylor).

Mistle Thrush
Turdus viscivorus
Fairly common resident.

Whitlock described Mistle Thrushes as common in Derbyshire and abundant in the lower valleys of the Peak. He said that the

number of breeding pairs varied according to the mildness or severity of the preceding winter. Jourdain confirmed these vicissitudes, and, interestingly, suggested that Mistle Thrushes overcame their shyness and nested close to houses for protection against Magpies.

There is no information to suggest any great subsequent change in numbers. At present Mistle Thrushes are quite common in farmland, parks, cemeteries, towns and villages and woodland edges. The BTO Atlas project proved breeding in every square. They are greatly outnumbered by Song Thrushes. The average number of territories on the Common Birds Census plots was one at Hilton gravel pits, Shiningcliff Wood and Tibshelf, two at Barrow Hill and Hathersage, and five at Mapleton – a total of twelve territories compared with seventy-six Song Thrush territories in the same areas. The only exception was at Fernilee where there were seven pairs of Mistle Thrushes but only two pairs of Song Thrushes. Cold weather now appears to affect them less than before and these thrushes survived the severe 1962–3 winter well.

Mistle Thrushes often band together after the breeding season and flocks can sometimes be seen as early as June, though the largest gatherings are generally found between September and November. Three-figure flocks have been seen on occasions and Tong (1972) has recorded a roost of up to 500 at Elvaston Country Park. Midwinter numbers are smaller suggesting partial emigration. Whitlock suggested that foreign immigrants visited us in autumn: this is still possible but is unproven.

Fieldfare
Turdus pilaris
Common winter visitor and passage migrant. Rare breeder.

Although there are August records as early as 14th (1975) and several for September, the first Fieldfares generally arrive in October and in favourable weather conditions our hedges and thickets may soon be alive with their chattering. Many pass on to other parts, leaving smaller flocks to winter. Cold weather may drive many away, though Fieldfares are not uncommon town visitors then, frequenting gardens and parks. Numbers increase in spring, when the largest flocks occur on the higher ground of the Peak District. Small parties often stay in the county until early May, and odd birds are sometimes seen later.

The largest flocks recorded were 8,000 roosting in conifers and rhododendrons at Osmaston in December 1976, and 3,000 roosting in Ling on Big Moor in April 1974. On 23 October 1970 an immense passage was briefly witnessed at Bradwell when flocks totalling 1,000 flew west in only ten minutes.

In 1921 a pair of Fieldfares was thought to be nesting at Hathersage but this was not proven. Five were seen in Wigley in June 1946 and a very few have been seen in Derbyshire most summers since 1967, with breeding proven in 1969–71. One breeding record came from a small dry limestone dale and another pair bred successfully in a ditch in a field in the gritstone part of the Peak.

Birds ringed in north-east Derbyshire in winter have been recovered in France (three weeks later), at Norrlangtrask (Sweden) in a subsequent May, in Varmland, Sweden, in a subsequent June, and at Hame, Finland, also in June.

Song Thrush
Turdus philomelos
Common resident and passage migrant.

The Song Thrush is a common bird in Derbyshire, breeding throughout the county in woods, parks, gardens and hedgerows and almost anywhere else where trees and bushes are present. However this species is much less numerous than the Blackbird and the total of eighty-one territories at the eight Common Birds Census sites indicated a ratio of about five Blackbirds to two Song Thrushes. Only at Hilton gravel pits were numbers similar, with nineteen Song Thrush territories to

50   *Song Thrushes breed commonly in hedges, gardens and woodlands, though they largely desert the woods in winter. (J. Russell)*

twenty-three of the Blackbird.

The species has almost certainly decreased since 1893 when Whitlock described it as extremely common, and like the Blackbird, breeding very close to the Ring Ouzel, occasionally nesting in stone walls. No recent instances of such a site have been recorded, though ground nests are found in most years.

In winter the Song Thrush generally deserts the woodlands and is more characteristic of built-up areas, town parks, hedgerows and fields. Probably some of our breeding stock moves away in winter but ringing records do not prove this. In January and February 1910 the species was said to desert the Ashbourne area entirely in cold weather. Evidence of passage is observed most years, and nocturnal passage is fairly common in September and October (the shorter call of this species being distinct from that of the Redwing). Larger than usual concentrations are sometimes recorded around the same time, and no doubt these birds are of Continental stock. They appear, however, to be less numerous now than in the days of Jourdain, or Whitlock who refers to typical migrant flocks of sixty or seventy birds.

Birds ringed in Derbyshire in late autumn or winter have been recovered in Portugal in January, in Sweden in May, and in France in October (twice). There are several recoveries in Britain from as far afield as Cornwall.

Redwing
Turdus iliacus
Common winter visitor and passage migrant.

Redwings are common winter visitors to Derbyshire though subordinate to Fieldfares in most years. A few are seen in September (earliest 3rd, 1977) but October and November are the chief arrival months. Many betray their nocturnal migration by their thin flight calls. As with Fieldfares many move on, but parties of Redwings, whether devouring hedgerow berries or feeding in pastures or parkland, are a common sight throughout the winter. Up to 8,000 have roosted together at Hayfield (South Pennine Ringing Group, 1977) and 5,000 were counted at Osmaston in December

1976. In cold weather many move off south, while some penetrate into built-up areas, though less readily than Fieldfares. An increase in numbers is often evident in March and early April, and some large flocks have been seen at this time, especially in the Peak District. Virtually all have gone by the end of April, with only a few May records as late as 30th (1975). In 1976 one was seen twice in June in the Derwent area (S. Jackson, *pers comm*). Subsong is often heard, especially in spring and early autumn.

One trapped at Hackenthorpe, formerly in Derbyshire, in 1972 belonged to the Icelandic race *T. i. coburni* (D. Atter, *pers comm*).

Redwings ringed at Darley Abbey, Bretby, and Staveley in winter have been recovered in Italy in subsequent winters. One ringed at Hackenthorpe in February 1967 was found in East Flanders, Belgium, eight months later.

Ring Ouzel
Turdus torquatus
Scarce summer visitor.

The Ring Ouzel's Derbyshire range has undoubtedly contracted during the present century. Whitlock wrote that they were common spring visitors to the Peak, found as low as 'The Fabric' near Ashover. They also bred in Dovedale and Storrs-Fox found them breeding in Lathkill Dale and Coombs Dale near Stoney Middleton. At none of the last four localities are Ring Ouzels found today. At present they are very rare on limestone – a survey organised by D. Alsop, the results of which were published in *The Derbyshire Bird Report 1974*, proved breeding only in Dowel Dale. Alsop considered the population of the Derbyshire Peak to be 200–250 pairs, with perhaps an annual fluctuation of fifty pairs. It seems likely that, in view of Whitlock's remarks, numbers were formerly higher. At Abney Moor, H. C. B. Bowles, recording their total absence in 1941, said that probably twenty to thirty pairs used to breed there. On the other hand, however, there seemed to be a small increase in the High Peak in the 1950s. Alsop considered the decrease on limestone to be the result of human disturbance and more intensive farming.

Alsop (*loc cit*) gives the altitudinal limits as 700 to 1,800 feet with an average of 1,100 feet. The chief habitat is rocky, broken, steep slopes with well-defined cloughs or gulleys (often formed by running water), and adjacent pastureland where earthworms may be obtained. For a long time Ring Ouzels and Blackbirds have been breeding almost side by side in some areas. The species' Derbyshire strongholds are the north-west edges, and central regions from Longdendale in the north to Combs Moss in the south, and the eastern edges from the Yorkshire border to the East Moors further south, with the Snake area the most densely populated of all. BTO Atlas records involve nine squares.

Away from the Peak, Ring Ouzels are but rare passage migrants in Derbyshire, not averaging a sighting a year. Most of these reports are in April (especially), March, September and October.

Most arrive in late March and April, sometimes later. The earliest recorded date is 23 February (1941). After the breeding season birds may move to slightly lower altitudes to feed on berries, especially Rowan, sometimes forming small parties. Rather exceptionally, up to 100 have been seen at Chunal (Mrs A. Shaw, *pers comm*). September and October records are quite common, and there are three November records, the latest being on 14th (1976).

Two Derbyshire-ringed birds were recovered in France in October and March.

Blackbird
Turdus merula
Abundant resident, passage migrant and winter visitor.

The Common Birds Census helps to reveal the true abundance of the Blackbird in Derbyshire. At Mapleton this was the most numerous species, while it ranked second at Barrow Hill and Tibshelf (after Skylark) and likewise at Hathersage, Shiningcliff Wood and Broadhurst Edge Wood (after Willow Warbler). Only the Sedge Warbler was more numerous at Hilton gravel pits but

on the upland farm at Fernilee the Blackbird was fifth. The average of 203 territories a year for these eight areas made it the most numerous species overall. Kitchen (1976) found eleven pairs in fourteen acres of suburban Somercotes. The BTO Atlas scheme proved breeding for every ten kilometre square in the county.

The Blackbird's success is no doubt largely due to its adaptability to a great variety of habitats, for it breeds from the town gardens to the edge of treeless moorland where its habitat overlaps with that of the Ring Ouzel. It has been suggested that the co-existence of these two thrushes is a recent phenomenon, but Whitaker and Jourdain both make mention of it. Both authors described the species as very common.

It seems likely that most of the Derbyshire breeding population is resident, but some certainly move to milder areas in winter, since four birds ringed in the county (two of them as nestlings) were found in Ireland between December and March. Many Continental birds winter here, and birds found at that season have borne rings from Sweden, Finland, Germany, Denmark, and Holland. One ringed in Derbyshire in November was found in Spain two months later. Sometimes the arrival of winter visitors is obvious because of the sudden appearance of large numbers, often in hawthorn scrub: 130 were seen in two such areas at Brimington on 26 October 1963. Birds flocking in winter, such as the fifty roosting in bracken at Kinder Bank in February 1974, are no doubt also of Continental origin. These immigrants arrive from late September to November, but their departure period is unknown.

Wheatear
Oenanthe oenanthe
Fairly common summer visitor and passage migrant.

In 1789 and 1829 Pilkington and Glover regarded Wheatears as common. By 1893 Whitlock thought the species had decreased, both in the Peak, where it was fairly common in a few localities, and on low ground. He quoted J. J. Briggs' statement relating to the

Melbourne area that 'enclosure and cultivation are fast banishing the Wheatear from our fauna; formerly they abounded on the rabbit warrens of the common, and bred in the deserted holes'. In 1906 Wheatears were described as common summer visitors to Thorpe Cloud, Bunster, and the whole upland country to the north. This still applies wherever suitable habitat exists in the form of rocky outcrops, scree-covered hillsides, quarries, stony moorland and the drystone wall country. They are much more numerous on Carboniferous Limestone than Millstone Grit, though in parts of the latter area Wheatears have certainly increased in recent years. Writing in 1957 C. M. Swaine said that only a very few pairs nested in the Glossop area, perhaps not annually. However J. E. Robson (*pers comm*) found over forty pairs within a three mile radius of the town in 1970.

Wheatears are now almost confined to the Peak District. The only post-war lowland breeding records came from two sites at Staveley in the 1950s and 60s, (R. A. Frost, Dr I. Newton, *pers comm*) and Church Gresley in 1967. This species possibly bred at Foremark in 1946 and summered at Drum Hill, Breadsall, in 1962. The BTO Atlas enquiry of 1968–72 proved breeding in thirteen ten kilometre squares.

In 1976 one was seen on 26 February, a very early arrival. Most arrive in March and April and vacate their breeding grounds between July and October. 11 November (1961) is the latest recorded date. Migrants, sometimes in small groups, may be seen on almost any kind of open ground throughout the county. Birds belonging to the Greenland race *O. o. leucorrhoa* have been identified several times between 13 April and 12 May and twice in mid-September.

One ringed as a chick in the Goyt valley in June 1966 was recovered at Alconbury, Huntingdonshire in August of the same year.

51   *Wheatears are common in parts of the Peak District, especially on the Carboniferous Limestone. (H. A. Hems)*

52　*The Stonechat is a very erratic breeder and is much more familiar as a passage migrant and winter visitor in increasing numbers. (H. A. Hems)*

Stonechat
Saxicola torquata
Scarce winter visitor and passage migrant. Rare breeder.

In 1789 Pilkington described Stonechats as common in the hilly parts of Derbyshire, especially the High Peak. By 1893 they were extremely local, according to Whitlock, who thought enclosure and the destruction of gorse had led to the decline. Thus for probably rather more than a century Stonechats have been uncommon or rare breeding birds in the county. This century there are breeding records for 1907, 1916, 1938, 1955 and 1975, though the 1955 record seems likely to have referred to Whinchats (Hollands, unpublished). In 1975 three pairs held territory on widely-scattered gritstone moorlands, two of them breeding successfully: none returned in 1976. J. Wright (*pers comm*) has also found Stonechats breeding at Dove Holes in recent years.

As winter visitors and migrants, Stonechats have greatly increased in the 1960s and 70s, probably as a result of the sequence of mild winters. As examples of this, only two were seen in 1964, yet in 1975 over 100 were reported with loose gatherings of up to ten. Such birds occur on a variety of open ground including heather moors, railway embankments, colliery tips and even waste ground in towns. They arrive in September and October and depart in March and April. It would be most interesting to know the origins of these birds.

Whinchat
Saxicola rubetra
Fairly common summer visitor.

Whitlock described Whinchats as abundant spring visitors to Derbyshire, most common 'in the rich meadows of the southern portion of the county, where it simply abounds'. They were fairly numerous in parts of the hills but almost absent from the moorlands.

As late as 1942 they were still numerous in parts of the south but by 1948 had virtually disappeared from Bretby and by 1956 from the Ashbourne district where they had been numerous ten years previously. The decline in low-lying regions has continued, with few pairs breeding south of Derby now. In eastern Derbyshire they are not so rare, but quite local, found on a variety of waste ground including rough grassland and railway embankments. Improved cultivation seems likely to be the main cause of their decline.

The Peak District now holds the bulk of Derbyshire's Whinchats. They breed quite commonly in parts of the stone wall country of the Carboniferous Limestone and on the Millstone Grit moors where bracken beds occur, especially below the rocky edges. Thirty-two pairs were found on 2,700 acres of moorland near Baslow in 1965. Howe (1972) stated that the upper Goyt Valley population is some six to ten pairs. They are quick to colonise most areas of new coniferous plantations. In view of Whitlock's comments, there appears to have been a population shift this century. Only four ten kilometre squares lacked Whinchats, according to the BTO Atlas.

The earliest recorded arrival was on 8 April (1952). Most arrive in the second half of April and the first half of May, and depart in August and September. October sightings are not rare and there is a November record of one shot on 10th (1921). Migrants occur on a variety of open ground, sometimes forming small groups.

One ringed as a chick at Moscar in June 1953 was recovered on the Portuguese Algarve three months later.

Redstart
Phoenicurus phoenicurus
Fairly common summer visitor and passage migrant.

Whitlock reported that Redstarts were well-diffused throughout the county, apparently being most common in parts of the Peak District but numerous also at Sutton Scars-dale. A few pairs bred in the pollard willows of the Trent and lower Dove valleys.

Redstarts are still common in parts of the Peak, especially in some of the gritstone oak-woods and in certain limestone dales. They are quite numerous in the limestone stone wall country though requiring belts of trees nearby. Coniferous woodland is sometimes accepted. The fifty-six acres of Shiningcliff woods surveyed by T. A. Gibson held an average of five pairs. At the Hathersage census area numbers fell from ten pairs in 1967 to as low as one in 1973, but Lomas's Mapleton figures were more stable, averaging five pairs a year.

In the lowlands there has certainly been a decrease and contraction of range this century, and in south and east Derbyshire Redstarts are distinctly local. Extensive field work for the BTO Atlas project failed to find the species in six lowland squares. The most likely reason is the felling of old timber where the birds found an ample supply of food and nesting sites. Probably the African drought conditions since 1968 have also had an adverse effect.

Generally, Redstarts arrive from mid-April to mid-May and may be seen until September. Extreme dates are 27 March (1943) and 2 November (1958). Migrants are not uncommonly seen, especially in hedgerows, and sometimes occur in urban gardens.

A juvenile ringed at Fernilee in July 1964 was found at Baena, Spain, three months later. One ringed as a nestling at Taxal in June 1962 died in the French Pyrenees in the following April. Others ringed as chicks in the Goyt valley area were found in Morocco and on the Portuguese Algarve in subsequent autumns. Two interesting British recoveries involve one which moved from Chatsworth (ringed, June 1963) to Taunton, Somerset, (August 1963), and another, from Lady-bower (ringed June 1971) was found dead under strawberry netting near Norwich, Norfolk in April 1974.

Black Redstart
Phoenicurus ochruros
Rare passage migrant and winter visitor.

Rare breeder.

The only records known to Whitlock concerned two, one of them trapped, at Melbourne in November 1856. Two were seen in Deep Dale in March, 1927 (Armitage, 1927), and there was one just over the borders of Staffordshire in 1948. In 1949–50 one apparently wintered at Findern. In 1954 came an undated record from Calver but there have been over thirty individuals since 1960, including records from the Goyt Valley in March 1962 (Howe, 1972) and Pleasley in January 1974 (T. Rodgers, *pers comm*), neither published by DOS. Most of these later records refer to migrants seen fleetingly in such places as gravel pits, quarries and a variety of waste ground and open country. Though there are records for all months of the year, there are peaks in March and May.

Sightings have come from many parts of the county but especially from Drakelow Power Station where breeding took place in 1970 (T. Cockburn) and was rumoured in other recent years. One sang in an urban street in Derby in June 1963 and apparently there have been other summer sightings in Derby more recently. This species is currently nesting in at least four adjoining counties and is likely to be breeding, overlooked, in urban areas of Derbyshire.

Nightingale
Luscinia megarhynchos
Rare summer visitor. Former breeder.

Derbyshire is just outside the regular British range of Nightingales, and these superb songsters have never been numerous here. However they are clearly much less regular now than formerly. Both Whitlock and *VCH* described Nightingales as regular spring visitors to those areas south of Derby and sometimes to the Nottinghamshire border area near Sherwood Forest. Since 1905 breeding has been reported at Melbourne in 1911, South Derbyshire in 1947, and at Clay Cross between 1910–20 (*Birds of the Chesterfield Area 1870–1970*). Meanwhile records of singing birds have become distinctly rare, with only four isolated records in the past twenty-two years (from Ticknall, Foston, Coxbench and Scarcliffe).

Records span the period 22 April (1944) to 31 August (1951).

Bluethroat
Luscinia svecica
Rare vagrant.

R. S. Beale saw a male of the Red-spotted form, *L. s. svecica*, in a small garden at Mickleover on 23 May 1977.

Robin
Erithacus rubecula
Common resident.

This is a common species throughout Derbyshire, nesting in gardens, hedge banks, and woodland of all sorts, including closed-canopy coniferous woodland.

In the two woodland plots censussed for the BTO it was found to be the third commonest species (after Willow Warbler and Blackbird) with an average of eighteen pairs at Shiningcliff and twelve at Broadhurst Edge. In the farmland areas it was fourth in abundance at Hathersage (twelve pairs), and sixth at Mapleton (forty-nine pairs), and Tibshelf (seven pairs). However only three pairs were found on the Fernilee hill farm (where stone walls replace hedges) and two at The Breck, Barrow Hill. The thirteen pairs at Hilton gravel pits made it the eighth commonest species there, while five pairs were found in fourteen acres in the suburbs of Somercotes (Kitchen, 1976).

In winter more are noted in towns, parks and gardens, and it is likely that this represents a partial exodus from woodland sites. However a count of fifty-one in a two hour transect of Scarcliffe Park Wood on Christmas Day 1961, shows that, even in winter, numbers in this habitat may be considerable. The Robin's habit of singing by the light of a street lamp during darkness is increasingly recorded.

It seems unlikely that much change has occurred since the days of Whitlock. He suggested that the number of birds found in Trent Valley osier beds in autumn suggested immigration. This may well still occur but has not been documented since. However that movements do occur is shown by two interesting ringing records from Breck Farm, Barrowhill. One ringed there in June 1973 was killed near Bridlington, Yorkshire in the following June, while a juvenile ringed in August 1974 was killed by a cat in May 1975 at Oostvoorue, Zuid, Holland.

Grasshopper Warbler
Locustella naevia
Scarce summer visitor.

There appears to have been little change in the status of Grasshopper Warblers since Whitlock's and Jourdain's publications. Both authors stressed these warblers' erratic appearances. Jourdain said that in some years they could be found all over the county, even on grouse moors. He had met with breeding pairs at 1,200 to 1,300 feet at Derwent. As examples of their irregularity six or seven pairs bred in the Ashbourne district in 1898 and 1901 but none in the intervening years, while the Flash Dam area held eight singing males in 1972 but only one in 1973. There is no evidence of any long term change in numbers, except those resulting from habitat alterations, as at Whitwell Wood where a population of thirty pairs in 1937 disappeared as the trees matured.

Only five ten kilometre squares, generally of high ground, lacked Grasshopper Warblers between 1968 and 1972 when the BTO Atlas investigation took place. That proof of breeding was obtained in only three squares reflects the skulking nature of this species which would doubtless be greatly overlooked but for its distinctive 'reeling' song.

Grasshopper Warblers inhabit a variety of habitats including scrubby woodlands and woodland clearings, young plantations, marshy ground, moorland and not uncommonly waste ground, even in suburban areas – for example several were heard singing in disused allotments at Normanton, Derby, in May 1967.

Most arrive in late April and early May and depart from July onwards. The extreme dates recorded are 8 April (1949, 1974) and 26 September (1964). One, ringed as a nestling at Broadbottom in June 1973 was recovered from Sandbach, Cheshire, two months later.

Reed Warbler
Acrocephalus scirpaceus
Scarce summer visitor.

The Reed Warbler's preferred habitat, beds of Reed and osiers, occurs in Derbyshire only in very small quantity, mainly in the south and east. Reed Warblers are accordingly very locally distributed although up to fourteen pairs have nested colonially at suitable sites. Sometimes they frequent marginal habitats such as areas of Reed-grass, Reedmace, or Nettles, willowherb, and various other tall weeds. Since the last war breeding has been recorded from Sawley, Sudbury, Melbourne, Weston on Trent, Shardlow, Barrow, Willington, Staveley, Bradbourne Brook, Scropton, Egginton sewage farm, Williamthorpe, Radbourne, Langley Mill, Brinsley, Hilton, Drakelow, Cotmanhay and Spondon sewage farm. There are no breeding records from high ground. Eleven ten kilometre squares had Reed Warblers definitely or probably breeding according to BTO Atlas findings, and the population probably lies between twenty and forty pairs a year. With the loss of so many marshes it seems highly likely that numbers have declined since the nineteenth century when Whitlock described them as local in the area of the Trent and its tributaries. E. Brown said that 'scores' frequented the osier beds around Burton on Trent.

Reed Warblers are not commonly recorded on passage, though they may well be overlooked. Migrants might be found at any wetland area and sometimes in rather drier sites. An unusual record was of one singing in a suburban garden at Newhall in May 1972. The locality is close to Winshill where last century H. Tomlinson always had 'a pair or two' breeding in Lilac bushes in his garden (Whitlock). The only published Peak District record is of an autumn migrant at Fernilee in September 1958.

They are rather late to arrive, 20 April (1968) constituting the earliest occurrence.

53 *Reed Warblers are scarce birds in Derbyshire because of a lack of suitable nesting habitat. (Derick Scott)*

Most arrive at the end of April and in May. The majority probably leave in August and September. A late bird was seen until 17 October (1974).

Two ringing recoveries are of interest. An adult ringed at Fairburn, Yorkshire, in June 1968 was caught at Drakelow in August of the same year. A juvenile ringed at Willington in July 1969 died at Goulmina, Morocco, in August 1972.

Sedge Warbler
Acrocephalus schoenobaenus
Fairly common summer visitor.

Sedge Warblers are far more catholic than Reed Warblers in their choice of habitat and are thus considerably more common; nevertheless they are still rather local. They are found in Reed beds, sometimes alongside Reed Warblers, as well as in osier beds and areas of Reedmace, Reed-grass and other aquatic vegetation. Increasing numbers are found in drier habitats such as young forestry plantations, industrial waste-land and even cereal fields. Though they are not as colonial as Reed Warblers, several pairs may nest in close proximity.

Sedge Warblers have decreased this century. Whitlock said that they were extremely common except in the Peak where they nested only in the broad dales. Common below 1,000 feet and exceedingly common in the Trent Valley was Jourdain's description of their status. Today they are 'exceedingly common' in very few places and virtually absent from the Peak District and high ground. There can be little doubt that wetland drainage is the reason for their demise. However in recent years a more marked decline occurred. This was well exemplified at Drakelow Wildfowl Reserve where the population fell from thirty pairs in 1970 to six in 1974, but recovered well by 1976. M. W. Pienkowski found twenty-six territories at Hilton gravel pit in 1967 making it the most numerous species there: current numbers are thought to be much lower. A similar decline has been noticed in the Glossop area where they have not bred since 1969 (J. E. Robson, *pers comm*). It seems possible that the drought conditions in Africa since 1968 have affected this species.

Most arrive in late April and May and depart from July onwards. The earliest and latest dates are 7 April (1966) and 13 October (1974). Small numbers occur on passage in non-breeding areas, though Peak District records are scarce.

One ringed at Willington in July 1966 was found at Lavadores, Portugal, in September of the same year. One caught at Radipole Lake, Dorset on 5 August 1976 had been ringed at Staveley only five days earlier.

Aquatic Warbler
Acrocephalus paludicola
Rare vagrant.

One was seen and later trapped and ringed at Clay Mills gravel pits on 20 August 1976. It remained in the area until 26 August (R. S. Beale, D. Budworth *et al*).

Blackcap
Sylvia atricapilla
Fairly common summer visitor. Rare winter visitor.

Whitlock said that the Blackcap was rather local though 'fairly distributed' throughout Derbyshire. In the Peak District it was confined to the wooded dales and small copses. Both he and Jourdain considered it less common than the Garden Warbler. The reverse is true today, though when the change occurred is insufficiently documented. Detailed information from Mapleton, Shiningcliff Wood and Scarcliffe woodlands suggests a ratio of nearly three Blackcaps to each Garden Warbler. Thirty Blackcaps were heard singing in a walk along the Wye from Ashwood Dale to Monsal Dale in June 1974. Both of these warblers were present in each ten kilometre square in the county (BTO Atlas). Habitat distinctions are discussed under Garden Warbler.

This species usually arrives in April, with 4th (1968) probably the earliest genuine arrival date. Their departure is veiled by the presence of potential wintering birds. October and November records are not uncommon and since 1959 the Blackcap has been seen in the county every winter. Such birds typically occur singly in suburban gardens but up to three have been noted together, and birds have occurred in rural areas. Numbers have generally increased and between December 1976 and February 1977 over twenty were reported. Though the opposite was once true, the majority of these wintering birds are males: their origin is unknown.

Garden Warbler
Sylvia borin
Fairly common summer visitor.

Glover did not include the Garden Warbler in his list of Derbyshire Birds and Briggs, Wood, Mosley and Brown all considered it outnumbered by the Blackcap. However Whitlock thought this generally the more numerous species. This opinion was confirmed by Jourdain who said that 'in some seasons (in 1901 for instance) it is exceedingly common'. As with so many common species little subsequent information on status changes was published until recently. In 1933 Garden Warblers apparently 'bred plentifully' near Hazelwood but notes in 1941–3 suggested a decrease. These may merely have referred to particularly good and bad years, for numbers vary from year to year like some other summer migrants. For many years now Garden Warblers have been less common than Blackcaps: this is discussed more fully under the latter species.

Though both the Garden Warbler and the Blackcap may be considered typical of deciduous and mixed woodlands throughout Derbyshire there are slight habitat differences between the two. The former is more typical of the woodland edges or the vicinity of a broad ride, whereas the Blackcap likes more cover, for example in the form of scrub and rhododendrons. The Blackcap is more likely to be found in parks and shrubberies close to urbanisation.

Though there are two March records as early as 19th (1960), Garden Warblers generally arrive later than Blackcaps, with some territories not occupied until the second half of May. After the breeding season little is seen of the former species. September sightings are rare, and there is but one October record, of a bird trapped and ringed on 18th (1969). One ringed in Northumberland in May 1969 was found at Melbourne in May 1973.

Whitethroat
Sylvia communis
Fairly common summer visitor.

Woodland edges and clearings, scrub, hedgerows and waste places comprise the chief habitats of the Whitethroat in Derbyshire. Whitlock described it as an abundant visitor to all low-lying portions of the county. Most of the few reports before the formation of DOS refer to increasing numbers. However in 1969 probably more than three quarters of Derbyshire's usual Whitethroat territories remained untenanted throughout the summer. This collapse was noticed nationally and was considered to be the result of drought conditions in west Africa, the wintering or migrational area of many of our summer visitors. The population has not recovered. As an example the combined farmland Common Birds Census plots at Hathersage, Mapleton and Tibshelf held 34 territories in 1968, nine in 1969 and eight in 1972. In contrast Scarcliffe's woodlands held 22 pairs in 1971 and 32 pairs in 1974.

As a measure of its former abundance, G. T. Walker estimated the 1912 population of Whitwell Wood at fifty pairs (compared with about six in 1972) and in 1938 he found sixty-six nests in the parish (J. Ellis, *pers comm*).

27 March (1968) was the earliest recorded arrival. Most are seen from mid-April onwards. Last dates are usually in late September with 6 October (1966) the latest.

A juvenile ringed at Hackenthorpe in August 1959 was found at Portland Bill, Dorset, in the following month. One found at Alvaston in May 1958 had been ringed at Leerdam in the Netherlands in the previous August. One ringed at Broadbottom in August 1970 travelled 200 miles to reach Shoreham, Sussex, six days later.

Lesser Whitethroat
Sylvia curruca
Scarce summer visitor and passage migrant.

The Lesser Whitethroat is a regular summer visitor to Derbyshire but varies greatly in numbers annually. This pattern is discernible throughout the literature back to the days of Whitlock who described it as 'fairly numerous in the cultivated portions of the county. Being partial to small copses and gardens, it is pretty sure to be found where such exist.' Presumably Whitlock was referring to rural gardens. Tall hedgerows, thickets and spinneys and sometimes the edges of woodland form its main habitats today. It is thus found mainly in lowland regions and is rather rare in the Peak District. An increase was recently noted at Mapleton; the first pair bred in 1968, and by 1972 there were four pairs. Generally numbers have increased since 1938, especially in the northern half of the county.

The BTO Atlas project showed the Lesser Whitethroat probably or definitely breeding in seventeen ten kilometre squares in the county, with birds present in another two. Eight squares lacked the species.

The bird arrives quite regularly in late April and early May. 9 April (1937) was an exceptionally early arrival date. Migrants occur regularly in non-breeding areas from July to September. The latest date is 25

September (1970).

Dartford Warbler
Sylvia undata
Rare vagrant.
A pair was shot off the top of a furze bush on Melbourne Common during severe winter weather in 1840. Whitlock, recording this, postulated that Charnwood Forest in Leicestershire may have been a suitable breeding ground at that time.

Willow Warbler
Phylloscopus trochilus
Abundant summer visitor and passage migrant.
Willow Warblers are the most common of all summer visitors to Derbyshire, nesting almost everywhere where there are a few trees or bushes for cover. Thus they occur in a variety of habitats, from large gardens, to hedgerows, to moorland cloughs, but probably reach their greatest density in deciduous woodland. Robin Wood had twenty-three territories in fifty-four acres in 1963 whilst a fractionally larger area of Shiningcliff averaged thirty-seven pairs in 1964–8. Anne Shaw found an average of twenty-four pairs in the nineteen acre Broadhurst Edge Wood (Sessile oak and birch) in 1974–5, making it the most abundant species there, as it was on the farmland plot at Hathersage where it averaged eighteen pairs.

It was much scarcer on the lowland farm plots at Barrow Hill and Tibshelf but averaged sixty-one pairs a year at Mapleton where it ranked as the second commonest species, while it was fourth at Fernilee with twenty-four pairs in 1972 and Hilton gravel pits in 1967 with eighteen pairs.

Willow Warblers usually arrive in the first half of April, often in large numbers simultaneously, when suddenly the familiar cascading song comes from every clump of trees. There are several March records with 18th (1967) the earliest on record. Arrival may continue into May. Return movement takes place from July onwards, and last records are usually in late September. There have been a few October sightings with one very late

record on 11 November (1962). *Phylloscopus* warblers seen in winter are invariably thought to be Chiffchaffs and the present species has not certainly been recorded in that season. Willow Warblers are very common on passage, often moving in distinct migrational waves which bring birds to a variety of sites ranging from town gardens to bracken beds on high moorland.

Birds ringed in Derbyshire in June and August were recovered in Morocco and Mali in subsequent Aprils. Of several recoveries inside Britain the most interesting was of one ringed on the Isle of May, Scotland in May 1954 and found dead at Staveley a fortnight later.

Chiffchaff
Phylloscopus collybita
Fairly common summer visitor. Rare winter visitor.
Chiffchaffs need more cover than Willow Warblers and are thus much more local. They occur throughout the county in a variety of woodland where the undergrowth is rank enough for feeding and breeding, and are especially fond of areas containing Rhododendrons.

Numbers are quite variable with some notably good and bad years on record, though even then there may be imbalances between different areas. Scarcliffe Wood held ten territories in 1973 but only four in 1974. Shiningcliff Wood and Mapleton census areas averaged three and four pairs a year, and there were four territories at Hilton gravel pits in 1967. Howe (1972) gave the usual Upper Goyt Valley population as five to seven pairs. No evidence exists to suggest any real change since the previous avifauna was published in 1893, when the bird was described as not numerous but 'fairly diffused' over the whole county.

According to the weather situation Chiffchaffs usually arrive in March and April, with some territories unoccupied until early May. 1 March (1972) is the earliest recorded date, though possibly this referred to a wintering bird. There are also records for 6, 9 and 10 March. Departure occurs from July to early October but later the situation is confused by potential wintering birds with several records for November and December and one for January, invariably from aquatic habitats such as reservoirs and gravel pits. Passage Chiffchaffs occur in the same places as migrant Willow Warblers but in smaller numbers.

Wood Warbler
Phylloscopus sibilatrix
Scarce summer visitor.

Whitlock thought the Wood Warbler fairly well distributed throughout Derbyshire, confined to, but fairly common in, woods or well-timbered parks. Jourdain described it as rather local and thinly-distributed, probably most common in the north but numerous in some southern districts. Although numbers are subject to annual variation, this indicates a decrease this century, at least in the south as the bird is decidedly local there. The Wood Warbler's stronghold is in the 'hanging' woods of the Peak District, especially those on the gritstone where several pairs may breed in fairly close proximity. At present the two most favoured woods are Padley Gorge and Manners Wood, Bakewell. Many other deciduous woods, especially those of oak and beech, support Wood Warblers and sometimes birds are found in pure coniferous woodland. This species needs less ground cover than the other *Phylloscopus* warblers. The BTO Atlas project proved breeding in nine squares, with presence or likely breeding in a further seven.

Late April and May is the general arrival time, with 13 April (1963) the earliest of all. Few are seen after the males cease their trilling songs. Thus Wood Warblers are not often seen after July, neither in breeding areas nor on passage elsewhere. The latest record was dated 16 September (1966).

One ringed as a chick at Dore in July 1962 was recovered at Mosorrofa, Italy, in August, 1964.

Goldcrest
Regulus regulus
Fairly common resident and winter visitor.

Found in twenty-five of the twenty-seven ten kilometre squares by the BTO Atlas project of 1968–72, the Goldcrest can be said to breed throughout the county wherever conifers are present. It is especially fond of spruces and Yews and may be found in settlements containing a single Yew. However the bird will also nest in broad-leaved woodlands, as at Darley Bridge where six out of eight territories in 1976 were in deciduous areas. As coniferous woodland is most frequent in the Peak District the bird is more numerous there than in the east and south. However it did not show up well in any Common Birds Census area with none of them averaging a pair a year.

The Goldcrest's numbers are limited to a considerable degree by severe winters. Captain W. K. Marshall recorded six nests at Radbourne in most years until 1940 when the bird disappeared following a cold winter. Numbers generally were high in the mid-1970s in consequence of a run of mild winters.

Increased numbers of Goldcrests, noticeable in many years from September onwards, are presumed to involve Continental immigrants. In winter the bird often occurs in small groups, sometimes in conjunction with tits. Eighty were counted in the small Bradley Wood in December 1964 and ninety in Shiningcliff Wood in December 1967.

Firecrest
Regulus ignicapillus
Rare winter visitor.

One was shot near Melbourne in 1838 and one at Draycott in the late nineteenth century (Whitlock). Several were seen at Calke Abbey in December, 1944 and one at Repton Shrubs on 11 March 1946, all by Repton School Field Club. Since then Firecrests have become much more common nationally both as breeding birds and at other times of year, but the only recent Derbyshire records concern singles at Combs Reservoir from 23 November 1974 to 23 March 1975, Hope on 31 March 1975, Edale on 9 April 1975 (P. J. Bacon, *pers comm*) and Sunnyhill allotments, Derby, on 21–23 April 1977.

Spotted Flycatcher
Muscicapa striata
Fairly common summer visitor.

This quietly attractive bird is common in parkland, large gardens, open woodland and woodland edges, and similar habitats. It is most numerous in some of the larger parks and limestone dales. Some evidence of its numbers came from Stanton by Bridge where fifteen pairs nested in only thirteen acres of mixed deciduous woodland in 1964, and at Glossop eight nests were found in ten acres of unspecified habitat in 1944. The BTO Atlas showed the species to be present throughout the county. Birds have been reported as high as 1,500 feet in moorland valleys.

There seems to have been little change since 1893 when Whitlock described this species as abundant in most parts and especially numerous in the Derwent Valley around Matlock and Cromford. However, of the various Common Birds Census sites the only one holding more than a pair a year was

Mapleton where the average was three pairs.

The Spotted Flycatcher often shows a remarkable tenacity to certain nest sites. For twenty years a pair bred on the branch of a tree nailed to a house at King's Newton (Whitlock) and Captain Marshall found a door-hinge site at Radbourne occupied in most years between 1920 and 1957. Not uncommonly this flycatcher takes over the old nest of another species, including, in recent years, House Martin and Hawfinch.

This is one of the later summer visitors, generally not arriving until May, though occasionally seen in April, with 8th (1944) very early. The latest date is 5 October (1957) but last dates are usually in September.

Pied Flycatcher
Ficedula hypoleuca
Rare summer visitor and passage migrant.

Whitlock and Jourdain thought it likely that the Pied Flycatcher formerly bred in the dales of north-west Derbyshire. Jourdain re-

54 *Female Pied Flycatcher photographed at Padley Gorge where breeding was first confirmed in 1945. 'Hanging' woods of oak and birch are preferred, especially those with running water nearby. (H. A. Hems)*

ported that two nests were found at Matlock in 1892 but was later sceptical about the record. Early this century there were spring and summer records from suitable nesting localities but it was not until 1945 that breeding was confirmed. In that year Ralph Chislett found a nest at Padley Gorge, which has been the bird's county stronghold ever since. The population increased to over ten pairs in the 1960s (most nesting in boxes erected for them) but with fewer in the 1970s. A pair bred at Ford Hall in 1946; Chatsworth has occasional breeding records since 1949, likewise the Goyt Valley since 1961. Since then Pied Flycatchers have bred in several widely-scattered localities in the Peak District, with evidence of a recent southward extension of range. Exceptionally a pair bred in the lowlands, at Whitwell Wood, in 1948–9 (Walker diaries).

Hanging woods, especially of oak and birch are preferred, especially if running water is nearby. However some Pied Flycatchers have sung their undulating spring songs from quite level woodlands.

They usually arrive in the latter half of April and May (earliest, 11 April, 1966). In most springs and autumns migrants, usually males in spring, are seen or heard singing in non-breeding areas. Especially in autumn these are likely to be Continental birds as our own populations very quickly vacate their territories after breeding. 1 October (1962) is the latest recorded date (DOS Bulletin no. 83).

There is an interesting ringing recovery of a bird ringed as a chick in the Goyt Valley in June 1961 from Souzelas, Portugal, three months later.

Dunnock

Prunella modularis
Common resident.

Described by Whitlock as abundant everywhere, this remains one of our commonest species today. It is found throughout the county from town gardens to even the tidiest farmland hedges and woodland of all sorts. Only our moors are without good populations of Dunnock and even then occasional pairs are found in beds of Bracken and in cloughs up to 1,600 feet.

On the two studied Coal Measures farms at Barrow Hill and Tibshelf this species was third in abundance, averaging ten and twelve pairs. It was fifth at Mapleton with fifty-one pairs, and equal eighth, with eight pairs, at Hathersage. There were seven pairs at Hilton gravel pits in 1967 but it was relatively scarce in the two woodland plots, both holding only two pairs, and on the Fernilee hill farm site with one pair. In 1934 G. T. Walker had eleven nests in his one and a quarter acre garden at Whitwell, and there were nine pairs in fourteen acres of suburban Somercotes in 1976 (Kitchen, 1976). 110 were seen in five hours of woodland transects at Scarcliffe on 25 December 1975.

In most autumns, especially during September and October, small numbers of this species exhibit 'migratory restlessness' when they fly much higher than usual, sometimes calling, as if on passage. A bird ringed at Barrow Hill on 2 November 1969 was considered by R. A. Frost and M. J. Wareing to belong to the Continental race, *P. m. modularis*.

One ringed at Darley Abbey in February 1964 was found dead ten miles to the east at Toton, Nottinghamshire three months later.

Meadow Pipit

Anthus pratensis
Common summer visitor, passage migrant and winter visitor.

The Meadow Pipit is much the dominant breeding species of the Peak District moors, being abundant from 600 feet to the highest tops. It also breeds in rough grassland throughout the hill country but in the lowlands of the south and east is generally scarce, and largely confined to waste ground such as rubbish tips, colliery spoil heaps and gravel pit margins. Only three ten kilometre squares lacked the species during 1968–72. A. W. Jones found twenty-eight pairs on 200 acres of upland farmland at Fernilee in 1972, while the rough field by Broadhurst Edge Wood held an average of four pairs in

1974–5. It was sixth in order of abundance on the Hathersage farmland plot, with nine pairs a year, but averaged only a pair at Barrow Hill, and was irregular or absent from Tibshelf and Mapleton. Breeding birds generally return to occupy territories in March and April, and remain numerous on the moors until September or October. A post-breeding flock of 400 was estimated around the perimeter of Barbrook Reservoir on Big Moor in September, 1962.

Assessment of any numerical change is difficult in so common a bird. Populations on high ground are unlikely to have undergone much change. In the lowlands, however, tidier cultivation must have caused a decrease, though the creation of colliery tips and similar sites has partly offset this.

A familiar passage migrant in Derbyshire, this species often performs striking spring and autumn movements. Autumn passage, most evident in October, is usually between south-east and west. Northward movement in early spring is nowhere more evident than in the Derwent Valley where flocks of some hundreds are sometimes seen: on 10 April 1960 an observer saw over 800 on a walk from Ladybower to Hathersage.

In winter a few may be found on the moors in mild weather but the great majority move to low ground frequenting cultivation, sewage farms and other open ground. Exceptionally winter flocks may reach three figures, but gatherings of up to thirty or so are much more usual at that season.

Birds ringed in the High Peak in spring have been recovered in Spain in November, December and March. One ringed at Ilkley, Yorkshire in December 1958 was recovered at Matlock a month later, and one found dead in Longdendale in April 1972 had been ringed at Nottingham two months earlier. Another, ringed at Hathersage in April 1974, was killed when it flew into a window in Somerset in March 1975.

Tree Pipit
Anthus trivialis
Fairly common summer visitor and passage migrant.

Tree Pipits are quite common summer visitors to woodland throughout the county, preferring the edges or more open sites. Even restricted areas such as copses and scrub-covered railway embankments may hold them. They are relatively numerous in young conifer plantations given a scatter of taller trees for song posts.

Both Whitlock and Jourdain considered them common, and there has probably been no great change since then except where ecological conditions have altered, though J. E. Robson (*pers comm*) states that this pipit has decreased in the Glossop area since 1967. The Common Birds Censuses show an average of three pairs in Broadhurst Edge Wood, though only one in the larger but denser Shiningcliff Wood census area. The well-timbered farmland sites at Hathersage and Mapleton averaged six and thirteen pairs a year. Only four squares were without Tree Pipits during the Atlas investigations of 1968–72.

An early record was on 29 March (1968). First arrival dates are invariably in April, with many territories not occupied until the following month. Our birds seem to leave in August and September. Occasionally there are October records, as late as 26th (1976) and Whitlock recorded a November sighting in 1833.

Migrants, usually identified by their hoarse flight calls, are seen in small numbers on passage.

Rock Pipit
Anthus spinoletta petrosus
Scarce passage migrant. Rare winter visitor.

Not until 6 March 1965, when R. A. Frost saw one at Westhouses 'flash', was this sub-species identified in Derbyshire. The degree to which Rock Pipits had been overlooked may be gauged by the fact that over 200 have since been recorded. As one observer identified over two-thirds of these it may be assumed that they are still being overlooked except by those who know the distinctive sibilant call note.

Spring passage occurs from February to April (latest 21st, 1975) and is usually on a smaller scale than autumn movement which may begin in late September (earliest 21st, 1972) and lasts until November. October is the main month of the year for records. A recent tendency has been for a few to winter in the Trent Valley, perhaps in response to the sequence of mild winters.

Numbers are never large. Most occur singly with occasional groups of up to six (Barbrook in October 1974 and Willington in October 1975). Records have come from numerous 'wet' localities, especially the larger reservoirs, certain sewage farms, gravel pits, and flood water. *Spinoletta* pipits considered to be Scandinavian Rock Pipits, *A. s. littoralis*, have been seen on a very few occasions since 1969, chiefly in spring, when they are most easily distinguishable from Water Pipits.

Water Pipit
Anthus spinoletta spinoletta
Scarce winter visitor and passage migrant.

The small reservoirs at Press, near Ashover, produced Derbyshire's first record of *spinoletta* Pipits when J. F. C. Kent and Mrs M. H. Mills identified three Water Pipits in November 1953. The next record followed in 1965 and since then this native of Alpine pastures has been found wintering every year. Probably more critical observation is responsible for this spate of records, though numbers certainly vary: at least twenty wintered in 1971–2 but before and since the county total has been closer to ten. The largest recorded gathering is of ten in March 1972 at Old Whittington.

Water Pipits winter at a variety of wetland habitats, especially subsidence 'flashes,' sewage farms and gravel pits. Passage birds frequent the same areas and are not uncommonly seen at reservoirs also. They arrive in October (earliest 7th, 1974). Many have attained the grey and creamy-pink of summer plumage before departure, usually in April, with 19th (1974) the latest date.

Pied Wagtail
Motacilla alba yarrellii
Common resident, summer visitor and passage migrant.

Described by Whitlock as abundant, the Pied Wagtail remains a familiar bird breeding throughout the county by streams and rivers (up to at least 1,500 feet in the Peak District), around farmsteads, and in quarries and built-up areas, commonly, but not essentially, close to water. Small parties often congregate in areas of short grass (such as lawns and tennis courts), and even more so at sewage farms and water margins. Birds may be found in urban habitats, especially in hard weather.

There were seven pairs at Fernilee in 1972: otherwise the Common Birds Census areas revealed only very small numbers. However the Waterways Bird Survey found an average of nineteen pairs on nineteen kilometres of the Derwent, and four pairs on six kilometres of the Wye, making it the third and eighth commonest species on these rivers.

Pied Wagtails roost gregariously for the greater part of the year, Reed and Reedmace beds are favoured sites, but there are records involving such sites as a factory roof and a young larch plantation while up to 220 utilised a single Rhododendron tree at Ashbourne in the 1930s. Roosts of up to 400 have been recorded, though a record of 500–750 at Bakewell on 3 October 1943 may well have referred to a roosting flock. The largest gatherings are usually seen in autumn.

Although many are found throughout the year, some of our birds are summer visitors, especially to upland territories. Pied Wagtails ringed in Derbyshire between March and August have been recovered four times in France and four times in Portugal, all between November and February. Diurnal passage is sometimes witnessed, most often in October and usually between south-east and south-west.

White Wagtail
Motacilla alba alba
Scarce passage migrant.

White Wagtails are regular spring migrants through the county in rather variable numbers. Probably they are regular, too, in autumn but are then much more difficult to identify with certainty from Pied

55　*Grey Wagtails nest widely on Peakland streams and occasionally in lowland regions.*
(H. A. Hems)

Wagtails.

Spring passage usually occurs from late March (earliest 1st, 1970) to early May. Stragglers have been claimed for late May and even June but are more likely to have been misidentified. Autumn records have occurred in the period 13 August to 9 October (1972). The largest flock occurred in autumn when twenty-four were seen at Fernilee Reservoir on 19 September 1956. However a ratio count of *alba* Wagtails roosting in a reed bed at Staveley in April 1966 suggested that about thirty were White Wagtails. More normally records concern one or two and occasionally up to about eight birds.

White Wagtails are most often seen in wetland areas such as reservoirs, subsidence pools and sewage farms.

Whitaker suspected that White Wagtails occasionally bred in Derbyshire, and though one or two records suggesting breeding have recently been submitted, none are sufficiently authenticated.

Grey Wagtail

Motacilla cinerea

Fairly common resident.

The status accorded this delightful bird by Whitlock and Jourdain agrees reasonably well with the present situation. The bird breeds widely on Peakland streams and rivers, more abundantly in the limestone region than on the gritstone. Relatively fast-flowing water is preferred, the nest usually being placed on adjacent rock ledges or below bridges, though occasionally nesting has taken place up to a quarter of a mile away from water. The Waterways Bird Survey revealed an average of sixteen territories on a total of twenty-five kilometres of the Derwent and Wye, compared with twenty-three of the Pied Wagtail. However five kilometres of the River Noe above Bamford held seven pairs in 1975, compared with only five pairs of Pied Wagtails. Fifteen ten kilometre squares held the species during 1968–72.

Whitlock and Jourdain reported breeding

on the Trent but the only recent such record was from Weston in 1955. However in 1969 a pair nested south of the river at Hartshorne. The bird suffers in hard winters and not until about 1971–2 did the Peak District's breeding stock recover from the severe weather of 1963. That the species has subsequently spread to more lowland sites such as two of the Magnesian Limestone streams is considered to be the result of very mild winters in the present decade. In 1977 a pair bred in urban Derby.

The Grey Wagtail may be found in small numbers in the Peak in winter but many more frequent lowland waterways, sewage farms and other wet areas, sometimes well inside urban areas. In these areas they are usually seen from about October (though sometimes as early as July) until March. The species does not flock like other wagtails and the largest gathering was of thirteen roosting on a factory roof in Chesterfield in November 1976. (DOS Bulletin No. 236).

One found dead at Pilsley, near Alfreton, in November 1956 had been ringed as a nestling at Appleby, Westmorland in July 1954.

Yellow Wagtail
Motacilla flava
Fairly common summer visitor. Rare winter visitor.

The race of the Yellow Wagtail familiar in Britain, *M. f. flavissima*, was abundant on all low-lying ground but local in the Peak, according to Whitlock. *VCH* stated that it occurred in considerable numbers below 500 feet, a few nesting in corn up to 600 feet. Stuart Smith in his monograph *The Yellow Wagtail* said in 1950 that this still adequately summed up the bird's status in Derbyshire.

The species remains typical of low-lying ground, especially water margins, damp water meadows and sewage farms. However it nests in arable fields and grassland to over 1,000 feet in the Peak District, mainly in the Carboniferous Limestone region. Numbers in the hills have certainly increased, since in 1957 Swaine (*in litt* to F. G. Hollands) said the bird was nowhere common around Glossop whereas J. E. Robson now finds it com-

mon in that area; other notes in the past thirty years refer to increased numbers at Hathersage, Parwich, Baslow and elsewhere, while lowland populations are thought to be stable. The average population of the Common Birds Census areas was three pairs at Barrow Hill, four at Mapleton and two at Fernilee with less than one elsewhere. The nineteen kilometres of the Derwent south of Bamford held an average of six territories in 1974–5 but none were found on the more gorge-like Wye. The bird was present in twenty-six ten kilometre squares during 1968–72.

Though there are three March dates, as early as 15th in 1961, the bird usually arrives in early or mid-April. Migrant flocks of up to thirty or so are occasionally seen in April and early May. Before and especially after breeding flocks roost in Reed beds. At Drakelow there were 300 roosting in September 1971 but three figure gatherings are uncommon. Most are gone by late September but birds have recently been seen in all of the winter months, with over-wintering proved in 1975–6. Most of these winter birds are seen at sewage farms.

A Yellow Wagtail ringed at Hathersage in July 1968 was found in Portugal two months later. One ringed as a nestling at Bretby in June 1972 was caught at Radipole, Dorset, two months later.

Blue-headed Wagtails, *M. f. flava*, the race inhabiting much of Europe, have been satisfactorily identified in Derbyshire about ten times, (and claimed many more times) since 1895, some of them possibly interbreeding with Yellow Wagtails. Additionally, a few variants, not easily ascribed to any race have been recorded: a male which bred with a female Yellow Wagtail at Ogston Reservoir in 1963 had some characters of the Syke's Wagtail *M. f. beema* of south-eastern Russia (R. A. Frost) as did an individual at Drakelow Wildfowl Reserve in the summer of 1977 (T. Cockburn *et al*).

Waxwing
Bombycilla garrulus
Rare winter visitor.

Whitlock and Jourdain (*VCH*) considered Waxwings to be erratic winter visitors in parties of up to fourteen. Though seen in the county every winter, they are still highly irregular in their appearances. In some winters only a handful are recorded; in others large flocks visit the county. In recent years large invasions occurred in 1959–60, 1965–6 and 1970–71. In the last-mentioned winter flocks included 280 at Bamford and some 400 in hawthorns at Dinting, Glossop (J. E. Robson, *pers comm*).

The earliest arrival date on record is 26 October (1970, 1974) and the latest departure date 25 April (1965). All intervening months have produced Waxwing records. They may occur practically anywhere in the county from scattered Hawthorns on the moors to urban parks and gardens.

A Waxwing ringed at Bamford in December 1970 was recovered at Stalybridge, Cheshire two months later. One found at Dinting in December 1970 had been ringed a month earlier in Sheffield. Birds ringed in the Dinting flock were later found in Cheshire, Yorkshire and Nottinghamshire.

Sir Oswald Mosley alluded to possible breeding at Rolleston in 1868 (*The Zoologist*, 1868) but it seems more likely that his butler, who made the observations, had a vivid imagination.

Great Grey Shrike
Lanius excubitor
Scarce winter visitor and passage migrant.

Both Whitlock and Jourdain knew of several Derbyshire records of Great Grey Shrikes and it seems likely that they were then, as now, scarce visitors in winter. Numbers vary but Great Grey Shrikes are of regular occurrence, 1963 being the last year without a record. In some years perhaps twenty individuals are seen, always singly. They are sometimes baffling in their distribution, apparently holding large territories and disappearing from some places for weeks before reappearing or else they may be seen in midwinter on one date only.

Great Grey Shrikes occur in a variety of habitats, the common denominator being the presence of scattered trees, bushes or other perching posts. Thus records have come from limestone dales, light woodland, moorland fringes, sewage farms and so on: quite a large proportion are seen close to water. Usually the first are seen in October, with an early record for 30 September (1972). There are further arrivals in November, and December has had more records than any other month. March usually provides the last record, though a few have stayed into April, as late as 17th (1967).

Woodchat Shrike
Lanius senator
Rare vagrant.

J. J. Briggs recorded one eating a Yellowhammer in the Melbourne district on 19 May 1839 (Whitlock), and J. H. Horobin saw one at Clay Mills gravel pits on 20 April 1968.

Red-backed Shrike
Lanius collurio
Rare passage migrant. Former breeder.

Whitlock thought this fine shrike a regular breeding species in small numbers in south and east Derbyshire, principally south of Derby. Breeding was also reported from Sutton Scarsdale. Jourdain said they bred below 500 feet, penetrating along the Dove and Derwent as high as Thorpe and Curbar. Breeding was reported in several years in the first half of this century, specified localities being the Dovedale area, Spondon, Repton, Cromford, the Matlock area, and Parwich. The last nest was found in 1942 close to Cromford railway station. This species has declined greatly and contracted its range in Britain this century (Parslow, 1973).

Since 1942 Red-backed Shrikes have been seen only rarely. There were single birds near Matlock in July 1951 and August 1960. In the 1950s a male was seen at Robin Wood, Ingleby (T. W. Tivey, *pers comm*). The last three records also concern single birds, at Sawley in June 1962, Langley Mill in May 1975 and Taddington as late as 26 October 1976.

Starling
Sturnus vulgaris
Abundant resident, passage migrant and winter visitor.

The Derbyshire status of this familiar bird is probably little-changed since 1893 when Whitlock wrote that it was extremely abundant. It nests almost anywhere where nesting sites are to be found, including buildings and structures in towns, tree holes in woodlands, and in rock faces in the Peak and north-east Derbyshire. Even small woods on moorland may hold nesting Starlings and on Big Moor a hole in a certain alder has been occupied every year from 1961–76. Sometimes birds are found breeding in winter: young were found in the nest in January in 1898 (*VCH*) and 1975 (P. Hancock, *pers comm*).

In Common Birds Census areas the species averaged a pair a year at Broadhurst Edge Wood, four at Fernilee, five at Barrow Hill and Hathersage, seven at Tibshelf (making it the seventh equal in abundance) and fifty-nine at Mapleton, where it was fourth after Blackbird, Willow Warbler, and Chaffinch. In surburban Somercotes it was possibly the most numerous nesting bird with twenty-seven pairs in fourteen acres (Kitchen, 1976).

Starlings roost communally at almost any time but especially in winter. Roosts vary in size from the twenty-five which L. Harris found roosting in a Magpie's nest (DOS Bulletin no 53) to the million-plus utilising the dark conifers of Markland Grips in 1959–60. Roebuck (1934) found some twenty roosts in the county in the winter of 1932–3. The favourite sites are conifer plantations and Hawthorn thickets; much less commonly other trees, and Reed-beds are used. Some roosts are used for several years in succession, while others last for one season or less.

That considerable numbers of Starlings are winter immigrants is well-shown by ringing. There are five recoveries involving Germany, four from the USSR, two each from Finland and Denmark, and one from Sweden, Poland and Ireland. Numbers are high from October or November, when west to north-west movement is evident on many mornings, until April.

Rose-coloured Starling
Sturnus roseus
Rare vagrant.

Five were recorded between 1784 and 1866, all in the Weston on Trent–Melbourne area, except for one at Matlock (Whitlock). *VCH* adds an undated Allestree record. September and October are the only months mentioned.

Hawfinch
Coccothraustes coccothraustes
Scarce resident.

In the early part of the nineteenth century Hawfinches were known only as uncertain winter visitors to the county, but by 1893 breeding had occurred in several places, including Aldercar, Little Eaton, the Trent Valley, Bakewell and in the Derby area (Whitlock). Jourdain (*VCH*) reported them as breeding locally, but in considerable numbers, in well-wooded parks and gardens all over Derbyshire excepting the High Peak. He found six nests in one small area of a wood at Yeldersley in 1901 (Jourdain diaries) and knew of seven nests in an Ashbourne garden in the same year (*VCH*).

Since that time Hawfinches have continued to breed almost throughout the county. Although High Peak nesting records have been few, these finches are not uncommon in some of the limestone dales. The BTO Atlas project suggested that they occurred only in seven squares. While greatly overlooked because of their stealthy habits, their metallic calls betray their presence to discerning ornithologists. Numbers vary annually, but there has clearly been a decline this century. These birds prefer clumps or woods of mature deciduous trees and it seems likely that the replacement of much of our native woodland by conifers has had an adverse effect. Certainly this was the case at Scarcliffe where a population of some fifty pairs in the early 1960s crashed to just one pair by 1976: fuller details were given by R. A. Frost in *The Derbyshire Bird Report 1969*.

Outside the breeding season Hawfinches

are found in widely-scattered localities: they are most likely in Hawthorn thickets and areas containing Hornbeams. Groups of up to a dozen or so are not rare: thirty-five at Chatsworth on 4 December 1977 was an exceptionally large concentration.

Greenfinch
Carduelis chloris
Common resident.

The Greenfinch is now, as in the days of Whitlock and Jourdain, a very common bird in almost all sorts of country where trees and hedges occur. Thus it nests throughout the county in open woodland, woodland edges, shrubberies, and the like, often deep into urban areas. It prefers unkempt hedges; not surprisingly, therefore, of the Common Birds Census areas it was most numerous at Mapleton, averaging sixteen pairs a year. At Tibshelf the average was four pairs but the number was very low at all the other sites, and there were none at all at Fernilee (where stone walls replace hedges). G. T. Walker's one and a quarter acre garden at Whitwell held fifteen nests in 1945.

Outside the breeding season the Greenfinch feeds largely on the seeds of various plants and forms large flocks, often in association with Linnets, Chaffinches and Tree Sparrows. Egginton sewage farm is a favourite locality and up to 2,000 have been counted on its weedy fields. Elsewhere flocks of some hundreds are not rare.

The Greenfinch roosts communally in winter, often in rhododendrons with Chaffinches and Bramblings. 2,000 were estimated at the well-known Shiningcliff Wood roost in December 1966, and there are several records of smaller numbers elsewhere.

Though the species is numerous in the county at all times of year, ringing recoveries show that at least part of the population is mobile. Greenfinches ringed in the county (particularly at Barrow Hill) have been recovered in Hertfordshire, Yorkshire, Cheshire, Hampshire, Lancashire, Northamptonshire, Lincolnshire and near Dublin, Eire. Birds ringed in Lincolnshire, Hampshire and Worcestershire have subsequently been found in Derbyshire.

Goldfinch
Carduelis carduelis
Fairly common resident and summer visitor.

The Goldfinch is now a fairly common bird almost throughout Derbyshire, and only in one of the twenty-seven ten kilometre squares was the species not found by Atlas workers. However it was not always so widespread. Whitlock reported that it was mainly a local autumn visitor, with a few pairs breeding in the south; it was formerly far more common but enclosure and better cultivation had seriously affected its numbers. Jourdain was of a similar opinion, adding that good numbers bred in damson orchards in the Dove Valley, but mainly on the Staffordshire side. He thought numbers had recently increased.

Since then there are many reports of an increase in numbers, which continues at the present time. The Goldfinch is now a familiar bird, breeding in trees and large bushes at the edges of woods, and inside open woodland, in spinneys, parks, shrubberies and increasingly in gardens. The species has a long breeding season, and young have been found in the nest in October. The Mapleton Common Birds Census figures reflect the trend: the population increased from one pair in 1964 to about nine by 1972 while at Scarcliffe woodlands there were two pairs in 1961 but eleven or more in 1976. At least part of the upsurge may be explained by the prohibition of finch trapping, which was formerly a popular activity, especially in mining areas.

In spring and autumn the Goldfinch forms small parties or flocks, feeding on the seeds of thistles, teasels and other weeds. There were 200 in Cunning Dale in September 1975 and other three-figure flocks have been seen. At Ashbourne up to 120 roosted in a single Holly tree in March 1959, while at the nearby Bradley Dam a roost in Alders and Hollies held 200 birds in March 1964. Numbers in winter are lower than at other seasons, indicating that a proportion of the county's Goldfinch population emigrates.

56 *Goldfinches have shown a great increase in recent years. (J. Russell)*

Siskin
Carduelis spinus
Fairly common winter visitor. Rare summer visitor.

Though still erratic in their numbers, Siskins are more regular winter visitors now than they were last century, though even then large flocks sometimes occurred. Usually the first arrivals are in October (occasionally September) and the last birds seen in April. In some years the largest numbers are in autumn indicating passage to other parts; more normally, though, the biggest flocks occur in February and March.

While typically found in Alders lining rivers and streams Siskins commonly inhabit woodlands, especially of conifers and birch. The largest gatherings are usually found in the Peak District though in a good winter they are scattered throughout the county. Flocks of up to sixty or so are normal, and gatherings of up to 200 occasional, with the largest count 700 at Derwent in March 1970.

As in many other counties these finches now often visit peanut bags in gardens. In Derbyshire the habit was first noticed in the 1971–2 winter.

Neville Wood considered that Siskins bred near Foston in 1831 and subsequently (Whitlock). In *VCH* Jourdain accepted a record of breeding at Repton in 1902, but his diaries show that he was sceptical and the record cannot be endorsed. Birds were seen in likely breeding habitat in the Peak in 1962, 1965 and most years since 1970 and fledged young were seen at Derwent in June 1971. Breeding was proved beyond all doubt in 1977 when D. Gosney and D. Herringshaw found a nest, also at Derwent. The breeding population seems likely to consolidate.

There are two interesting ringing recoveries. One ringed at Chapel en le Frith in November 1961 was found in Belgium three months later, and one trapped in Monsal Dale in November 1970 was found at Vasterbotten, Sweden, in May 1972.

57 *Linnets are common birds of open country throughout the county.* (*J. Russell*)

Linnet
Acanthis cannabina
Common summer visitor and resident.

The attractive Linnet is a bird of open country, nesting in hedgerows, bushes, small trees (especially young conifers), gorse patches and other vegetation. It is a common bird in the lowlands, especially on farmland, and not uncommon on higher ground: on the moors it may be found in places up to 1,400 feet or more, nesting in Bracken and heather, sometimes alongside the Twite. Breeding was proven or thought probable in every ten kilometre square in the county in 1968–72. In the Common Birds Census areas it was fifth and sixth in abundance at Tibshelf and Barrow Hill (eight and seven pairs) and eleventh at Mapleton (seventeen pairs) and fifteenth (four pairs) at Hathersage. The total at the other sites averaged thirteen pairs a year.

There are some signs of a slight decrease in numbers during the present decade; otherwise there is nothing to suggest any great change since the days of Whitlock, who considered that the increase in cultivation had caused a decline, though it was still 'pretty common in the wilder parts of the county'.

The Linnet is chiefly a summer visitor to Derbyshire, arriving in March and April, and leaving by November. In spring and more so in autumn large flocks may be found. Egginton sewage farm, a favourite haunt of several species of finch, attracted 3,500 in October 1964: elsewhere gatherings of up to a few hundred are usual. In winter numbers are much smaller, though even then flocks of 100 or more are not rare.

The destination of our emigrating Linnets is well-proven by ringing with three recoveries affecting Spain and seven from France, all between October and April.

Twite
Acanthis flavirostris
Scarce summer visitor and passage migrant.

Rare winter visitor.

Francis Jessop of Broom Hall, Sheffield, was the first man to identify the Twite as a separate species. That he did so in the Peak District is fitting as this interesting finch is one of the typical inhabitants of Peakland moors. Whitlock stated that the bird could be found throughout Derbyshire at one time or another, breeding on moors (especially around Castleton) and formerly on lower ground, at sites including Foston and Anchor Church.

Records suggest that the Twite continued to nest in small numbers in north-west Derbyshire until 1953. Apart from a single sighting in June 1957 there were no further breeding season records until 1965 when the species was found in four separate areas in summer. While it seems unlikely that Twite totally disappeared from 1953 to 1964, especially in view of a record of two nests at Edale in 1958 (N. W. Orford, *pers comm*), the fact that there has been a great increase since the mid 1960s is beyond dispute. Orford (1973) who carried out the Twite investigation on behalf of the BTO said that the principal breeding grounds were between Glossop and Hayfield, on Combs Moss and the Cat and Fiddle Moors. On the eastern side of the Peak breeding was proven only on Big Moor. However, during the 1970s the species has increased markedly east of the Derwent, now nesting on all suitable moors. While breeding takes place among moorland vegetation the presence of pasture or other grassy areas nearby is necessary for feeding purposes. J. E. Robson (*pers comm*) says there are several colonies of up to fifty pairs around Glossop.

Twite usually return to our moors between April (sometimes earlier) and June, and may be seen in some numbers until October. Autumn numbers may be augmented by arrivals from elsewhere. Sometimes large flocks of up to 400 (Big Moor in October 1973) are formed.

Between September and April these finches may be seen in the lowlands, usually as passing migrants but occasionally wintering in small parties. They frequent farmland and waste ground.

Good numbers of these birds have been trapped in Derbyshire: this has produced recoveries involving The Wash (twice), Spalding in Lincolnshire, Essex, Kent, Belgium and Italy.

Redpoll
Acanthis flammea
Fairly common resident, passage migrant and winter visitor.

The Redpoll bred in small numbers throughout the county but most commonly in northern woods, according to Whitlock. It was most numerous in the valleys of the upper Derwent, Ashop and lower Dove. Numbers appear to have been maintained in the first half of this century though with some fluctuations. There was apparently an increase around 1908 and 1944–5, and a much more notable upsurge in numbers since the mid 1960s, generally considered to be the result of new conifer afforestation. However Dr Ian Newton, author of the New Naturalist book, *Finches*, referring to the Chesterfield area said in 1973 (*pers comm*) 'Up to 1938–40, used to breed much more commonly than today, especially on overgrown pit yards and slag heaps. Old bird catchers regarded it as the commonest finch, except for Linnet. Then a big decline in numbers, though still common in winter. Now breeds thinly and in fluctuating numbers, though has almost certainly increased in young conifer plantations.'

At present the Redpoll is a fairly common bird in a variety of woodland (but especially coniferous), areas of scattered bushes, and hedgerows on farmland and in gardens, even those in towns. At Scarcliffe most of the estimated thirty-eight territories in 1976 were in young Corsican pines. At Broadhurst Edge Wood this was the fifth equal commonest species, with nine pairs a year in nineteen acres. Elsewhere only up to three pairs were found at Common Birds Census sites.

The species occurs in erratic numbers outside the breeding period: sometimes few are to be found anywhere and at other times there are large flocks in our birch and conifer woods, and in waterside Alders. Three figure flocks are on record for all months between September and May, with 500 at Spring Wood, near Staunton Harold Reservoir, in February 1971, the greatest concentration.

The larger, greyer Scandinavian subspecies *A. f. flammea* known as the Mealy Redpoll is seen in the county most winters (between October and March) but only in very small numbers, with seven at Williamthorpe in December 1972 the largest party.

A Redpoll ringed at Alnwick, Northumberland in September 1971 was caught in Derby in August 1972, and one ringed as a chick at Whitwell Wood in June 1977 was caught at Dungeness Bird Observatory, Kent, four months later.

Bullfinch
Pyrrhula pyrrhula
Common resident.

Whitlock thought the Bullfinch a fairly common resident, breeding commonly in the south but confined to wooded valleys in the Peak. His own sighting of ten together in January was considered to be an unusual sight. According to Jourdain gardens were favourite nesting sites.

Very little was subsequently written about the species until 1943–4 when increased numbers were reported in a few places, and an autumnal flock of thirty was seen. Thirteen nests were found at Dore in 1944. A more notable increase was recorded from 1957, accelerating from 1963 but this has now greatly slowed, or ceased. However the Bullfinch remains a quite common bird nesting in woods, spinneys, hedgerows and gardens and it was found by the Atlas in every square in the county. However, the bird did not show up well on local Common Birds Censuses except at Mapleton (averaging six pairs a year) and Hilton gravel pits (seven pairs). There was a pair a year at Shiningcliff but less than one at the other sites. An estimated minimum of twenty-four pairs were breeding at Scarcliffe woodlands in 1974.

The generally agreed reasons for the increase are the decline of the species' chief enemy, the Sparrowhawk, and legal protec-

tion – formerly the Bullfinch was a favourite quarry of birdcatchers, as mentioned by Whitlock.

Though most often seen in pairs or small groups, larger flocks, but rarely of more than twenty, may congregate in favoured feeding areas. In addition to berries, the Bullfinch will eat the seeds of various weeds, especially orache. Parties are sometimes found feeding on heather seeds high on the moors, even in mid winter.

Though this finch is thought to be largely sedentary, there is an interesting ringing recovery of one caught in Northamptonshire in October 1962 being found at Whaley Bridge in June 1963.

Crossbill
Loxia curvirostra
Rare visitor, mainly in late summer. Rare breeder.

To Derbyshire, as to most parts of England, Crossbills are extremely erratic in their visitations. In some years there are no records; in others large flocks may occur – as in 1936, 1942, 1957–9, 1962–3, 1966 and 1972. The general pattern of these irruptions is the appearance of excited parties of Crossbills in our coniferous woodlands in late summer, usually late June or July. Many leave but some may stay into the autumn (at times augmented by fresh arrivals), or even into the following year. Most Crossbill records come from the gritstone parts of the Peak District, especially Longshaw, though the largest flock was seen at Ladybower where there were sixty-five in July 1972.

Some of the birds which have stayed in the county following their irruption have showed signs of breeding: this has been proved three times, at an unspecified locality in 1916 (*The Handbook*), at Longshaw in 1958 (Trevor Marshall, *pers comm*) and near Ladybower in 1977 (J. W. Atter, K. Clarkson, *pers comm*). Crossbills have been seen in Derbyshire in all months of the year with most in July, March and August.

The earliest recorded Crossbill irruption in Derbyshire was in 1758 when Pilkington said many of those visiting orchards around

Derby were taken with birdlime at the end of long poles. There is no reason to suppose that Crossbills occur much more or less frequently nowadays than in Whitlock's time.

Two-barred Crossbill
Loxia leucoptera
Rare vagrant.

One was shot at Mickleover on 21 November 1845 (Whitlock).

Chaffinch
Fringilla coelebs
Common resident, passage migrant and winter visitor.

Today, as in Whitlock's and Jourdain's time, the Chaffinch breeds throughout the county wherever it can find suitable clumps of trees, woods, or hedges for nesting. Thus its distribution extends from surburban areas to the edges of the moors. In 1918 in *DAJ* it was stated that they were 'to be seen and heard everywhere, more plentiful than Sparrows. On 23rd April three nests were found in a lane in under 100 yards.'

Though still common, the consensus of opinion is that the Chaffinch has decreased, possibly because of toxic chemical usage. The lowland farms at Barrow Hill and Tibshelf had a yearly average of only three pairs each but the more upland farm sites at Mapleton, Hathersage and Fernilee averaged ninety pairs in total (it was third, third and sixth in abundance). In the two small woodland plots there were six pairs at Shiningcliff and four at Broadhurst Edge.

Like some other finches, the Chaffinch roosts communally in winter, especially in clumps of rhododendrons, and up to 3,000 have used the well-known Shiningcliff roost. However, at Osmaston there was a much larger roost in the 1960s: unfortunately it was not adequately counted but 4,900 flew over Bradley towards this roost in only thirty minutes on 2 January 1964.

No doubt some of these winter Chaffinches are Continental immigrants; Whitlock thought that the rich colouring of some of the male Chaffinches frequenting the Trent margins in spring indicated this. Many pass over the county in autumn, heading usually between south and west: there can be little doubt that these are European birds, too.

A Chaffinch ringed as a chick in Norway in May 1954 was caught in Holland in October of the same year, and was later found dead at Clowne in February 1958. One ringed at Darley Abbey in February 1967 was found in Essex in March 1970, and one caught at Egginton in November 1973 was retrapped in Holland nearly a year later.

Brambling
Fringilla montifringilla
Fairly common winter visitor and passage migrant. Rare in summer.

Whitlock spoke of Bramblings as winter visitors in small numbers from October to March. Jourdain said they were very irregular but occasionally seen in large flocks. This sums up their status today.

In some winters Bramblings are found only in small groups. For example in 1967–8 the largest gathering was of only sixty, at a Rhododendron roost in Shiningcliff Wood; yet the same roost had attracted some 5,700 in the previous winter. Smaller four-figure flocks have been seen on a very few occasions, though gatherings of some hundreds are not rare in a 'good' Brambling winter. In some years they feed on Beech mast, but more commonly they frequent such places as ploughland, stubble and kale fields and weed-covered colliery tips. Birds have been reported from gardens in hard weather. Largest numbers tend to occur in north Derbyshire.

September arrivals, as early as 13th (1975), are rather rare: October records are usual, and arrival sometimes continues into December. Last records are usually in April: May sightings are uncommon, with 10th (1974) the latest of all.

Singing Bramblings were noted in the Goyt Valley in June and July 1956, at Gleadless for most of the summer of 1970 (Smith, 1974) and in north Derbyshire in midsummer 1976. No evidence of breeding was found in any of these instances.

Birds ringed in winter at Breck Farm, Barrow Hill were found at Kilpisjarvi, Finland, in July of the following year, and in Rheinland-Pfalz, Germany, in the following October.

Corn Bunting
Emberiza calandra
Scarce resident.

Whitlock and Jourdain were at variance regarding the Corn Bunting's Derbyshire distribution. The former said that it was very common in the valleys of the Trent, lower Dove and Derwent but somewhat local elsewhere, and scarce in the Peak. However the stone wall country of the north-west, for example between Tideswell and Brough, was the bird's stronghold according to Jourdain. He said that small numbers occurred in south, central and north-east Derbyshire.

In 1934 the species was stated to be very local in the county, and three years later it had become rare or had disappeared from the Trent Valley and Winster areas, though it still bred 'in one locality in the north'. In 1943 Arthur Whitaker thought its decrease in the north-east was due to better cultivation. There were other reports of diminished numbers in the 1940s. Since then the species has disappeared from some areas but increased in others, for example south of the Trent where T. Cockburn counted some thirty singing males in 1976. At the southern end of the Carboniferous Limestone region, Miss K. M. Hollick has correlated an increase in the late 1960s and early 1970s with the increased acreage given over to barley (*Derbyshire Bird Report 1973*).

Overall the species has probably decreased this century: in few places is it relatively common, except south of the Trent and on the Magnesian Limestone plateau. Elsewhere it is generally scarce though with small scattered 'pockets' holding good numbers. The bird inhabits a variety of farmland, but prefers arable. The BTO Atlas scheme found it in sixteen squares, but of all the Common Birds Census areas only at Barrow Hill was it reasonably prominent, the average of six territories a year making this the seventh commonest species there.

Our Corn Buntings appear to be resident (the many ringed birds having produced only local recoveries), though in winter often forming small roaming flocks, sometimes of thirty or more. The bird favours Reed and Reedmace beds for roosting and at Bolsover, Williamthorpe and Killamarsh maximum counts have been 300, 180, and 120 respectively.

Yellowhammer
Emberiza citrinella
Common resident.

Yellowhammers are today, as in Whitlock's time, common birds, though it is generally agreed that some diminution of numbers has occurred in the past two decades. Suggested reasons for this include hedgerow destruction, and the tidying-up of untidy corners of farmland. They breed throughout the county frequenting farmland, thickets, open woodlands and scrub, and even some upland valleys. Young plantations, especially of conifers, are particularly favoured: in 1976 there were forty-six pairs in Scarcliffe woods, mainly in small Corsican pines. Matlock WEA class found a pair to every five acres of young coniferous plantation in Matlock Forest and only the Willow Warbler was more numerous in this habitat. This species was fourth in overall abundance at the two Coal Measure farms which were censussed averaging nine pairs a year at both Barrow Hill and Tibshelf. Eight pairs at Hathersage made it the eighth most common species there, while it was in seventeenth position with an average of thirteen pairs at Mapleton, where it declined from twenty-five pairs in 1965 to five in 1971.

Though largely summer visitors to upland territories, Yellowhammers are plentiful in Derbyshire throughout the year. In winter loose flocks of up to 250 have been seen on farmland (where newly-manured fields are often frequented) and in open woodlands, especially those where grain is left out for Pheasants. Sometimes these buntings may be seen moving south with other passerines in cold weather movements. Communal roosts of up to 200 have been found in Reed beds in the north-east.

One ringed at Staveley in February 1971 was killed by traffic in Derby in September of the same year.

Cirl Bunting
Emberiza cirlus
Rare vagrant.

There are about eight permissible records. One was seen at Bladon Wood, near Repton, around 1881 and A. S. Hutchinson met with it once or twice near Chellaston (Whitlock). Jourdain quoted E. A. Brown in recording its occurrence near Burton but it seems likely that this is a Staffordshire record. Clifford Oakes gave a good description of a male at Ashopton on 20 April 1926 (*in litt* to F. G. Hollands). F. N. Barker (*pers comm*) saw and heard a singing male at Hackenthorpe in 1950, but it did not stay. On 11 March 1956 in Peter Dale, near Tideswell, the male of a pair was singing (A. L. Hunter, P. Shooter). A male was at Snelston on 23 March 1960 (Miss K. M. Hollick) and a pair at nearby Osmaston in November and December 1965 (J. C. Wingfield). After further investigation a breeding record from Melbourne in 1942 is unacceptable.

Reed Bunting
Emberiza schoeniclus
Fairly common resident and passage migrant.

Reed Buntings are quite common in suitably damp areas throughout the county: thus habitats such as Reedmace and Reed beds, willow holts, swamps, and sewage farms usually hold good populations of the species, though it was as low as seventh in order of abundance at the Hilton gravel pits, with fourteen pairs. Whitlock found the bird very common in these habitats and also mentioned its breeding in hedgerows bordering fields. Additionally Reed Buntings now breed in quite dry habitats such as cereal fields, (as at Barrow Hill where there was an average of five pairs a year), young forestry plantations (young Corsican pines at Scarcliffe holding twenty pairs in 1976) and moorlands where territorial birds have been found up to 1,600 feet.

Outside the breeding season the bird is generally scarce on high moorland but may sometimes be found in some numbers lower down – for example at Leash Fen: Purple moor grass seems to be the main attraction in such areas. In the lowlands it is still quite common, sometimes visiting suburban gardens for food and it is not rare in open woodland, even in midwinter. The largest counts each year generally come from communal roosts in Reedmace and Reeds: flocks of 250–300 have been recorded at Bolsover and Killamarsh and there have been three-figure roosts elsewhere.

That Reed Buntings are passage migrants through Derbyshire may be proven at any well-watched locality. In March 1960 there were many at Egginton sewage farm where normally few are seen, and in a census area at Big Moor, where the count is usually under ten, there were no fewer than 123 on 14 October 1973.

Among many ringing recoveries those showing the furthest movements were from Killamarsh to Willington, Hathersage to Attenborough (Nottinghamshire) and Willington to Clifton (Nottinghamshire).

Lapland Bunting
Calcarius lapponicus
Rare passage migrant or vagrant.

Single birds were seen and heard on Big Moor on 26 October 1966 and 27 September 1973. (R. A. Frost).

Snow Bunting
Plectrophenax nivalis
Rare passage migrant and winter visitor.

Whitlock and Jourdain knew of many sightings of this attractive bunting, the former saying that considerable numbers sometimes occurred on the Sheffield side of the Peak District. After a 1911 record, many were seen from the 1930s and since 1957 only 1971 is without any sightings. Much the most interesting series of records was made in the 1930s when John Armitage of Buxton carried out investigations into buntings wintering on the Pennines. He found a definite link between the presence of Snow Buntings and Purple moor-grass infested with the larvae of the gall-midge *Cecidomyidae.* Armitage recorded many Snow Buntings in north-west Derbyshire including two flocks of fifty, one of forty and one of thirty (see *British Birds,* 1932, 1933, and 1935). In recent years the largest flock was of thirty-six on Totley Moss in 1965. Most are seen singly.

Snow Buntings have occurred in many habitats other than moorland, including gravel pits and reservoirs in the south and farmland and open-cast coal workings in the east. All have been observed between 2 October (1957) and 10 April (1977) (and in all intervening months) with the exception of a male holding territory on a drystone wall at Dove Holes on 18–19 June 1955.

House Sparrow
Passer domesticus
Abundant resident.

The House Sparrow is an abundant bird in settlements throughout the county except perhaps in a few isolated hamlets in the Peak District. The species may breed more rurally in thickets, quarries and other sites but at least in the breeding season is rarely found far from man. Although sixteen species were confirmed as breeding in each of Derbyshire's twenty-seven ten kilometre squares in 1968–72 the House Sparrow was not one of them – in the upper Derwent area where there are probably fewer than a dozen houses, the bird was merely recorded as present; it has, however, bred there since 1972 (D. Herringshaw *pers comm*).

In 1962 J. C. Wingfield found seventy-two nests at Bradley and at the same place in 1965 three acres of land, including a farmhouse, sheds and trees, held fifty-four occupied nests. Sometimes this species will nest in bushes like the Tree Sparrow. Wingfield found a strange double nest in 1961: it was a foot across with two hollows in it, each holding a clutch of House Sparrow eggs (DOS Bulletin no. 70). Jourdain (in *VCH*) reported winter-time breeding, and nests or young birds continue to be seen occasionally at that season.

From late summer until the following spring House Sparrows often form large flocks, (sometimes of four figures) characteristic of ripening corn in late summer and of stubble fields, ploughland and other open ground later.

This species is rarely seen on our moorlands and in certain other parts of the hill country. On Big Moor it occurs on very few occasions during the year, usually in October, when small, high flying parties sometimes cross the moor, generally between south-west and north-west. The House Sparrow thus behaves at this locality like several other migrant passerines at that time of year.

Tree Sparrow
Passer montanus
Fairly common resident.

Tree Sparrows are locally distributed throughout the county, though with only small numbers in the Peak where they are absent from moorland. However, the BTO Atlas project found them in all but one ten kilometre square. Though breeding principally in holes in old trees (in woods, parks and on farmland), they will also utilise cavities in rock faces and buildings and will sometimes build untidy open nests in trees or hedges. Where suitable nestboxes are erected in woodland these sparrows may be quick to colonise. Forty of forty-five boxes at Scarcliffe in 1974 held this species and large numbers use boxes in nearby Whitwell Wood. This suggests that the lack of nesting places governs their distribution but A. B. Wassell, reporting on a nestbox scheme in *The Derbyshire Bird Report 1971*, said that the number of clutches laid by the species at Horsley for unknown reasons fell from thirty-six in 1968 to just two by 1972.

Mapleton had an average of twenty pairs on the Common Birds Censuses of 1965–71, making this the ninth species in overall abundance there. There was an average of one pair at Hathersage, Hilton and Broadhurst Edge. In 1962, farmland in southern Derbyshire held twenty-three pairs in 241 acres at Spondon and thirty-two pairs in 471 acres at

Stanton by Bridge (J. Robbins).

Perusal of Whitlock and other old records suggests little overall change in the breeding status of Tree Sparrows this century. However, Whitlock seems to have seen very few in winter, but now flocks are widespread at that season and the birds often associate with Greenfinches and other finches, mainly on farmland, sewage farms, rubbish tips, and in woodland. Flocks of 200 or so are not rare; over 500 have been reported from Dethick and Pleasley, with 1,000 or more at Egginton sewage farm on occasions.

One ringed at Barrow Hill in October 1971 was found dead near Huddersfield six months later; otherwise all ringing recoveries revealed very little movement.

Appendix 1

Species not fully admitted to the British List

Appendix 2

Unacceptable records

The British Ornithologists' Union created category D of their check list of British and Irish birds to include species reliably identified during the fifty years prior to 1971 but not fully admitted to the list because they may have been escapes from captivity, were found as tideline corpses (which may or may not have reached Britain alive), or because they are of feral species breeding in the wild but not yet considered to be fully established. Of the four species recorded in Derbyshire the pelican fits the first category and the others the last-mentioned category.

White Pelican
Pelecanus onocrotalus
On 4 November 1905 one was seen flying and later settled in a field in the Derwent valley: a more precise locality is not given.

Wood Duck
Aix sponsa
One was shot on the Derwent in 1853, and a young female was killed near Ogston Hall in October 1878. These were recorded under the name 'Summer Duck' by Whitlock who apparently overlooked a record of one killed on the Trent near Drakelow, apparently in the mid-nineteenth century in the *Natural History of Tutbury and Neighbourhood*. Jourdain accepted the latter record in *VCH*.

Bob-white Quail
Colinus virginianus
At least one estate in Derbyshire has released these small game-birds but they are not thought to have persisted.

Reeves's Pheasant
Syrmaticus reevesi
These beautiful pheasants have been released on at least one private estate in the county. Most have been subsequently shot and the rest 'caught up' for the summer.

King Eider
Somateria spectabilis
A female was said to have been shot by J. H. Towle on the Derwent near Draycott in November 1887. It was recorded in *The Zoologist*, 1879 p. 131 but was not accepted in *The Handbook*.

Gyrfalcon
Falco rusticolus
What was possibly an Iceland Falcon was shot at Spondon one November prior to 1789. This bird is described in Whitlock but the notes are inconclusive, as Whitlock rightly decreed.

Capercaillie
Tetrao urogallus
Glover included the Capercaillie in his list without any evidence to justify it (Whitlock).

Crane
Grus grus
Glover included the bird in his list, saying that it was rarely found in the county. Whitlock thought the record may have referred to the Heron.

Sooty Tern
Sterna fuscata
Rare vagrant.
One killed near Tutbury in October 1852 was the first British record and is recorded for Derbyshire by Whitlock and Jourdain (*VCH*). However *The Handbook* and *The Status of Birds in Britain and Ireland* both attribute the record to Staffordshire.

Passenger Pigeon
Ectopistes migratorius
J. J. Briggs reported one near Melbourne in *Field* for 10 September, 1869. Jourdain placed the record in square brackets in *VCH*, while Whitlock did not mention it.

159

Tree Swallow

Tachycineta bicolor

One is supposed to have been killed near Derby in the summer of 1850. Discussing this Whitlock did not think the evidence strong enough to warrant the species' admission to the British List.

Chough

Pyrrhocorax pyrrhocorax

Whitlock stated that Charles Doncaster recorded an example in his list of birds seen within ten miles of Sheffield (p 504 of Gatty's edition of *Hunter's Hallamshire*), possibly from the Derbyshire moors.

White's Thrush

Zoothera dauma

DAJ recorded one at Priestcliffe, Taddington on 14 September 1935 but there is no mention of it in *The Handbook* nor in *The Status of Birds in Britain and Ireland* (1971) and thus it must be regarded as unacceptable.

Marsh Warbler

Acrocephalus palustris

In 1952 two observers found the nest of a pair of *Acrocephalus* warblers in willowherb at Sudbury. The nest had basket handles but as the birds concerned were feeding young little song was heard. The record was 'square bracketed'.

Red-eyed Vireo

Vireo olivaceus

Two 'Red-eyed Flycatchers' were said to have been caught by a birdcatcher at Chellaston in May 1859 and the male was preserved. Whitlock was happy about the identification but doubted that the birds were genuine vagrants.

Pine Grosbeak

Pinicola enucleator

VCH stated that two birds in Derby Museum were said to have been obtained locally but no further details were available. An unsatisfactory sight record from the Buxton area was mentioned in the *Field* of 4 February 1860 (*VCH*).

Appendix 3

The fossil birds of Derbyshire

Bird osteology is a somewhat neglected science which the writer was forced to study in order to identify the many finds of birds' remains from Peak District caves during archaeological excavations. The opportunity was thus provided to study certain changes in distribution from the later phases of the Ice Age up to recent times. A few of the species are no longer met with in the county and some are now very rare vagrants to Britain. The chief factor affecting bird distribution has been the fluctuations in temperature of the Pleistocene Ice Age, during which phenomena temperate warmth has passed to arctic conditions and then back again to temperate. These warm intervals are known as interglacial or interstadial phases, the interglacial of some 80,000 years ago being the earliest one to yield a few bird species, from the fissure at Hoe Grange Quarry, Longcliffe. The site has long since been quarried away. The species recorded are few: Short-eared Owl, Robin and Redwing, which would be more in place under cooler conditions and suggests that these small bones could have mingled with the interglacial mammals by being washed in at a later date.

This interglacial was followed by glacial conditions lasting about 70,000 years but this period was relieved by at least three milder oscillations during which the vegetation must have changed and influenced the fauna. During this final glacial the ice did not reach the Peak District, being diverted by the high ground around Buxton. The proximity of the ice sheet did, however, cause our area to experience periglacial conditions, resulting in a tundra type of vegetation in which only dwarf Willow, dwarf Birch, Juniper and perhaps Crowberry, Bilberry, Cloudberry and Heather were the main trees and shrubs. There was extensive marsh and grassland and many herbs which we now call weeds, colonising the rather unstable sheets of glacial débris and frost-disturbed ground.

A number of caves provide sediments belonging to this tundra period, the best-known being those in the Creswell Crags, particularly the Pin Hole cave where the excavations of the late A. L. Armstrong produced some 90 species of birds along with the remains of mammoth, reindeer, horse, hyena, lion, arctic fox and other mammals. The lion and hyena appear to have been very adaptable carnivores and were not then confined to the tropical lands. It is unfortunate that the notes left by the excavator do not allow us to sort out the birds of the colder and milder phases of the final glacial. A similar state of affairs exists with the list of birds from another East Derbyshire cave, at Langwith, where Eagle Owl and Ptarmigan are listed alongside fowl and Pheasant. Fortunately a very carefully-conducted excavation at Robin Hood's Cave, Creswell, (Campbell, J. B., 1969), has produced an accurate picture of the bird life on the tundra, though the excavator was hampered by the small amount of undisturbed ground left after the earlier explorations of the cave. The activities of The Peakland Archaeological Society have also provided securely-dated material from Dowel Cave and Fox Hole Cave, both near Earl Sterndale, in the upper Dove area.

With the final retreat of the British glacial ice, about 10,000 years before the present, the temperature rose and forest began to cover the former tundra areas, first with taller species of Willow and Birch, then Pine, Alder, Hazel, Elm, Ash, Oak and Lime. In the early Post-Glacial the forest was only light but by the time the people of the Late Neolithic/Beaker culture became established, dense woodland covered all but the higher peaks and plateaux.

The earlier or light forest phase is covered by bird remains from a higher stratum in Dowel Cave and by a group of birds from an inhabited rock shelter in Demen's Dale, near Taddington. Following forest clearance by the early agriculturalists, temperate open ground species would increase at the expense of the woodland forms, while predators would be hunted in the interests of the domestic animals and birds. The Late Neolithic levels at Dowel Cave show that woodland species were still plentiful in that area but the birds are generally of small size and were evidently derived from pellets of Owls and Falcons. A few larger birds have been recovered in recent years from the excavations carried out at barrows or burial mounds of this age, and it may be noted that the Victorian antiquary, T. Bateman, records the finding of beaks of hawks in four of the barrows opened by him. Perhaps falconry has an earlier history than is at present imagined.

With the introduction of game preserving and use of fire arms, and the collecting of specimens for cabinets, further species are found to fade out from the historic levels of the caves; ravens and buzzards being the most obvious. With our help these two species could be the first to return to our district.

Sub-fossil bird remains from Derbyshire cave sites

Geological Period: Late Pleistocene
AGE: about 12 to 10,000 years before the present.
ROBIN HOOD'S CAVE, CRESWELL
Mallard (*Anas platyrhynchos*) ?
Goldeneye (*Bucephala clangula*) ?
Goshawk (*Accipiter gentilis*)
Kestrel (*Falco tinnunculus*)
Grouse (*Lagopus lagopus*)
Ptarmigan (*Lagopus mutus*)
Black Grouse (*Lyrurus tetrix*)
Plover sp (*Charadriidae* sp.)
Short-eared Owl (*Asio flammeus*)
Woodpecker, cf Great Spotted (*Dendrocopos major*)
Ring Ousel (*Turdus torquatus*) ?
Fieldfare (*Turdus pilaris*)
Large Bunting or Finch
Jay (*Garrulus glandarius*) ?
Magpie (*Pica pica*)
Jackdaw (*Corvus monedula*)

Reference: Campbell, J., 1969, *DAJ*, Vol LXXXIX, pp49–58
This account does not mention the above

bird fauna but features the mammalian remains and the flint tools of late upper Paleolithic culture. A later comprehensive work on the British late upper Paleolithic will include this and other bird faunas and will provide more detailed dates and vegetation studies. The Robin Hood's Cave birds were identified by D. Bramwell.

DOWEL CAVE, EARL STERNDALE
Kestrel (*Falco tinnunculus*)
Grouse (*Lagopus lagopus*)
Ptarmigan (*Lagopus mutus*)
Black Grouse (*Lyrurus tetrix*)
Capercaillie (*Tetrao urogallus*)
Partridge (*Perdix perdix*)
Crake sp (*Porzana pusilla or parva*)
Lapwing (*Vanellus vanellus*)
Knot (*Calidris canutus*)?
Short-eared Owl (*Asio flammeus*)
Woodpecker, cf Great Spotted (*Dendrocopos major*)
Tit sp. (*Paridae* sp.)
Wren (*Troglodytes troglodytes*)?
Fieldfare (*Turdus pilaris*)
Pipit or Wagtail sp. (*Motacillidae* sp.)
Bullfinch (*Pyrrhula pyrrhula*)
Jay (*Garrulus glandarius*)
Jackdaw (*Corvus monedula*)

Reference: Bramwell, D., 1959, *DAJ*, Vol LXXIX, pp97–109
This archaeological report does not list many of the birds. It describes the late upper Paleolithic occupation zone from which the above species were collected. The age will be around 10,000 years before the present. D. Bramwell identified the birds, which are kept at Bakewell on behalf of the Peakland Archaeology Society.

Geological Period: Early Post-Glacial
DEMEN'S DALE ROCK SHELTER,
   TADDINGTON
Mallard (*Anas platyrhynchos*)?
Teal (*Anas crecca*)
Gadwall (*Anas strepera*)?
Wigeon (*Anas penelope*)?
Pochard (*Aythya ferina*)?

Tufted Duck (*Aythya fuligula*)
Goosander (*Mergus merganser*)?
Kestrel (*Falco tinnunculus*)
Grouse or Ptarmigan (*Lagopus* sp)
Partridge (*Perdix perdix*)
Corncrake (*Crex crex*)?
Moorhen (*Gallinula chloropus*)
Coot (*Fulica atra*)
Golden Plover (*Pluvialis apricaria*)
Turnstone (*Arenaria interpres*)
Green Sandpiper (*Tringa ochropus*)?
Eagle Owl (*Bubo bubo*)
Tawny Owl (*Strix aluco*)
Mistle Thrush (*Turdus viscivorus*)
Hawfinch (*Coccothraustes coccothraustes*)
Jay (*Garrulus glandarius*)

The above excavation is unpublished. The bird identifications were by D. Bramwell in whose collection the specimens remain.
Probable date is between 10,000 and 8,000 years before the present.

Birds recovered from Late Neolithic/ Beaker Period sites
AGE: about 4,000 years before the present.
DOWEL CAVE, EARL STERNDALE
Mallard (*Anas platyrhynchos*)
Teal (*Anas crecca*)
Goshawk (*Accipiter gentilis*)
Kestrel (*Falco tinnunculus*)
Partridge (*Perdix perdix*)
Sandpiper sp (*Scolopacidae* sp)
Stock Dove (*Columba oenas*)
Barn Owl (*Tyto alba*)
Tawny Owl (*Strix aluco*)
Skylark (*Alauda arvensis*)
House Martin (*Delichon urbica*)
Great Tit (*Parus major*)
Tit sp (*Paridae* sp)
Wren (*Troglodytes troglodytes*)
Dipper (*Cinclus cinclus*)
Mistle Thrush (*Turdus viscivorus*)
Fieldfare (*Turdus pilaris*)
Song Thrush (*Turdus philomelos*)
Redwing (*Turdus iliacus*)
Ring Ousel (*Turdus torquatus*)?
Blackbird (*Turdus merula*)
Wheatear (*Oenanthe oenanthe*)

Chat sp (*Turdidae* sp)
Redstart (*Phoenicurus phoenicurus*)
Robin (*Erithacus rubecula*)
Warbler sp (*Sylviidae* sp)
Goldcrest (*Regulus regulus*)
Dunnock (*Prunella modularis*)
Pipit or Wagtail sp (*Motacillidae* sp)
Starling (*Sturnus vulgaris*)
Hawfinch (*Coccothraustes coccothraustes*)
Greenfinch (*Carduelis chloris*)
Goldfinch (*Carduelis carduelis*)
Linnet (*Acanthis cannabina*)
Bullfinch (*Pyrrhula pyrrhula*)
Chaffinch (*Fringilla coelebs*)
Bunting sp (*Emberizidae* sp)
Tree Sparrow (*Passer montanus*)
Raven (*Corvus corax*)
Crow or Rook (*Corvidae* sp)
Jackdaw (*Corvus monedula*)
Magpie (*Pica pica*)
Jay (*Garrulus glandarius*)

Other Birds of the Late Neolithic/Beaker period

FOX HOLE CAVE, EARL STERNDALE
Golden Eagle (*Aquila chrysaetos*)
Black Grouse (*Lyrurus tetrix*)
Capercaillie (*Tetrao urogallus*)
Great Spotted Woodpecker (*Dendrocopos major*)
Skylark (*Alauda arvensis*)
Nuthatch (*Sitta europaea*)
Mistle Thrush (*Turdus viscivorus*)
Fieldfare (*Turdus pilaris*)
Blackbird (*Turdus merula*)
Robin (*Erithacus rubecula*)
Finch or Bunting sp (*Fringillidae* or *Emberizidae*)
Crow or Rook (*Corvidae* sp)
Jackdaw (*Corvus monedula*)
Magpie (*Pica pica*)
Jay (*Garrulus glandarius*)

FROM BARROWS (Burial mounds):
Hindlow barrow: Black Grouse and Long-eared Owl
Tideslow barrow: Little or Baillon's Crake, Mistle Thrush and Hawfinch
Green Low barrow (Alsop Moor): Mallard and Raven
Green Low barrow (Aldwark): Blackbird, Finch sp and Jay

The full list of birds for Fox Hole cave is unpublished but details of the excavation appear as follows:
Bramwell, D., 1971, 'Excavations at Fox Hole Cave, High Wheeldon, 1961–1970', *DAJ*, Vol XCI, pp1–19
Radley, J., and Plant, M., 1971, 'A Neolithic Round Barrow at Tideswell', *DAJ*, Vol XCI, pp20–30
Marsden, B. M., 1963, *The Re-Excavation of Green Low – A Bronze Age Barrow on Alsop Moor, Derbyshire*, pp82–9
Manby, T. G., 1965, 'The Excavation of Green Low Chambered Tomb', *DAJ*, Vol LXXXV, pp1–24
Ashbee, P., 1959, *Archaeological Newsletter*, V, pp134–5 for a report on Hindlow Barrow.

All the above identifications were by D. Bramwell.

D. Bramwell
Nov 1975

Appendix 4

Names of plants mentioned in the text

Both vernacular and scientific names follow those used in Clapham, Tutin and Warburg's *Flora of the British Isles* (1952) except in the case of those trees not included in this work; in this case I have followed A. Mitchell's *A Field Guide to the Trees of Britain and Northern Europe* (1974). Agricultural plants are not listed.

Alder *Alnus glutinosa*
Ash *Fraxinus excelsior*
Beech *Fagus sylvatica*
Bilberry *Vaccinium myrtillus*
Birch *Betula pendula/pubescens*
Bent-grass, Common *Agrostis tenuis*

Bracken *Pteridium aquilinum*
Cotton-grass *Eriophorum angustifolium/ vaginatum*
Crowberry *Empetrum nigrum*
Elder *Sambucus nigra*
Elm *Ulmus glabra/procera/carpinifolia*
Fir *Abies* spp. or *Pseudotsuga* spp.
Furze/Gorse *Ulex europaeus/gallii*
Hawthorn *Crataegus monogyna*
Hazel *Corylus avellana*
Heather/Ling *Calluna vulgaris*
Holly *Ilex aquifolium*
Hornbeam *Carpinus betulus*
Ivy *Hedera helix*
Larch *Larix decidua/leptolepsis*
Lilac *Syringa vulgaris*
Lime *Tilia x europaea/platyphyllos*
Ling See Heather
Mat-grass *Nardus stricta*
Moor-grass, Purple *Molinia caerulea*
Nettle *Urtica dioica*
Oak *Quercus* spp.
Oak, Sessile *Quercus petraea*
Orache *Atriplex* spp.
Osier/Willow *Salix* spp.
Pine *Pinus* spp.
Pine, Corsican *Pinus nigra ssp. laricio*
Pine, Lodgepole *Pinus latifolia*
Reed *Phragmites communis*
Reed-grass *Glyceria maxima*
Reedmace *Typha angustifolia/latifolia*
Rhododendron *Rhododendron ponticum*
Rowan *Sorbus aucuparia*

Rush *Juncus* spp.
Sheep's Fescue *Festuca ovina*
Spruce *Picea* spp.
Sycamore *Acer pseudoplatanus*
Teasel *Dipsacus fullonum*
Thistle *Cirsium* spp.
Traveller's Joy *Clematis vitalba*
Water-lily, Yellow *Nuphar lutea*
Willow See Osier
Willowherb *Epilobium* spp.
Willowherb, Rosebay *Chamaenerion angustifolium*
Yew *Taxus baccata*

Appendix 5

Orders other than birds mentioned in the text.

These are listed in alphabetical order of vernacular names.

Earthworm Annelida: Oligochaeta
Fox *Vulpes vulpes*
Gall-midge Cecidomyiidae
Rabbit *Oryctolagus cuniculus*
Sheep *Ovis* (domestic)
Squirrel, Grey *Neosciurus carolinensis*
Trout *Salmo* spp.
Vole, Short-tailed *Microtus agrestis*

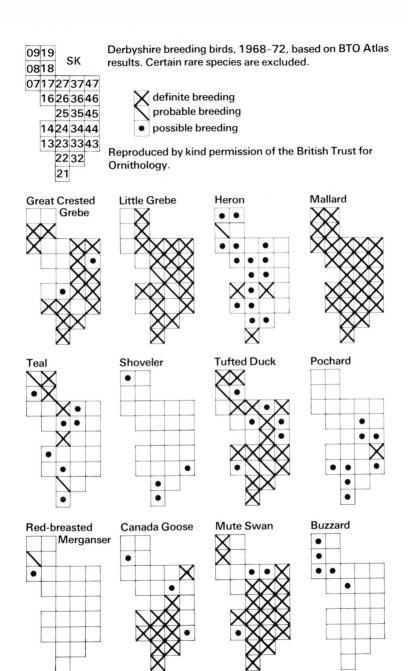

Derbyshire breeding birds, 1968-72, based on BTO Atlas results. Certain rare species are excluded.

SK

X definite breeding
\ probable breeding
• possible breeding

Reproduced by kind permission of the British Trust for Ornithology.

Great Crested Grebe

Little Grebe

Heron

Mallard

Teal

Shoveler

Tufted Duck

Pochard

Red-breasted Merganser

Canada Goose

Mute Swan

Buzzard

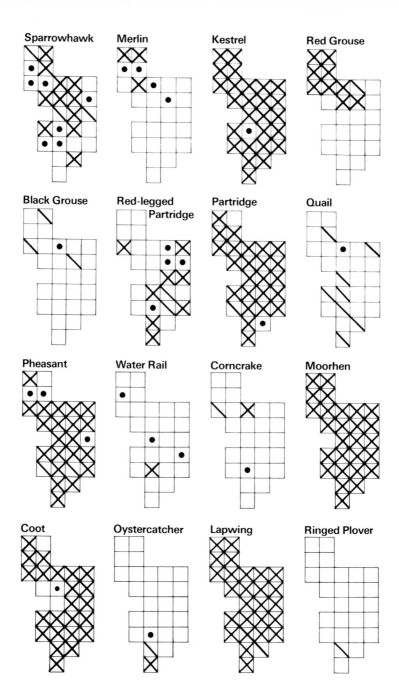

Sparrowhawk

Merlin

Kestrel

Red Grouse

Black Grouse

Red-legged
Partridge

Partridge

Quail

Pheasant

Water Rail

Corncrake

Moorhen

Coot

Oystercatcher

Lapwing

Ringed Plover

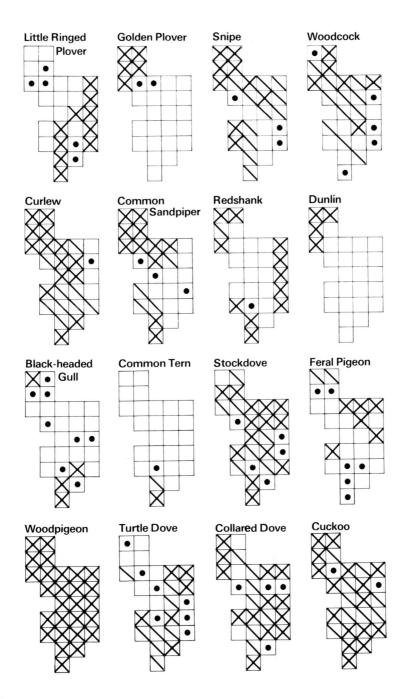

Little Ringed Plover

Golden Plover

Snipe

Woodcock

Curlew

Common Sandpiper

Redshank

Dunlin

Black-headed Gull

Common Tern

Stockdove

Feral Pigeon

Woodpigeon

Turtle Dove

Collared Dove

Cuckoo

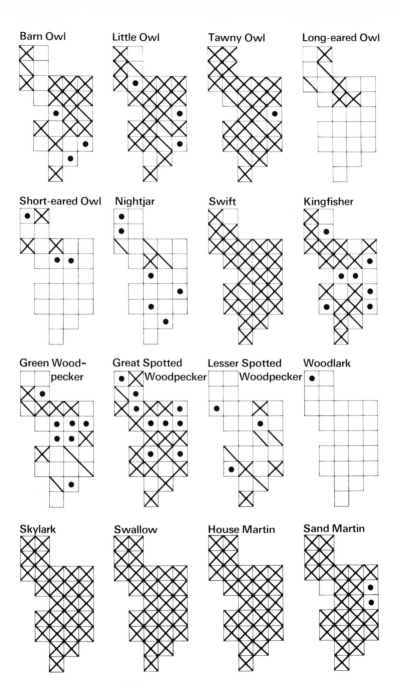

Barn Owl Little Owl Tawny Owl Long-eared Owl

Short-eared Owl Nightjar Swift Kingfisher

Green Wood-pecker Great Spotted Woodpecker Lesser Spotted Woodpecker Woodlark

Skylark Swallow House Martin Sand Martin

168

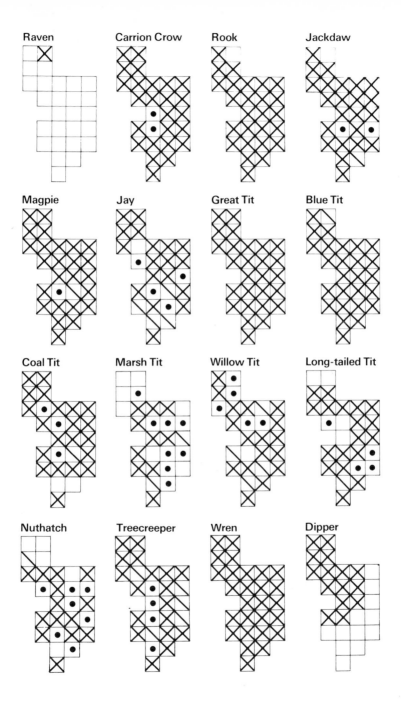

Raven   Carrion Crow   Rook   Jackdaw

Magpie   Jay   Great Tit   Blue Tit

Coal Tit   Marsh Tit   Willow Tit   Long-tailed Tit

Nuthatch   Treecreeper   Wren   Dipper

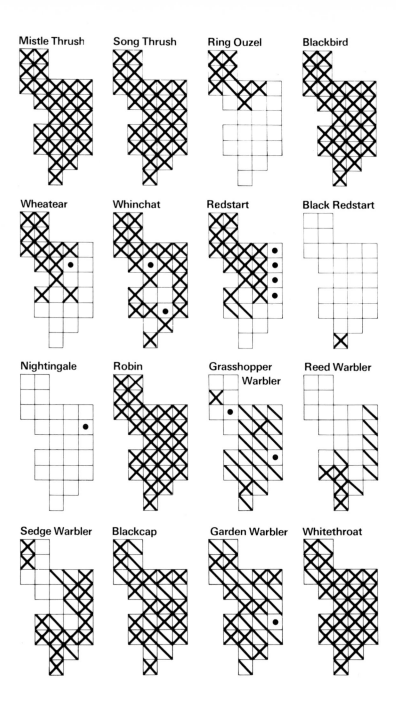

Mistle Thrush

Song Thrush

Ring Ouzel

Blackbird

Wheatear

Whinchat

Redstart

Black Redstart

Nightingale

Robin

Grasshopper
Warbler

Reed Warbler

Sedge Warbler

Blackcap

Garden Warbler

Whitethroat

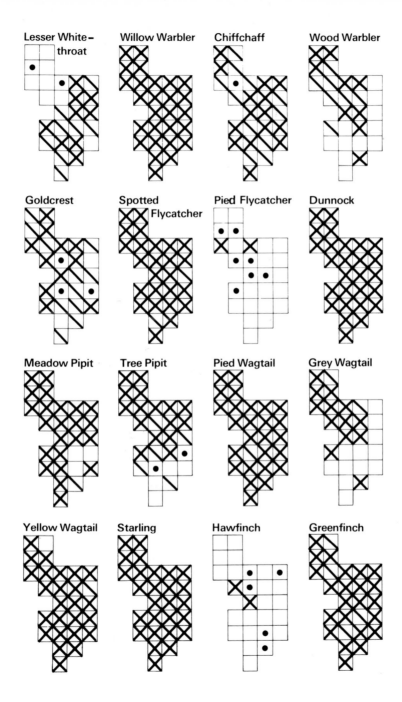

Lesser White-throat

Willow Warbler

Chiffchaff

Wood Warbler

Goldcrest

Spotted Flycatcher

Pied Flycatcher

Dunnock

Meadow Pipit

Tree Pipit

Pied Wagtail

Grey Wagtail

Yellow Wagtail

Starling

Hawfinch

Greenfinch

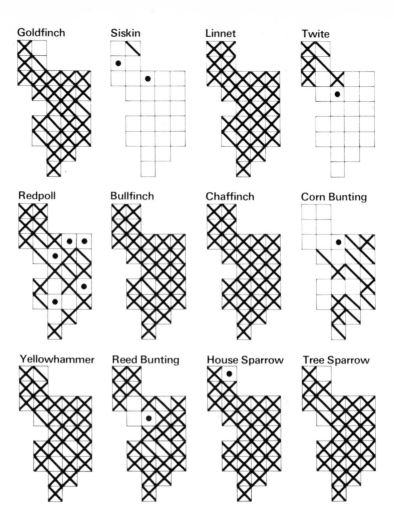

Goldfinch   Siskin   Linnet   Twite

Redpoll   Bullfinch   Chaffinch   Corn Bunting

Yellowhammer   Reed Bunting   House Sparrow   Tree Sparrow

Bibliography

The five main sources were:-
Journal of the Derbyshire Archaeological and Natural History Society, 1893–1954. (*DAJ*)
Derbyshire Ornithological Society (DOS). Annual Reports, 1955–76 (Derbyshire Bird Report). Bulletins 1954–January, 1978
Whitlock, F. B., 1893 (Whitlock) *Birds of Derbyshire*
Jourdain, F. C. R., 1905, (Jourdain or *VCH*) 'Birds' in *The Victoria County History of Derbyshire*. Vol 1, 119–45. Addenda and corrigenda, XXIX

The abbreviations or names used in the text are shown in brackets.

OTHER BOOKS
Banks, F. R., 1975, *The Peak District*.
Bell, T. Hedley, 1962, *The Birds of Cheshire* (Altrincham)
British Ornithologists' Union, 1971, *The Status of Birds in Britain and Ireland* (Oxford and Edinburgh)
Bryden, H. A., 1907, 'Shooting' in *The Victoria County History of Derbyshire*, Vol 2, 293–5.
Chislett, Ralph, 1952, *Yorkshire Birds*
Clapham, A. R., 1969, *The Flora of Derbyshire* (Derby)
Clapham, A. R., Tutin, T. G., and Warburg, E. F., 1952, *Flora of the British Isles* (Cambridge)
Coward, T. A., 1910, *The Vertebrate Fauna of Cheshire and Liverpool Bay*
Dixon, Charles, 1900, *Among the Birds in the Northern Shires*
Dury, G. H., 1963, *The East Midlands and the Peak*
Edwards, K. C., 1962, *The Peak District*
Edwards, K. C., 1966, *Nottingham and its Region* (Nottingham)

Gruson, Edward S., 1976, *Checklist of the Birds of the World*
Hudson, W. H., 1913, *Adventures among Birds*
Linton, D. L., 1956, *Sheffield and its Region* (Sheffield)
Millward, R. and Robinson, A., 1975, *The Peak District*
Parslow, John, 1973, *Breeding Birds of Britain and Ireland* (Berkhamstead)
Patten, C. J., 1910, 'Aves' in *Handbook and Guide to Sheffield*, pp455–68
Sharrock, J. T. R., 1976, *The Atlas of Breeding Birds in Britain and Ireland* (Tring)
Smith, Harold, 1974, *Birds of the Sheffield area* (Sheffield)
Smith, Stuart, 1950, *The Yellow Wagtail*
Tudor, T. L., 1903, *Derbyshire*. Revised by E. Carleton-Williams, 1950
Wareing, Mike J., 1973, 'Farmland' in *Birdwatchers' Year*, pp191–242 (Berkhamstead)
Witherby, H. F., *et al*, 1938–41, *The Handbook of British Birds*

OTHER SOURCES
Alsop, Derek, 1974, 'The Ring Ouzel (*Turdus torquatus*) in Derbyshire', *Derbyshire Bird Report, 1974*, pp10–14
Alsop, G. H., *et al*, 1971, Ornithological Survey of the Sutton Scarsdale area.
Armitage, J., 1927, 'Note on Black Redstarts in Derbyshire', *British Birds*, **20**, p275
Armitage, J., 1932, 'Snow Buntings inland in Lancashire in winter', *British Birds*, **26**, pp206–7
Armitage, J., 1933, 'The Association of Birds and a Moor-grass on the Pennines in winter', *British Birds*, **27**, pp153–8
Armitage, J., 1935, 'Lapland and other Buntings on the Pennines in winter', *British Birds*, **28**, pp230–3
Atlee, H. G., 1948, 'Breeding of Hobby in

North Midlands', *British Birds*, **41**, p87

Bacon, P. J., 1972, Derbyshire Grebe Survey

Birklands Ringing Group, Reports 1973, 1974

Boyd, Hugh, 1954, 'The wreck of Leach's Petrels in the autumn of 1952', *British Birds*, **47**, pp137–63

Buxton Field Club, Reports, 1969–74

Derbyshire County Council, 1972, Countryside Plan

Derbyshire County Council, 1975, Structure Plan

Derbyshire Naturalists' Trust, Newsletters, 1962–77

Derbyshire Ornithological Society, 1955, Bird Distribution Survey

Drakelow Ringing Group, Reports, 1970–5

Ellis, John, 1973, Birds of Whitwell and District

Frost, R. A., 1967, 'Birds of the Peak District', *Birds*, July–August, 1967

Frost, R. A., 1969, 'The Hawfinch at Scarcliffe', *Derbyshire Bird Report 1969*, pp9–10

Frost, R. A., Shooter, P., and Stoyle, M. F., 1969, A Check List of The Birds of Ogston Reservoir

Gillham, E., Harrison, J. M., and Harrison, J. G., 1965, A study of certain *Aythya* hybrids. *Wildfowl Trust, Seventeenth Annual Report*, pp49–65

Hawley, R. G., 1968, 'Birds' in *The Natural History of the Sheffield District*, pp39–44

Herringshaw, D., and Gosney, D., 1977, 'Recent changes in status of some birds in the Sheffield area', *The Magpie*, **1**, pp7–18

Hollands, F. G., The Stonechat in Derbyshire since 1893 (unpublished)

Howe, G., 1972, A check list of the birds in the upper Goyt Valley

Hudson, Robert, 1971, *A species list of British and Irish Birds*, BTO Guide 13

Hudson, Robert, 1973, *Early and late Dates for Summer Migrants*, BTO Guide 15

Hulme, Derek C., 1962, Index of Derbyshire Localities

Kitchen, A., 1976, 'A Suburban Bird Census at Somercotes', *Derbyshire Bird Report 1976*, pp11–14

Lomas, P. D. R., 1968, 'The decline of the Rook population of Derbyshire', *Bird Study*, **15**, pp198–205

Lovenbury, G. A., Waterhouse, M. and Yalden, D. W., *In press*, 'The Status of Black Grouse in the Peak District'

Macdonald, J. D., 1953, 'Black-browed Albatross in Derbyshire', *British Birds*, **46**, pp110–111, 307–10

Marsland, Michael, 1974, 'Birds of the Peak District', *Bird Study*, **21**, pp135–40

Matlock Field Club, Reports, 1969 and 72

Minton, C. D. T., 1968, 'Pairing and breeding of Mute Swans', *Wildfowl*, **19**, pp41–60

Minton, C. D. T., 1971, 'Mute Swan Flocks', *Wildfowl*, **22**, pp71–88

Nicholson, E. M., 1929, 'Report on the *British Birds* Census of Heronries 1928', *British Birds*, **22**, pp270–323, 334–72

Ogilvie, M. A., 1969., 'The Status of the Canada Goose in Britain 1967–69', *Wildfowl*, **20**, pp79–85

Ogston Hide Group, Annual Reports, 1969–75

Orford, Noel, 1973, 'Breeding Distribution of the Twite in Central Britain', *Bird Study*, **20**, pp51–62, 121–26

Raynor, Michael, 1963, 'The Lesser Black-backed Gull in Derbyshire', *Bird Study*, **10**, pp211–18

Robson, J. E., and Shaw, Anne, 1976, Some Birds of Glossop.

Rodgers, Hester C., 'The Extension of the Breeding Range of the Nuthatch in Derbyshire', *Derbyshire Bird Report 1974*, pp7–9

Roebuck, A., 1933, 'A survey of Rooks in the Midlands', *British Birds*, **27**, pp4–23

Roebuck, A., 1934, 'Starling Roosts in the East Midlands', *British Birds*, **27**, pp325–32

Roworth, Peter C., 1971, 'Notes on the occurrence of the Little Owl (*Athene noctua*) in Derbyshire', (unpublished)

Roworth, Peter C., 1974, 'The Little Owl in Derbyshire', *Derbyshire Life and Countryside*, May 1974

Sheffield Bird Study Group, Sheffield Bird

Reports, 1973–6; Bulletins, 1974–7

Shooter, Philip, 1970, 'The Dipper population of Derbyshire, 1958–68', *British Birds*, **63**, pp158–63

Sorby Natural History Society, *Sorby Record*, 1958–76; Newsletters, 1964–77

South Pennine Ringing Group, 1977, Birds of the Southern Pennines

Swaine, C. M., 1943–4, 'Barnacle Geese in Derbyshire', *British Birds*, **37**, p 199

Tong, Michael, 1972, 'Birds of a Country Park', *Derbyshire Bird Report 1972*, pp10–11

Wassell, A. B., 1971, 'A report on the first six years of a Derbyshire Nest Box Scheme', *Derbyshire Bird Report 1971*, pp8–14

WEA, Alfreton, 1971, Birds of the Alfreton Area 1870–1970

WEA, Alfreton, 1975, Birds of Matlock Forest and Beeley Moor

WEA, Chesterfield, 1971, Birds of the Chesterfield Area 1870–1970

WEA, Matlock, 1973, Birds of Shiningcliff Woods

Whitaker, Arthur, 1929, 'Notes on the Birds of the Sheffield District', *Proceedings Sorby Scientific Society*, **1**, pp16–33

Whitwell Wood Natural History Group, 1977, First Report

Wigglesworth, George, Survey of the Birds of the Matlock Urban District 1945–66

Wilson, D. R., 1958, 'The Birds of the Sheffield Area', *Sorby Record*, **1**, pp54–62

Yalden, D. W., 1972, 'The Red Grouse (*Lagopus lagopus scoticus*) in the Peak District', *Naturalist*, **922**, pp89–102

Yalden, D. W., 1974, 'The status of the Golden Plover (*Pluvialis apricaria*) and Dunlin (*Calidris alpina*) in the Peak District', *Naturalist*, **930**, pp81–91

The following journals were also abstracted:
British Birds, 1907–77
Bird Study, 1954–76
The Naturalist, 1960–76
The North West Naturalist, 1926–75
The Zoologist, 1843–1916
The Magpie, 1977

Index

English names are indexed under the last word. Scientific names are indexed under the generic name, and are printed in italics. Numbers in bold type refer to the first page of an entry in the systematic list, and roman type to entries elsewhere.